Minorities and
Family Therapy

Minorities and Family Therapy

George W. Saba
Betty M. Karrer
Kenneth V. Hardy
Editors

The Haworth Press
New York • London

Minorities and Family Therapy has also been published as *Journal of Psychotherapy & the Family*, Volume 6, Numbers 1/2 1989.

The Haworth Press, Inc., 10 Alice Street, Binghamton, NY 13904-1580
EUROSPAN/Haworth, 3 Henrietta Street, London WC2E 8LU England

Library of Congress Cataloging-in-Publication Data

Minorities and family therapy / George W. Saba, Betty M. Karrer, Kenneth V. Hardy, editors.
     p.   cm.
    "Has also been published as Journal of psychotherapy & the family, volume 6, numbers 1/2, 1989" – T.p. verso.
    Includes bibliographical references.
    ISBN 0-86656-777-1
    1. Minorities – Mental health – United States. 2. Family psychotherapy. I. Saba, George William. II. Karrer, Betty M. III. Hardy, Kenneth V.
RC451.5.A2M54   1989
616.89'156'08693 – dc20
                                      89-26981
                                       CIP

Minorities and Family Therapy

CONTENTS

ABOUT THE EDITORS

George William Saba, PhD, teaches systems-oriented treatment to family physicians at San Francisco General Hospital where he is the Director of Behavioral Sciences. He is also an Adjunct Assistant Clinical Professor in the Department of Family and Community Medicine at the University of California, San Francisco. Dr. Saba was previously Director of Training at Midwest Family Resources in Chicago. Working primarily with urban under-served families, his clinical and research interests include family therapy, eating disorders, family violence, substance abuse, family therapy training, and minority health care.

Betty MacKune Karrer, MA, began work at the Institute for Juvenile Research in 1971 as director of an early intervention program for kindergarten aged children. She obtained her training in family therapy at the Institute of Juvenile Research, and joined the Family Systems Program of IJR in 1982 as a trainer/supervisor in family therapy. Her areas of interest and expertise are training and supervision, as well as cultural and minority issues in family therapy. Presently, she is involved in a three-year study with families in the process of cultural transition (both immigrants and refugees). She has lectured on these topics extensively, throughout the United States, Mexico, and South America.

Kenneth V. Hardy, PhD, is Executive Director of the Commission on Accreditation for Marriage and Family Therapy Education of the American Association for Marriage and Family Therapy (AAMFT). A family therapist by training, Dr. Hardy also maintains a part-time practice in marital and family therapy in Washington, D.C. He is the former director of Group and Family Treatment with the East New York Psychiatric Outpatient Clinic in Brooklyn, New York. Dr. Hardy is a Clinical Member and Fellow of the American Association for Marriage and Family Therapy. He currently serves on the editorial boards of several professional journals in the family therapy field. He is also an accomplished speaker, having presented numerous workshops and papers on family therapy and minority family issues.

Preface

As I assumed the Editorship of the *Journal of Psychotherapy &
the Family* it was my intention to commission a special issue and
book which focuses on underserved clients, particularly poor people and minorities. Family therapy, like psychiatry, is viewed by
many as treatment for the privileged. Yet there are millions of underprivileged who could benefit significantly from family therapy
services.

At the same time, many family therapists are ambivalent in working with certain client populations distinguished by their minority
status, race, ethnicity, cultural, and economic status. As an illustra-
tion of this underservice and ill-preparation, there are very few
books which address family therapy services to minority families.
None, in my judgment, effectively capture the challenges of working with these populations while, at the same time, provide a useful
array of family therapy/systemic approaches to treatment. I am
pleased to say that this major gap in the literature is now filled by
this fine collection.

We are very fortunate to find such a distinguished group of editors. George W. Saba, PhD, is Director of Behavioral Sciences at
San Francisco General Family Practice Program, the University of
California School of Medicine, Department of Family and Community Medicine in San Francisco. He has written numerous scholarly
works in the area of family therapy. Betty M. Karrer is a member of
the faculty of the highly celebrated Family Systems Program at the
Chicago Institute for Juvenile Research. She is a nationally-recog-
nized authority on ethnic minority family systems and a popular
lecturer at home and abroad on this and many other topics in the
family therapy area. Kenneth V. Hardy, PhD, has served for many
years as the Executive Director of the national Commission on Accreditation for Marriage and Family Therapy Education. This important Commission is sanctioned by the U.S. Department of Edu-

cation and is affiliated with the American Association for Marriage and Family Therapy. Perhaps more than any other, Dr. Hardy has enlightened the profession of family therapy about the challenges and opportunities of comprehensive family therapy training that includes sensitivity to family characteristics such as race, ethnicity, culture, and class.

This important work is the culmination of nearly four years of continuous effort. Located on both coasts and the midwest of the U.S. continent, the co-editors' collaboration was remarkable and, from all indications, highly successful. They were able to attract a rich assortment of papers written by nationally respected scholars. What emerges throughout this fine collection is an exciting opportunity to apply proven family therapy methods to an important, underserved population. They have not only helped insure that the underserved will be understood and helped more effectively, but they have, collectively, pushed the field of family therapy toward greater sensitivity to context and, in the process, made the field more relevant to modern American life.

Charles R. Figley, PhD
Editor, *Journal of Psychotherapy & the Family*

Acknowledgments

Many people have worked together to produce this work. First, we would like to thank the families who have educated us by allowing a look into their lives, strengths and struggles.

We are extremely grateful to Charles Figley, whose steadfast commitment to this project helped bring it to fruition. Through continued support, editorial wisdom, and remarkable flexibility, Charles helped us avoid organizational disasters and move beyond delays caused by acts of God.

As we know, the support of one's context is crucial to allowing an editor to devote time and to utilize needed resources. We thank Peter Sommers, MD, the Family Practice Residency Program, San Francisco, and the Department of Family and Community Medicine, University of California, San Francisco (in particular, Paul Bailiff, Virginia Lax and Ken Law); and the American Association for Marriage and Family Therapy.

An exciting dimension of editing this volume was the opportunity for dialogue about the work with expert colleagues in the field. The reviewers whom we contacted, to a person, were prompt and provided excellent reviews of the papers. We wish to thank the following members of the editorial board of the *Journal of Psychotherapy & the Family* and ad hoc reviewers: Carol Anderson, Doug Breunlin, Lee Combrink-Graham, Guy Diammond, Celia Falicov, Shotsy Faust, Lawrence Fisher, Bernard Guerney, William Hiebert, Florence Kaslow, Judith Landau-Stanton, Kitty LaPerriere, Jay Lappin, Grace Laurencin, Howard Liddle, Gayla Margolin, William Nichols, Denise Rodgers, Dick Schwartz.

Betty Karrer wishes to acknowledge the helpful editorial comments of Nancy Burgoyne, Leslie Davis, and Jerry Lockhart. George Saba would like to thank his wife, Teresa Rebeiro Saba, who taught him that the acceptable, if immoral, is unacceptable.

Introduction

George W. Saba
Betty M. Karrer
Kenneth V. Hardy

I don't deny that these sociological formulas are drawn from life. But I do deny that they define the complexity of Harlem. They only abstract it and reduce it to proportions which the sociologists can manage. I simply don't recognize Harlem in them. And I certainly don't recognize the people of Harlem whom I know. Which is by no means to deny the ruggedness of life there, nor the hardship, the poverty, the sordidness, the filth. But there is something else in Harlem, something subjective, willful, and complexly and compellingly human. It is that "something else" that challenges the sociologists who ignore it, and the society which would deny its existence. It is that "something else" which makes for our strength, which makes for our endurance and our promise.

— Ralph Ellison
On White observers of Harlem life (1967, March)

This novelist's grave concern for how Blacks in Harlem are observed and portrayed by the dominant culture holds as much relevance today as it did twenty years ago. It is time for the "something else" of minority families to be examined by therapists who struggle mostly with that "something subjective, willful, and complexly and compellingly human." In order to move our field away from the deficit, pathological focus that currently prevails, we need to capture that "something else." To this end, we present an exploration of how systems-oriented clinicians, who search for strengths, presently work with ethnic and racial minority families.

The field of family therapy (a field which began with a strong concern for social issues) has paid little attention to the clinical needs and strengths of minority families. With the exception of a few important works (e.g., McGoldrick, Pearce, & Giordano, 1982; Falicov, 1983; Ho, 1987), the family therapy literature offers limited discussion of clinical approaches for minority families. In addition, training programs generally neglect minority studies (Hardy, 1989).

As the field continues to evolve, this benevolent neglect is clearly an attempt to reduce the "something else" of minorities to a manageable level. Unwittingly, we may enter the therapy room carrying a mixture of clinical stereotypes and a can of whitewash. Without sufficient exploration and training, we risk treating minority families from a narrow, incomplete perspective. We may filter out their inner resources, values, intelligence, spirituality, and wisdom; and most importantly, we may underestimate the influence of the social settings in which they live.

A therapist interested in caring for minority families from a more sensitive and expanded perspective must consider several societal trends that will accompany us into the 21st century.

THE CHANGING COMPLEXION OF THE UNITED STATES

The 1980 Bureau of Census indicated that one out of every five persons in the United States is a member of a minority group. Of the total population in this country, 11.5% are Black, 6.4% are Latino, 1.6% are Asian/Pacific Islanders, and less than one percent are Native Americans (Heckler, 1985). Most likely, these percentages are even higher since minorities tend to be underrepresented in the census data. In addition, the number of minorities will soon increase. For example, in the year 2000, 46% of the population of California will be Latino, Asian and Black. By the year 2010, this percentage will rise to 55. Perhaps most remarkable is that 92% of Californians will live in counties where the "minority" population is more than 30%. Similar changes are occurring in most central cities and metropolitan areas in this country (i.e., Baltimore, Philadelphia, Chicago, Miami, Atlanta, Denver, San Antonio, Houston, Dallas, New York). These increases seem related to lower birthrates and aging of traditional populations and the explosion of numbers, immigration, and birthrates in minority populations (Cisneros, 1988, August 28; 1988, September; Lufkin, 1988, August 23). Thus, family therapists will likely treat greater numbers of minority families in the coming decades.

THE TIMES THEY ARE A'CHANGING – FOR BETTER AND WORSE

These demographic changes will be compounded by economic, social, and political trends which profoundly influence the lives of these families.

For example, the economic life of minority families has undergone dramatic changes. In 1985, the top 20% of Americans earned 43% of the national income, the largest percentage earned by this group since World War II. The bottom 20% earned 4.7% of the national income, the smallest percentage in 25 years (Cisneros, 1988, August 28). In 1987, 32.5 million Americans, both minority and non-minority, lived below the poverty line ($11,600 for a family of four). During that year the proportion of White Americans living in poverty declined while the proportion of Black and Latinos increased. In 1986, 8.98 million Blacks lived in poverty; in 1987 the number rose to 9.68 million. The numbers also rose for Latinos during that year – 5.11 million in 1986 to 5.47 million in 1987 (Tolchin, 1988, September 1). Of American children under the age of 18 who live in poverty, 43% are Black and 37% are Latino. Nearly one in three Black children is without a working parent. In 1987, total federal spending for public assistance programs (e.g., welfare, housing, food stamps, Medicaid) had grown 800% ($85 billion) since 1970. Nearly 2.6 million Black adults currently receive some form of welfare. In 1985, 10% of Black females (15-19 years old) had children compared to 4% of White teens (Cisneros, 1988, August 28; Futrell, 1988; Ralston & Hollister, 1988, Spring). In contrast to these troubling economic trends, some positive changes are occurring. For example, an increasing number of Blacks, Latinos, and Asians are entering the middle class (Robotham, 1988, Spring; Sellers, 1988, September). Given the profound impact of economics on families, clinicians will need to consider class as a critical dimension in their therapy.

Therapists are keenly aware of the importance of education as a key to a family's options in society. The current state of education of minorities is as complex as the financial picture. For example, education in inner city schools (with high minority enrollment) is in trouble; the national drop-out rate is 7%. In some ghettos, the drop-out rate reaches frightening dimensions (e.g., Detroit's 81%). Blacks in college represented 34% of the student body in 1976; in 1986 the number has dropped to 29%. The college drop-out rate among Blacks is twice that of Whites. School performance for recent Latino (e.g., Central American) and Asian (e.g., Southeast Asian) immigrants is handicapped by language barriers. However, these two groups are the only ones who have increased their number in public schools. Whites and Blacks have decreased in numbers (Coro, 1988, September).

Minorities vary in how healthy they are when compared to Whites and to each other. Blacks, Latinos, Native Americans, and Native Hawaiians trail the health statistics of Whites by decades. For example, in 1983 the life expectancy for Whites reached 75.2 years. The life expectancy for Blacks in that year was 69.6 years which matched the life expectancy for Whites in the early 1950s. Presently, infant mortality in Blacks is twice that of Whites and at a level similar to White deaths in 1960. While in aggregate, Asians and Pacific Islanders tend to be healthier than all others in the United States, including Whites, group statistics can be misleading. For example, as a group they have a greater life expectancy than Whites. However, there are specific diseases for which they are at higher risk and significant subgroups for which national data is inadequate (e.g., Southeast Asians and other recent immigrants) (Heckler, 1985).

Drug and alcohol abuse is a much greater problem among Blacks, Latinos and Native Americans than Whites; diseases and deaths related to these problems are similarly higher. Blacks represented 44% of the murder victims in the United States in 1986. Suicide rates among the Native Americans are 20% greater than the general population. Native Americans also have the highest rate of death from unintentional injuries or "accidents." Chinese women have a higher suicide rate compared to White women (Heckler, 1985; Ralston & Hollister, 1988, Spring). With increasing health costs, the epidemic of AIDS, the rise of homelessness, and the lack of a National Health Program, the health of some minorities will continue to suffer.

Perhaps the most compelling positive trend for minorities has occurred in the political arena. At the 1964 Democratic convention, considerable controversy arose about seating the Mississippi Freedom Democratic Party. This party was formed to challenge Mississippi's regular Democratic party which, in practice, excluded Blacks. Twenty-four years later, a Black man headed the Mississippi delegation to the 1988 Democratic convention. In fact, Mississippi is the only state whose Democratic party is led by a Black, Ed Cole. During the 1988 presidential campaign, the Reverend Jesse Jackson became a major contender for the Democratic party's nomination. For the first time in the nation's history, there are 23 Black members of the United States Congress and 303 Black mayors. Presently, there are eight Latino members of Congress (i.e., one Puerto Rican and seven Mexican). An increasing number of Latinos are mayors of major cities (e.g., Henry Cisneros [San Antonio], Federico Pena [Denver] and Xavier Suarez [Miami]).

This brief "minority" glimpse of the State of the Union yields a complex picture. While we can identify certain positive trends, we must consider others quite disturbing. The conservative agenda during the last decade has dismantled many of the foundational programs which facilitated the advancement of all minorities. Compared to 20 years ago, the vision of equal opportunity is both closer for some and further for others. On the threshold of the 21st century, we risk becoming a country of "haves" and "have nots."

In light of these current trends, family therapists will encounter considerable complexity in the minority families they treat. For example, a Cuban-American middle class family in Miami will be both different and similar to a non-documented family from El Salvador in Los Angeles. Stereotypes will fit less well than before. Generalizations and comparisons will need to be done with care.

A ROSE BY ANY OTHER NAME
MAY SMELL EVEN SWEETER

As we know, our words used to describe people both reflect how we think about them and influence how we treat them. The term "minority" deserves attention, since we employ it to describe millions of people.

The word "minority" can conjure up the notion that "there are fewer of them than us, and hence we need to pay them less attention." However, as the percentage of Blacks, Latinos, Asians, Pacific Islanders, and Native Americans increase, the statistical aspect of "minority" becomes less valid.

In addition, the word permits us to ignore the differences, the similarities, and the humanness of the people we wish to describe. Perhaps one of the most oppressive features of this description is that it can encourage a poor self image. Malcolm X reflected, "By thinking we're a minority, we struggle like a minority, we struggle like we're an underdog. We struggle like all the odds are against us. This type of struggle takes place only because we don't yet know where we fit into the scheme of things" (X, 1965, p. 117).

As an alternative descriptor to "minority," Meyers (1984) suggests the use of "oppressed groups." This definition addresses the destructive impact of poverty, lack of education, and institutional racism that minority families experience. The term "minority," for most of us, fails to communicate the experience that oppression connotes, thus allowing us to more easily ignore our social responsibilities. The term "oppressed group" seems preferable since it encourages one to examine the interactional relationship between the oppressor and the oppressed and the context in which it occurs.

However, focusing on oppression may also organize us to view minorities in a limited way, and keep us from understanding the "something else" about minority families. The "something else" refers to the strengths, legacies, values, history, accomplishments, and wisdom these families show as they struggle to adapt. We rarely celebrate these positive aspects. Despite our best intentions, we often narrowly define minority families.

Nonetheless, we must push beyond limited and/or degrading stereotypes. The images of Charlie Chan and the Dragon Lady need to be replaced by Ellison Onizuka and Maxine Hong Kingston. Aunt Jemima and Stepp'nfetchit need to be buried by Maya Angelou and the Reverend Dr. Martin Luther King, Jr. The genius and courage of Manuela Saenz, who helped Simon Bolivar liberate six Latin American countries, need to erase the forced subjugation of La Malinche, a concubine of Hernan Cortez. The leadership of Chief Joseph and the pottery of Nampeyo must be substituted for the subservience of Tonto and the songs of Hiawatha.

To better describe "minority" families, we need a multifaceted definition which would capture the neglected "something else." Unfortunately, we are unable to suggest an alternate term. A single word seems inadequate. Thus, we will, reluctantly, use the word "minority" throughout this collection. However, we ask that it triggers the reader to think broadly, complexly and humanly. Similarly, we hope therapists who think in rich and varied ways will see "minority" families with fresh eyes and a multidimensional approach.

EPISTEMOLOGIC BLINDSPOTS

Family therapists are both guided and handicapped by their epistemologies. The dominant epistemology in society (i.e., dualism) encourages us to develop blindspots to and or discount unacceptable phenomena. Even when our intentions are otherwise, our epistemology can still trick us into familiar patterns.

For example, a recent special issue of *Life* magazine (1988, Spring) examined the state of affairs in Black America since the early 1960s. The editors tried to avoid dealing with Blacks according to stereotypes. One can see by looking at the front cover that their good intentions became derailed quite early. The top half displays a compelling picture of Martin Luther King. Below are six photos: a little girl, an L.A. Laker, Jesse Jackson, a ballerina, and a Navy seaman. While clearly these people are remarkable, they nearly all fit stereotypes of Blacks: an athlete, a preacher, a dancer, and a military man. "Something else" was missing (e.g., pictures of doctors, lawyers, teachers, astronauts, and business owners).

The contemporary epistemologies in the family therapy field have discouraged significant attention to minority studies (Hardy,

1989). For example, the family therapy field has successfully de-emphasized the issues of oppression both with women and minorities (Goldner, 1985; Taggert, 1985; Saba, 1984, November-December).

This neglect may reflect a spirit of dualism operative in our society and in our professional work. Hodge, Struckman, and Trost (1975) suggest that oppression is epistemologically based in the dualistic tradition. For example, Plato, a foundational contributor to dualism, believed that one could find the highest form of knowledge in the intelligible world. A person could obtain this knowledge through intelligence and pure thought. A lower form of knowledge related to the physical world which consisted of physical things, shadows, images, and sense perception.

In the third century, the religious leader Mani bolstered Platonic dualism. He preached that the world consisted of two opposing forces: good and evil, or Light and Dark. The Light is to be victorious, while the Dark captured and confined.

Early Christianity and Western European civilization incorporated such dualistic thinking. From Augustine to Freud, dualistic leaders helped shape an epistemology that valued certain qualities of life which included lightness, good, mind, ideas, intellect, and science. The less desired qualities included darkness, evil, body, emotions, intuition, passions, and nature. Out of this tradition, a hierarchy evolved in which the good, enlightened, intellectuals were to control the evil, darker, emotional ones.

As this epistemology took root, White European males moved to the top of the hierarchy, while women and people of color were subjugated to the bottom. Men were encouraged to negate emotions, "evil" thoughts, and physical labor; to live in the world of ideas; and to assert authority. Women and people of color became identified with sex, physicality, stupidity, irrationality, and craziness; they were to be dominated and controlled. Racism, sexism, colonialism and imperialism in Western societies are aspects of this group oppression which have been deemed necessary in order to control evil (Hodge, 1975).

In the family therapy field, the feminists have critiqued the prevailing epistemology. Recently, some have challenged family therapy's descriptions of abuse and domestic violence which can lead one to think the victim asks for and/or enjoys the abusive situation (Goldner, 1985, 1987, 1988; Luepnitz, 1988; Taggart, 1985; Ault-Riché, 1987; Goodrich, Rampage, Ellman, & Halstead, 1987; Hare-Mustin, 1978, 1987).

Similarly, a contextual cybernetics can be employed to erase the notion of oppression and its effects on minority families. From a cybernetic perspective, a complementary relationship (between oppressed and oppressor) would suggest that the participants are equally locked in a mutually reinforcing pattern. "Oppression" becomes a linear, problematic myth that evaporates when one perceives an equal involvement of the perpetrator and victim. What we miss in this description is the experience of each of the people in this relationship, and the options that each has in starting, maintaining, and escaping the cycle of oppression.

An example of the risks one faces by ignoring broader contexts when applying cybernetics involves Gregory Bateson's challenge to the notion of power. From his perspective, power is a troublesome construct that should be discarded. He tried to poke holes in the widely held belief that Goebbels, Hitler's minister of propaganda, was an extremely powerful person in Nazi Germany. Bateson reports that Goebbels had spies who continually ascertained what the German people thought of his ideas. If he discovered that they did not support his policies, he would change them (Bateson, 1972; Luepnitz, 1988). While this recursive loop of communication explains a part of the political process, one must wonder if his spies polled any of the Jews, Catholics, gays and others in the concentration camps for their opinions.

One may also neglect minority needs by applying concepts of constructivism (Watzlawick, 1984) out of context. To consider that one's reality is solely related to one's perceptions can lead clinicians to assume minority families "construct" poverty, injustice, slavery, and violence. Dr. King's "dream" takes on a different meaning, if one assumes oppression is the fruit of fantasy.

While a systems framework provides a view that can lead to cooperation, shared power, and equality, we are far from having clinical theories that address sexism, racism and oppression. Perhaps, our lingering dualistic desire to have parsimonious, scientific explanations of behavior has encouraged the field of family therapy to ignore passion, violence, hatred, and discrimination. As we have seen, a dualistic perspective would advocate that these qualities should be overcome and discounted. Unfortunately, we cannot "think" away the tragedy that exists. We will need to be careful to avoid epistemologic fiddling while Rome burns, or perhaps Harlem and East L.A.

To move beyond this epistemologic impasse, we will need to incorporate such valuable notions of cybernetics, constructivism and systems into a broader canvas that includes an appreciation for context, a sense of history, a clarification of values, an understanding of politics, and the complexity of societal emotions.

It is perhaps in a *contextual* definition of oppression that the use of the word "minority" is most relevant. That is, while minority families do participate in their oppression they are a lesser and unequal participant, a minority, in altering the pattern (Luepnitz, 1988).

OUT OF SIGHT, OUT OF MIND

Our clinical contexts may also lead us to making errors of omission. For instance, as less money is available for reimbursing therapy with the poor, clinicians will economically be forced to see more middle and upper class families and perhaps fewer minorities. The conclusions one draws about family functioning, problems, and avenues for change will relate more to this selected population. We must exercise caution when generalizing to minority families.

PURPOSE OF THIS COLLECTION

As we have seen, family therapists will face new challenges in caring for minority families. Given the changing demographics, the social trends, the political conservatism, the epistemologic development of the family therapy field, and our contexts of practice, we may benefit from a fresh look at minority families.

This collection represents our attempt to share the work of experienced, sensitive clinicians who along with minority families have found creative solutions to the problems they present. The collection is written for the clinician and the student of therapy interested in working with such families.

ORGANIZATION AND CONTENT

Much of the sparse literature addressing family therapy with minorities has focused on the unique characteristics of these families as a means of enhancing the effectiveness of treatment. Ken Hardy abandons this traditional approach as he examines the seldom explored territory of the "world view" of the therapist as it is shaped through the structure and process of most family therapy training programs. Family therapy with minorities is often overshadowed by an epistemological view that is based on the notion that all families are the same; a view that is reified through the various components of family therapy training programs, professional organizations, and clinical practice. Several recommendations are provided for creating a new epistemology for working with minority families.

Many minority families often feel the world misunderstands them. Therapists are at risk of furthering the misunderstanding since they view the families' problems through very personal lenses. Through clinical vignettes and folk stories, Braulio Montalvo and Manuel Gutierrez suggest assumptions therapists can adopt to promote understanding and to improve care.

The strengths of minority families are often ignored by family therapists, particularly when these "strengths" deviate from what is considered "normative" by the larger society. Nancy Boyd-Franklin discusses the strengths of Black families and recommends five key concepts for working effectively with these families.

Terry Tafoya expands our views by introducing us to the rich, inner life of Native Americans. His stories, metaphors, and rituals are creative, clinical approaches that not only fit this population, but that will undoubtedly enrich your clinical practice with all families.

An increasing number of Chinese are emigrating to the United States. Evelyn Lee provides a cogent guide to understanding the similarities and differences in assimilation of these immigrants. She also provides specific assessment and treatment techniques for caring for the most recent of these arrivals.

Yvette Flores-Ortiz and Guillermo Bernal review the relevant empirical studies of Latino drug addicts and their families. They adopt a multiple context view of drug addiction which highlights intra-familial and external losses and intergenerational legacies. Their treatment approach, based on the Contextual Family Therapy Model (Boszormenyi-Nagy), is presented as a culturally sensitive treatment approach for Latino families. They view the strong sense of family interdependence that these families have not only as a strength, but as essential in the process of therapy and in overcoming drug addiction.

AIDS has tragically robbed us of many individuals, affecting families and communities. Blacks and Latinos bear a heavy burden in this epidemic. Mindy Fullilove, Robert Fullilove III, and Edward Morales present an exciting psychoeducational program designed to promote family and community behaviors aimed at curbing the spread of this disease.

Family therapy treatment models are often described as embracing the views of the White middle class. Paulette Hines, Deborah Richman, Karen Maxim, and Hillary Hays present a model of family therapy for working with a clinical population that they describe as suffering from triple jeopardy . . . "economically poor, politically weak, and discriminated against because of race." A detailed description of the model (which combines sensitivity, intensity, comprehensiveness and reality), its application, and case examples are presented.

Many minority poor families turn to health care settings for mental health care. In addition, increasing numbers of physicians are providing therapy. More family therapists are also working in health settings. These well-intentioned health care providers may unwittingly discriminate against the families they are attempting to heal. Through examining lessons from clinical practice, George Saba and Denise Rodgers describe pitfalls of discrimination and strategies to avoid them.

In the last chapter, Betty Karrer presents a multidimensional model for examining the interconnectedness between the culture of the minority family and that of the therapist. Through a critical review of the evolution of family therapy, she challenges therapists to adopt a relativistic perspective that considers the many contextual dimensions of values. The model, and its illustrations, have the potential for transforming the world views of the therapists who work with multicultural families.

As one can see, this collection attempts to provide a glimpse at the diversity of clinical work which currently occurs with various minority groups and from different clinical perspectives.

While we address a variety of issues in this collection, our scope has been limited by constraints of space. We recognize that there are many other minority families who have emigrated to the United States from the Third World (e.g., Indians, Arabs, Ethiopians) and Europe (e.g., Jews, Poles, Irish, Italians). They too have faced discrimination, oppression and prejudice and possess that "something else." Unfortunately, we are unable to present the special needs of all ethnic and racial minorities. In addition, we focused only on ethnic and racial minorities and did not include similar oppressed people such as women, gays and lesbians, and the handicapped. Clearly, there is a great deal of work yet to be done. We hope our collection will be another small step to alerting clinicians to the special needs of these families.

Throughout this effort, we have been concerned how the reader might perceive a focus on a specific clinical population (e.g., minority families). Historically, two reactions have emerged. On the one hand, one may argue that all families face adversity and that general theories of family functioning and treatment are sufficient to care for specific groups. Overfocusing on a particular population can risk reductionism, require therapists to accumulate considerable specialized knowledge, and hamper good care. On the other hand, one may consider existing knowledge inadequate to address the uniqueness of such families. Considerable harm could result from a wholesale application of generic models of treatment to specific groups of families. A fresh look is needed and special information supercedes existing skills.

We have attempted to address these concerns by shunning the urge to present generic discussion of "Black families," "Latino families," "Asian families," etc. . . . . Rather, we recruited clinicians who could present their work in a way that captured the similarities and differences between minority and non-minority families. In fact, many of the papers discuss the very issue of the danger of assuming minority families are like all families or that they are different. In this collection, we hope to provide information about working with all families, as well as, specific strategies for treating minority families. We will have failed if this work becomes pigeon-holed as "another cross-cultural" effort.

As you begin to read the following stories, let us now end by returning to our beginning:

> And, as I said before, a decision has been made. I'm shaking off the old skin and I'll leave it here in the hole. I'm coming out, no less invisible without it, but coming out nevertheless. And I suppose it's damn well time. Even hibernations can be overdone, come to think of it. Perhaps that's my greatest social crime, I've over-stayed my hibernation, since there's a possibility that even an invisible man has a socially responsible role to play. (Ellison, 1947, p. 568)

This collection hopes to encourage a "shaking off of the old skin," i.e., attitudes, beliefs, stereotypes and those clinical approaches that view minority families in limited ways. Perhaps under the old skin a "coming out" awaits us all, because whether "visible or invisible, we all have responsible roles to play."

REFERENCES

Ault-Riché, M. (Ed.). (1986). *Women and family therapy*. Rockville, MD: Aspen Systems Corp.

Bateson, G. (1972). *Steps to an ecology of mind*. New York: Ballantine.

Cisneros, H. (1988, August 28). The changing complexion of America's future. *San Francisco Chronicle*, p. B-1.

Cisneros, H. (1988, September). A new day for Hispanics. *The World & I*, pp. 69-72.

Coro, A. (1988, September). The new bilingual education. *The World & I*, pp. 38-45.

Ellison, R. (1947). *Invisible man*. New York: Vintage Books.

Ellison, R. (1967, March). A very stern discipline. *Harper's Magazine*, pp. 76-95.

Falicov, C. J. (Ed.). (1983). *Cultural perspectives in family therapy*. Rockville, MD: Aspen Systems Corp.

Futrell, M. (1988). *Minorities and education.* A paper presented at the 25th Anniversary of the March on Washington, Washington, DC, August 27.

Goldner, V. (1985). Feminism and family therapy. *Family Process, 24,* 31-47.

Goldner, V. (1987). Instrumentalism, feminism and the limits of family therapy. *Journal of Family Psychology, 1*(1), 109-16.

Goldner, V. (1988). Generation and gender: Normative and covert hierarchies. *Family Process, 27,* 17-31.

Goodrich, T. J., Rampage, C., Ellman, B., & Halstead, K. (1988). *Feminist family therapy: A casebook.* New York: W. W. Norton & Company.

Hardy, K. V. (1989). The theoretical myth of sameness: A critical issue in family treatment and training. In G. W. Saba, B. M. Karrer, & K. V. Hardy (Eds.), *Minorities and family therapy,* New York: Haworth Press.

Hare-Mustin, R. (1978). A feminist approach to family therapy. *Family Process, 17,* 181-94.

Hare-Mustin, R. (1987). The problem of gender in family therapy. *Family Process, 26,* 15-27.

Heckler, M. (1985). *Report of the Secretary's task force on Black and minority health.* Washington, DC: U.S. Department of Health and Human Services.

Ho, Man Keung. (1987). *Family therapy with ethnic minorities.* Newbury Park, CA: Sage Publications.

Hodge, J. L., Struckman, D. K., & Trost, L. D. *Cultural bases of racism and group oppression.* Berkeley, CA: Two Riders Press.

Luepnitz, D. A. (1988). *The family interpreted: Feminist theory in clinical practice.* New York: Basic Books.

Lufkin, L. (1988, August 23). How we'll live in the 90's: Minorities in the majority. *San Francisco Chronicle,* p. B-3.

Meyers, B. (1984). Minority group: An ideological formulation. *Social Problems, 32*(1), 1-15.

McGoldrick, M., Pearce, J., & Giordano, J. (Eds.). (1982). *Ethnicity and family therapy.* New York: Guilford Press.

Ralston, J., & Hollister, A. (1988, Spring). No relief. *Life,* pp. 78-82.

Robotham, R. (1988, Spring). A growing middle class is keeping faith in America. *Life,* pp. 46-50.

Saba, G. W. (1984, November-December). On gender and color blindspots in family therapy. *Family Therapy News,* p. 5.

Sellers, J. (1988, September). Economic power and problems. *The World & I,* pp. 28-37.

Taggart, M. (1985). The feminist critique in epistemological perspective: Questions of context in family therapy. *Journal of Marital and Family Therapy, 11,* 113-26.

Tolchin, M. (1988, September 1). Minority poverty on the rise even as White poor decrease in U.S. *The New York Times,* p. A-11.

Watzlawick, P. (Ed.). (1984). *The invented reality: How do we know what we believe we know? Contribution to constructivism.* New York: W. W. Norton & Company.

X, M. (1965). *Malcolm X speaks.* New York: Grove.

The Theoretical Myth of Sameness: A Critical Issue in Family Therapy Training and Treatment

Kenneth V. Hardy

Historically, the topics of race, culture, ethnicity, and gender have received scant attention in the psychotherapy literature. Even family therapy, with its emphasis on systems theory and the importance of understanding "the family in its context," also has been virtually inattentive to these issues. Taggart (1985), Hare-Mustin (1978), Rampage (1988), and Myers-Avis (1985, 1986) have written critiques regarding the impact of gender bias on family therapy theory and practice. The "feminist critique of family therapy" has not only resulted in a dramatic increase in the attention given to gender in family therapy literature, theory and practice, but has also challenged the field to re-examine traditionally held assumptions and suppositions regarding systemic theory and practice vis-à-vis women's issues.

While gender-related issues have begun to receive more attention in the family therapy field, little has changed in the case of minorities. Race, culture, and ethnicity still have not been fully incorporated into mainstream family therapy literature. Moreover, it is commonplace for family therapists to commence, maintain, and terminate treatment without having the slightest appreciation, knowledge, or respect for the larger contextual issues (e.g., race, culture, gender, ethnicity) that subsequently impact treatment. This over-

Kenneth V. Hardy, PhD, is Executive Director, Commission on Accreditation for Marriage and Family Therapy Training and Education, American Association of Marriage and Family Therapy; and is in private practice in Washington, DC.

17

sight often results in a process that I refer to as the "neglect of context."

The "neglect of context" is not relegated to the therapist-family relationship, but it is replete throughout the field of family therapy. Consequently, the lack of attention paid to minorities within the clinical arena parallels the lack of attention devoted to minorities throughout family therapy training programs, professional organizations, and practice. The "neglect of context" and the proclivity towards promoting sameness is a systemic issue that pervades the family therapy field.

Family therapy, despite emphasizing a systems epistemology, has embraced a rather narrow, if not lineal, view of systems theory with regard to the treatment of minorities. Efforts to engage and treat minorities in family therapy are done so repeatedly without regard for the larger context within which these families exist. This oversight is often exacerbated by the fact that many family therapy trainees have not been prepared adequately for clinical work with minority families.

Family therapy training programs have disregarded the importance of the training context. The disregard for the importance of context is often subtle, inadvertent, and pervasive, making it difficult to detect or rectify.

THEORETICAL MYTH OF SAMENESS

The relative inattention to the contextual importance of family therapy training has resulted in a universally monolithic model of training. Most family therapy programs subscribe to and reinforce a model of training that is based on a "theoretical myth of sameness." The theoretical myth of sameness (TMOS) is a belief system or "way of thinking" that is based on the notion that all families are virtually the same.

The TMOS asserts that "becoming a family therapist" requires one to become conversant with the rudimentary aspects of family functioning and a wide armamentarium of clinical interventions. Although somewhat overstated, this view postulates that once one has a firm grasp of family therapy theory and techniques, one is imminently prepared to treat "families" . . . since all families are virtually the same. Although the TMOS is rarely discussed in class lectures, or in supervisory sessions, it transcends every dimension of the training program. The "way of thinking" that is promoted by the TMOS becomes the major theoretical framework from which most family therapy with minority families is approached.

THE MYTH OF SAMENESS AS A WORLD VIEW

The TMOS is the epistemological foundation for practically all family therapy training and practice. It represents a "world view" that reinforces widely held conceptualizations about minority family functioning, and influences clinical practice with minority families. The TMOS as a world view influences how training programs are organized, what is ultimately taught, and by whom. Administrative decisions regarding faculty teaching assignments, committee appointments, and academic advisement are greatly influenced by the theoretical myth of sameness. Clinically, decisions regarding case assignments, treatment strategies, who gets invited to therapy sessions, the type of questions asked, and the use of negative and positive connotations are all governed by the TMOS.

Family therapists describing themselves by the family therapy model with which they identify, such as "structuralist," "systemic," etc., tend to embrace the TMOS as meta-model. Efforts to remain pure to the model of family therapy that one has been trained to do, or what one believes to be effective, is undoubtedly influenced by the TMOS.

The TMOS as a world view, is manifested in one of two predominant ideologies: the conventional and the contemporary. The conventional view is represented in much of the traditional literature addressing minority issues. The contemporary view, on the other hand, has emerged in reaction to the conventional view. Each of these views represents different sides of the same issue.

THE THEORETICAL MYTH OF SAMENESS:
A CONVENTIONAL VIEW

Conventional ideology regarding the TMOS asserts that minority families are no different than non-minority families. This view posits that "families are families" and emphasizing differences serves to construct differences where they don't exist. In terms of family therapy education, programs adopting this view emphasize the importance of theory comprehension and skill acquisition without punctuating differences that might be attributable to race, culture, ethnicity, and/or gender.

The majority of family therapy training programs has adopted the conventional view of the TMOS. These programs are extremely dedicated to training and producing well-trained competent family therapists, but do so in a milieu that fails to devote more than cursory attention to the importance of differences. The implicit message conveyed is, "if you understand the complexities of family theory and use this understanding as the basis for your clinical interventions . . . you will be a competent therapist, because all families are basically the same." Hence, the accentuation and appreciation of differences and the role of the therapist's use of self, are critical training issues that remain tangential to the core of family therapy training.

THE THEORETICAL MYTH OF SAMENESS: A CONTEMPORARY VIEW

The contemporary view is espoused by many, although not exclusively, minority family therapists and asserts that all families are not the same. This view is critical of the conventional view for understating the differences that exist between minority and non-minority families. Proponents of this view have played an instrumental role enlightening the family therapy community regarding the subtle and not-so-subtle differences existing between minority and non-minority families. For the first time in recent history of the field, the emergence of this view is encouraging family therapy trainees and educators alike to question, if not challenge, the assertion that all families are the same. The widespread use of McGoldrick's et al., *Ethnicity and Family Therapy* in many family therapy training programs, in one sense, has begun to revolutionize our thinking about the influences of differences in clinical practice.

The shift from the conventional to contemporary view of the TMOS represents a change of the first order. While the contemporary view has undoubtedly sharpened our sensitivity regarding differences, it has concomitantly perpetuated the TMOS by the relative inattention given to differences that exist among minority groups. Minorities are often described as if they were monolithic (e.g., Hispanics, Asians, etc.). Rarely, does this view attempt to examine the differences *within* minority groups that are attributable to geography and socio-economics, for example.

The *Ethnicity and Family Therapy* text, despite numerous disclaimers throughout the text, has become the widely accepted recipe in clinical training programs for "how to" treat specific ethnic minority families. Fortunately, the presence of the text calls into question the theoretical myth of sameness by emphasizing the importance of recognizing differences that might be attributable of one's ethnic identity. Unfortunately, the misuse of the text perpetrates the TMOS by generalizing the level of "sameness" that might exist among families sharing a common ethnic/racial background.

The recent proliferation of articles, books, seminars, and workshops on special topic areas such as "Family Therapy with Black Families," "Feminist Family Therapy," "Structural Family Therapy with Latin American Families," etc., has made major contributions to the field. These topic areas are critically important because they have served to "dehomogenize" family therapy at one level, while simultaneously providing a much needed clinical and theoretical supplement to most family therapy training programs. Unless special topic areas give acute attention to the differences that exist within any one group, be it women, gays or lesbians, or ethnic minorities, the inevitable consequence is a perpetuation of the epistemological error (TMOS) for which these areas have been designed to rectify. Can there be a family therapy model that is effective for and applicable to *all* Hispanics? Is it possible for feminist family therapy to address the needs of all women given the vast number of gender-related permutations that may be a function of the interaction between race, ethnicity, religion, social class, etc.? Can we assume that a given technique or therapeutic principle that applies to *this* Hispanic family or *this* woman can be applied globally to all Hispanics or women?

Although these special topics serve a viable function for a field that is rigidly oriented toward sameness, extreme caution must be exercised to ensure that they do not perpetuate the TMOS (Contemporary View) by ignoring "within group" differences.

ON SAMENESS AND DIFFERENCE

The conventional and contemporary views represent divergent manifestations of the TMOS. Both views insist on the dichotomization of sameness and difference, failing to recognize the interrelationship between the two concepts. As the family therapy field continues to grapple with how it can become more sensitive to minority issues, the question that unfortunately gets asked most frequently, is not the question to be answered. The question, "Are minority families different or the same as all other families?" merely reinforces the type of thinking that perpetuates the TMOS. Perhaps, the more appropriate, although seldom asked question should be: In what ways are minority and non-minority families different *and* similar? The question is not one regarding difference *or* sameness, but rather difference *and* sameness.

FAMILY THERAPY TRAINING

As far as the clinical treatment of minorities is concerned, if the family therapy field were a family, by most family therapy standards, it would deserve the label "dysfunctional family." The treatment of minorities is often characterized by rigidity, ambiguous communication patterns and mixed messages, fusion and lack of respect for differences, scapegoating, and failed and attempted solutions that exacerbate the problems for which they have been designed to resolve. The "system" that regulates the clinical treatment of minorities in the larger society is the vast number of family therapy training programs. In a sense, these programs assume an instrumental role in determining "how well" or "how poorly" families will be treated clinically. In the case of treating minority families, both the content and the context of the therapist's training are critical intervening variables.

Most clinical programs, including psychology, counseling, family therapy, psychiatry, and social work (to a lesser degree) are remiss in training aspiring clinicians to work effectively with minority families. The focus of this paper will be limited to family therapy, albeit the other disciplines have not made significant strides regarding clinical preparation for working with minorities either. The neglect of context with respect to family therapy treatment and training promotes the TMOS. Student and faculty compositions, curricular designs, and exposure to skewed clinical populations become the major subsystems within the field that facilitate the maintenance and perpetuation of the TMOS.

Student Composition

The overwhelming majority of family therapy programs are comprised of a racially, ethnically, and culturally homogenous student body. Students enrolled in family therapy programs are thus denied an opportunity to train and associate with peers whose life circumstances are vastly different in scope, meaning, and context. The opportunity to learn informally through interactions with peers from diverse cultural, ethnic, and racial backgrounds is virtually nonexistent in most family therapy programs.

In the few instances where the student body is comprised of minority students, the number is very small, rarely more than one. Flores (1979), a Chicano, noted that despite attending graduate school in southern California, only a "handful" of his several hundred classmates were Latinos, many of whom did not speak Spanish. The subtle pressures that the minority student encounters to "be like his/her classmates" often translates into the message: "to survive is to be the same." Consequently, the experiential, philosophical, and ideological diversity that they can add to a training program, is frequently suppressed by perceived and "real" forces to be the same as other students. The homogenous student body promotes a belief system or world view that is rigidly oriented toward a myth of sameness.

Faculty Composition

The faculty of most family therapy training programs are predominantly white and male, thus affirming the theoretical myth of sameness. Since many of these individuals were trained in settings that were isomorphic to the programs in which they now serve as faculty, rarely are old ideas and beliefs challenged.

When minorities join the faculty of family therapy training programs, they too reify the theoretical myth of sameness. Frequently, their teaching assignments are limited to teaching courses related to ethnic minority and cross cultural issues. Understandably, the decision to teach these courses is often with the approval of the faculty member. However, recruiting minorities to teach minority-related content, only reinforces the TMOS. The theoretical myth of sameness is further validated by the fact that the minority faculty member has probably had no formal training in ethnic minority or cross cultural studies. These faculty are often considered qualified to teach such courses on the basis of their membership in a specific minority group. The implicit messages embedded in situations of this type are considered "truth" and remain largely unchallenged.

Programs that hire minority faculty based on these assumptions or similar ones, should recognize the consequences embedded in such faulty logic. Enhancing the ethnic and cultural heterogeneity of family therapy training faculty can enrich the program in multitudinous ways. To do so, however, the roles and tasks assigned to minority faculty must extend beyond those activities that merely serve to perpetuate the TMOS.

Curriculum Design

As noted earlier, most family therapy training programs perpetuate the TMOS by limiting students' exposure to didactic coursework that focuses chiefly on the rudimentary aspects of family therapy theory and practice. Much of this coursework tends to fall short of exploring differences and similarities that may be attributable to race, culture, ethnicity, and/or religion. When minority-related content is taught, it is done so in a way that lends continued credence to the theoretical myth of sameness. Minority families are often described as homogenous entities (e.g. "Hispanics," "Asians," etc.).

The theoretical myth of sameness is also perpetuated through the academic requirements promoted by family therapy licensing and certification laws, and by national voluntary credentialing organizations such as the American Association for Marriage and Family

Therapy (AAMFT) and the Commission on Accreditation for Marriage and Family Therapy Education (COAMFTE).

There are currently 18 states with marriage and family therapy licensing or certification laws; of these, only California requires coursework in cross cultural studies. The educational requirements for the remaining 17 states reinforce the training model that most family therapists have been exposed to previously: that is, one that promotes a TMOS. Hopefully, the curriculum requirements from the California law will serve as a model and have a profound influence over other state laws.

AAMFT's standards for clinical membership are recognized frequently as rigorous and substantially equivalent to the educational requirements mandated by many family therapy state laws. These standards, unfortunately, have become the model by which many laws, particularly the educational requirements, have been developed. Both sets of standards reinforce the other and simultaneously validate the theoretical myth of sameness.

Similarly, training programs seeking accreditation by the Commission on Accreditation for Marriage and Family Therapy Education are not required to offer coursework addressing minority or cross cultural issues. Fortunately, the revised accreditation standards will require programs "to demonstrate that ethnicity and gender are taught throughout the entire curriculum or that there are two separate courses offered addressing these issues" (*Manual on Accreditation*, 1988). The inclusion of this standard is a major step for the family therapy field and for the treatment of minority families.

The student and faculty composition, and the design of the curriculum, are the major areas of family therapy training programs that perpetuate the theoretical myth of sameness. The training context where many trainees learn about family therapy and conduct their practica, embraces the theoretical myth of sameness and is oblivious to the critical issues of "difference" and "sameness." The perpetual and systemic transmission of the theoretical myth of sameness is reasonably guaranteed since many of these trainees, particularly at the doctoral level, later become key faculty members and supervisors in family therapy training programs. The cycle of family therapists who are poorly trained for treating minority families, and who in turn, train a new generation of poorly trained family therapists (for treating minority families) continues in perpetuity. Meanwhile, minority families continue to be underserved and labeled resistant and recalcitrant.

As pointed out earlier, the theoretical myth of sameness is not unique to family therapy training programs; instead, it permeates the field of family therapy. Professional family organizations (e.g., the American Association for Marriage and Family Therapy, the American Family Therapy Association, and the National Council on Family Relations) are homeostatic mechanisms for ensuring that the field maintains its current structure and function vis-à-vis minorities. As in the case of training programs, the theoretical myth of sameness is reified in these organizations by the dearth of ethnic and racial diversity that is commonplace throughout their membership, staff, and policy-making bodies.

Minorities participating in such organizations are very likely to be the same individuals who were the sole minority students in family therapy training programs. Their participation represents "more of the same" in two significant ways: (1) the perceived and "real" pressure to be "the same as other members" is as intense as a professional as it was as a student. This, feigning "sameness", ensures continued participation while "difference" is covertly discouraged. (2) Minority members are often assigned to committees, task forces, workshops, etc. that address minority issues. Admittedly, some minority members welcome the opportunity and challenge to pursue these issues of importance. The inherent danger, however, is that it nurtures the erroneous belief that it is the responsibility of the minority member only, to bring these issues into the mainstream of the organization and the field. The dearth of minority members participating in the major family organizations coupled with the nature of the participation of few who do, unfortunately, offer few discernible challenges to the theoretical myth of sameness.

CLINICAL IMPLICATIONS

The TMOS also organizes our thinking about minority families, how they function, and how therapists should be trained to treat them. The TMOS influences the type of questions that therapists ultimately ask or don't ask, who is invited to attend therapy sessions, and who are identified as potential referral sources for minority families.

Getting Stuck

Family therapists treating minority families have a proclivity towards "getting stuck." Family therapy with minority families is impeded frequently by the multitude of erroneous theoretical underpinnings that shape the clinical work of therapists. Most therapists, minority and non-minority, are ill-prepared to work effectively with minority clients. The clinical work of these therapists is hampered by their adoption of the TMOS. For many non-minority therapists, the assessment and treatment of minority families are influenced by the former's vacillation between the conventional ("all families are the same") and contemporary ("all minority families are the same") ideological views of the TMOS. The impetus for the "shift" is the realization that the therapist's orientation towards sameness is incongruent with the client's orientation towards difference. Many clients seek therapy with the belief that their problems are unique . . . different. References in the family therapy literature to "normalizing the problem" is predicated on the assumption that most clients think their problems are different from other clients. Minority clients, influenced by a variety of non-therapy experiences in which their differences are often highlighted, overtly or covertly, tend to believe that not only are their problems different, but so are they as human beings. The world view of the minority client is in direct conflict with the world view that pervades much of the family therapy field: a conflict that inevitably results in a major clinical impasse for both therapist and client.

Minority family therapists are also prone to have their work sabotaged by the TMOS. Minority family therapists tend to over-generalize the differences that exist between minority and non-minority families while simultaneously over-generalizing the similarities that exist among minority families. The adoption of the TMOS (contemporary view) encourages the therapist to make unwarranted, often precipitous, and ill-advised assumptions about the minority family and the problem that is presented.

The operationalization of the TMOS in the clinical context results in a variety of therapeutic blindspots. The TMOS shapes our views about "what therapists should look for" as well as "what therapists ultimately see." The recursive patterns that are often characteristic of family therapy with minority families are as follows: the therapists seeks to fit the family into the model by searching for sameness, and remaining oblivious to the interrelatedness of sameness and difference, while the family searches for clues from the therapist that their differences are recognized. These patterns are recursive in that the more the therapist pushes for sameness, the more the family searches for difference, and so on . . .

Strategies and Techniques Related to the TMOS

Family therapists trained in programs that are influenced by the TMOS experience considerable difficulty engaging minority families in the "real world." Since their training is designed to provide the rudiments of family therapy techniques and theory in a world that is largely conceived as homogenous, attempts to engage minority families in therapy is often a seemingly insurmountable task. When faced with such a challenge, most family therapists do exactly what there training has taught them to do: go back to the basics . . . even if the basics have proven to be ineffectual. The undying belief in sameness, coupled with inadequate training for treating minorities, encourages the perpetual utilization of these "same" strategies and techniques even when they are contraindicated. The other alternative is to "blame the victim" by noting that the family is resistant, hard to engage, or not amenable to treatment.

Referrals and Case Assignments

The referral and assignment of minority family cases are frequently influenced by the TMOS. Minority families, whether treated in community mental health centers, private practice settings, training centers, internship and practica sites, or other clinical settings, are virtually always assigned and/or referred to minority therapists, many of whom are no better trained to treat minorities than are their non-minority counterparts. Referrals and case assignments embrace the TMOS by promoting the view that all minorities are the same, and perhaps (poorly trained) minority therapists are more effective with minority families than (poorly trained) non-minority therapists. Referrals and case assignments that are guided by the TMOS are homeostatic functions that ensure the perpetuation of a major epistemological error. (Note: This point is not intended to include situations where the minority family may request a minority therapist.)

Many minority families, are underserved clinically. These families continue to provide on-the-job training for countless numbers of family therapists. For most therapists, it is infrequent clinical experience with minorities, as well as attendance at minority-focused workshops that provide most of the formal training that becomes the bases for all of their clinical work with minorities. Until the treatment of minorities is fully explored within the larger context of the family therapy field, both therapist and family will continue to be victimized by the TMOS.

SUGGESTIONS, SOLUTIONS, RECOMMENDATIONS

It is conceivable that the theoretical myth of sameness has been beclouded by the narrowly focused discussion contained throughout this paper. Repeated references to the "number" of minority faculty or the "number" of courses addressing minority-related content are illustrative properties of the concept rather than explanative ones. The theoretical myth of sameness has little to do with a quantitative assessment of minorities' participation in any one subsystem of the family therapy field. The detrimental impact that the TMOS has on family therapy training and clinical practice can not be remediated by solely addressing the number of minorities participating in various areas of the family therapy field. Excessive preoccupation with and reliance on such "first order" solutions are ill-advised, since they frequently only serve to perpetuate the theoretical myth of sameness.

The TMOS as a concept, is not synonymous with the myriad of terms such as "stereotyping," "discrimination," or "prejudice" that are frequently used to describe interactions with minorities. As it has been previously stated, the TMOS is a way of thinking, an epistemology. It pervades the family therapy field, particularly vis-à-vis minority families. Although it has been discussed in this paper almost exclusively in the context of treating minorities, it is also applicable to the treatment of women, gays, lesbians, and other groups.

The TMOS is symptomatic of a malfunctioning system rather than an indicator of an isolated individual pathology. Any recommendations/solutions that are designed to affect a "new" way of thinking about minority families must be multidirectional and global in scope. Potential recommendations for creating a new epistemology for treating minorities include structural, curricular/experiential, and epistemological remedies.

I. Structural Remedies

A. The structure of the family therapy field reinforces the myth of sameness. Increasing the participation of women and ethnic minorities in all aspects of the field is critical. The enhancement of minority participation in the following is crucial: (1) as faculty of academic and training programs, (2) as executive level staff and members of policy-making boards of the major family organizations such as the AAMFT and the NCFR, (3) as members of editorial boards of family therapy and family science journals, (4) as students in family therapy training programs, and (5) as therapists in agencies and other treatment centers.

Minority members should not be inculcated into these subsystems in ways that perpetuate the myth of sameness. The responsibility for teaching minority content, supervising and advising minority students, raising minority-related issues within an organization, or increasing the sensitivity of others to minority issues should not be assigned exclusively to minority members. Increased interactions with and consistent exposure to minority individuals can facilitate a greater appreciation for sameness and difference.

II. Curricular/Experiential Remedies

A. Family therapy curricula must be modified to take into account minority-related issues. To be effective, minority-related content should be integrated throughout the curriculum, rather than appearing as a single isolated course, taught by the minority faculty member. Relatedly, clinical populations must be broadened to include minority clients that ALL students will have exposure to and experience with, not just the minority student.

B. The Family of Origin and Person of the Therapist exercises that are used widely in family therapy training programs must be expanded to incorporate ethnic, racial, and gender-related issues. Family therapy students must be challenged to explore the potential impact that their ethnic, racial, and gender identity has on their work as clinicians. Moreover, expanded versions of the Family of Origin and Person of the Therapist exercises could be quite instrumental in encouraging students to examine various minority-related stereotypes.

C. Therapists must find ways to enhance their multicultural experiences. Minorities are expected, if not required, to become conversant with the values, mores, and idiosyncrasies of non-minorities. In so doing, minorities learn to interact with non-minorities with minimal difficulty. It should not be the continued burden of the family in crisis to teach a therapist the idiosyncrasies of one's culture, ethnic, or racial group. Admittedly, it is virtually impossible for therapists to know all there is to know about every possible minority, however, it is not impossible for one to reduce the level of ignorance through increased awareness. At the very least, an effort could be made to learn more about the specific minorities that comprise the catchment area of one's clinical practice.

III. Epistemological Remedies

A. Family therapy theorists and practitioners must broaden the traditional views of systems theory. Family therapy heretofore, has focused primarily on the "family system" to the virtual exclusion of examining how the family in treatment is affected by macro-systemic issues such as race, ethnicity, culture, and gender. The focus on "process" over "content" has nurtured both the narrow view of systems and the theoretical myth of sameness. Taggart (1985), in an article addressing the feminist critique of family therapy questioned whether rape can or should be looked at strictly in terms of process.

B. Family therapy educators, theorists, supervisors, and students must also broaden their views of systems theory by recognizing the interactional relationship between sameness and difference. Perhaps, one noteworthy area to start would be with the language that is used to describe minorities. Commonly used terms such as Hispanics, Asians, and Blacks reinforce the TMOS by constructing realities based on homogeneity.

C. Increased empirical inquiry regarding family therapy and ethnic minority families is sorely needed. The paucity of research in this area has impeded our ability to know what we don't know about minorities and family therapy.

These are a few suggestions, solutions, and recommendations for creating a process that will lead to a new way of thinking about minorities and family treatment. As the family therapy field continues to mature as a discipline, it is imperative that current efforts to homogenize the field be resisted. It is important that the next generation of family therapists be prepared clinically, theoretically, and experientially, to recognize and accept the multitudinous ways in which minority families specifically, and families in general, are "like all other families, like some other families, but like no other family."

REFERENCES

Commission on Accreditation for Marriage and Family Therapy Education. (1976). *Manual on Accreditation*. Washington, DC: Commission on Accreditation/AAMFT.

Flores, J.L. (1979). "Becoming a Marriage, Family and Child Counselor: Notes from a Chicano." *Journal of Marital and Family Therapy*, 5:4, 17-22.

Goodrich, T.J., C. Rampage, B. Ellman, and K. Halstead (1988). *Feminist Family Therapy: A Casebook*. New York: Norton.

Hare-Mustin, R. (1978). "A Feminist Approach to Family Therapy." *Family Process*, 17, 181-194.

McGoldrick, M., J.K. Pearce, and J. Giordano (Eds.) (1982). *Ethnicity and Family Therapy*. New York: The Guilford Press.

Myers-Avis, J. (1986). "Feminist Issues in Therapy." F. Piercy, D. Sprenkle, and Associates (Eds.), *Family Therapy Sourcebook*. New York: The Guilford Press, 213-242.

Myers-Avis, J. (1985). "The Politics of Functional Family Therapy: A Feminist Critique." *Journal of Marital and Family Therapy*, 11-2, 127-138.

Taggart, M. (1985). "The Feminist Critique in Epistemological Perspective: Questions of Context in Family Therapy." *Journal of Marital Family Therapy*, 11:2, 113-126.

Nine Assumptions for Work with Ethnic Minority Families

Braulio Montalvo
Manuel J. Gutierrez

The therapist's task of seeing a family's problem from their perspective rather than his or her own is full of possibilities for misunderstanding. Those possibilities multiply when working with minority families, because of the disruptive conditions impacting their sense of continuity and self-worth. The stresses of migration, unsuccessful relocation, uneven cultural assimilation, inadequate schools, family dismemberment, participation in unresponsive judicial and welfare systems, lack of job skills, relentless socio-economic obstacles, and frustrated opportunities often combine to shake the stability and sense of control of these families. Many feel the world around them just generally misunderstands what they are going through. When dealing even with the most stable of such families, therapists can use a set of assumptions aimed at lessening the possibilities of adding to the sense of being misunderstood. This paper offers nine such assumptions through brief case examples and stories.

Assume that:

1. Cultural assimilation exists unevenly within the same family.
2. Mourning and grieving are not only internal emotional processes but behaviors of social consequence.
3. Upholding continuity and lessening disparity between family members is frequently a basic goal.

Braulio Montalvo, MA, is on the faculty of the Family Medicine Department, School of Medicine, University of New Mexico, Albuquerque, NM.
Manuel J. Gutierrez, PhD, is affiliated with Aspira, Inc., Philadelphia, PA.

35

4. Misunderstandings can be solved by figuring how context explains the interpretation of behaviors.
5. The family's view of the world can be inferred from how it uses or misuses its beliefs and orientation systems.
6. Culturally endorsed intrafamily patterns of coercion must be met with extra alertness on the part of the therapist.
7. Obtaining the family's consent can be a means of preventing and correcting misunderstandings.
8. The therapist's openness to guidance from the family allows access to its cultural priorities and promotes therapist's modification.
9. Alertness to preconceptions, a generic tool in all therapy, is of critical importance in working with minority families.

CULTURAL ASSIMILATION IS UNEVEN

To gain appreciation and deliberate use of the strengths of different cultures, the therapist must keep in mind that a culture's influence is not evenly distributed among all family members. Expect to see earlier roots of that culture finding expression in some members and not in others. This differentiated understanding of the family is often of critical importance in the therapy of personal loss, mourning, and violence.

Jay Lappin saw a case of a grieving Hispanic woman who had a terrible tragedy. Her husband and young son stepped out of their car to fix a tire and an oncoming car hit both of them, killing the husband and throwing the son far into some bushes. After inspecting the accident, a policeman came to the house to report on her husband's death. He had no news about her son. She asked desperately about her child, but he was unable to provide an answer. Anxious, confused and grieved, she paced the house. For unspecified reasons the policeman followed her like a shadow. Because of his presence, she could not even change her bathrobe to go to the hospital. She felt she might be assaulted. She feared this stranger was planning to rape her. These consecutive violations could not be controlled. They were too sudden and went beyond her usual competence, driving her crazy, after a few days, with suicidal and homicidal rage. She was hospitalized.

Months went by, and her sadness continued. Nothing could snap her out of her depression. The family was trying to "take care of its own." Her younger and more outgoing sister pushed her to go out and be with other people. After sponsoring this sister to go on with her pressure tactic, the therapist shifted and urged the victim to defend herself: "What do you want? Tell your sister." "It is my life," the patient replied. "It is too soon. I feel as if he died yesterday. Going out now would be as if I was betraying him. I know I have to go out, but later. What I need is time."

The therapist helped this woman to protect her boundaries. He put her, not the relatives, in control. His emphasis on manipulating contemporary family forces was far removed from conventional grief work and its concern with the unfolding of affective stages. Those stages, after all, never occurred strictly inside a person, without an interpersonal and cultural context. The therapist had perceived quickly that the victimized woman was more old-fashioned; she needed a pace of mourning which was fitting to her roots in an earlier and slower Hispanic world not shared by her Americanized sister. His hunch was that the rhythm and pace of her grief work was being impaired by a sense of being rushed, trespassed upon once more. The trauma had already pushed her to extremes. It was essential for her not to let her sister push her too. By helping her to resist the culturally assimilated ways of her sister, the therapist enabled this woman, who had always been the slower, less outgoing sibling, to defend aggressively all her rights. The victim went on to control and modulate the pace of change to a rate that she considered within her means. The shift towards mental health accelerated when she demanded that her sister return to her care her remaining children. The sister had taken them over during the crisis, driven by the value placed by the Hispanic culture on "Our families must help their own."

Clearly, the clinician must be ready to observe the clash of cultures not only between the family and the surrounding host culture, but within the family itself.

GRIEF HAS SOCIAL CONSEQUENCES

In working with personal loss and grief related stress, the therapist who seeks to avoid misunderstanding of the culture must shift focus. S/he must observe not only emotions unfolding inside the surviving persons, but their outside conflicts as they modulate the pace of grieving and shape the image that the one they have lost will have in the memory of the community. This means the therapist needs to support the surviving relatives as they form the pace of mourning and structure or "edit" the remembered image of the lost one inside and outside the family. These are essential functions, buffering the impact of disruption and restoring some sense of control by preserving elements of continuity.

Sean has died. One by one everybody in the community approaches the mother, "Poor Sean. What did he die of?" Sobbing, she explains, "He died from the gonorrhea." People are appropriately taken aback. After their shocked "Oh's" and "Ah's," they move on. The parade of visitors goes on late into the night, and every questioner gets the same answer. The local therapist, a doctor who had known of Sean's illness, had been watching. Afraid that he may have been misunderstanding something, he pulls the mother aside and asks, "He died of the diarrhea! Why do you keep saying he died of the gonorrhea?" She looks up with a twinkle in her eye, "Well, doctor, I'd rather they think of him as a sporting fellow, not the shit he had become with booze."

This mother was coping with more than her own internal sense of loss. She was actually monitoring the external regard in which outsiders held her son, helping the community to reach agreement on a certain image. Her comments were aiming to influence the son's immediate community of peers as well as the friends of the family, protecting his reputation and hers.

The family and the community hold on to their members even after death. This is evident as well in the following anecdote:

> Jose, a Puerto Rican, became a widower after thirty years of marriage. Trying to overcome his sadness and loneliness, he retired to Miami. He began efforts to come out of his emotional retreat. While walking on the boardwalk, he was impressed with the colored shirts that "gringos" wore and by their cheerful attitude. He bought a wildly colorful shirt. He put it on and felt different. Then he saw a place advertising facial silicon implants. He made an appointment and firmed

up his cheeks. After the operation, the nurse suggested he should dye his hair blonde, since now he looked young. He also took an EST course and felt, not only a surge of confidence, but almost arrogance. He intended to take charge of his life. As he walked along the boardwalk, a beautiful Anglo blonde winked at him. Before he knew it, he was going arm in arm with her down the boardwalk. He was amazed. He had been a good husband, a good working man. He was sure he deserved all this. At that very instant, lightning came down from heaven and struck him dead. Angrily he showed up in heaven. God's imposing image peeked through the clouds. Jose complained, "Why me, God? Why now? I was a good husband, a good man. I worked hard all my life. For the first time I am having fun and thinking of myself. Why . . . why?" God looked carefully at him and hesitatingly said, "Is that you, Jose? Man, I did not recognize you, you look like a gringo!"

Many cultural groups have some version of such a story. It serves as a warning to their people to stay in line, not to lose their identities, forfeiting membership in their group's culture. You will pay dearly if you transform yourself too radically whether through alcoholism, like Sean, or through cultural assimilation, like Jose. The collective memory others have of you will be obliterated. The culture demands that its members maintain a certain integrity, and then the interesting features of your life and character are kept in mind. They live on in the minds of those who remember the past, and in the minds of those who will learn about them in the future.

UPHOLD CONTINUITY, LESSEN DISPARITY

The family is supposed to struggle against internal misunderstanding in order to protect the continuity of its social fabric. Those misunderstandings present routine problems for therapists who deal with members from family networks that are fragmented by political upheaval, wars, and forced migration.

Juan sends pictures of his family in Chicago to his relatives in Cuba. His hope is that the tie between them will be kept alive. An old neighbor comes from Cuba and Juan finds the results were not what he expected. The visitor informs him that his relatives over there are angry at him. Juan cannot understand. He had tried to keep the friendship alive despite the distance. When he showed this neighbor the Christmas pictures he sent to his relatives, the man's comment was, "Look at that table . . . that turkey looks delicious!" And looking at the next picture of the man's wife and son, he could not get over the brand new refrigerator in the background. Finally Juan realized suddenly how insensitive he had been. Unwillingly he had offended his relatives. They probably thought he was trying to show off his wealth and comforts, which those in Cuba had lost forever.

Such rifts develop painful intensity between family members, because they entail much more than rivalry over goods and status. They threaten the very core of family identity and unity. Relief from that threat comes when a friend or therapist helps the cutoff participants to repair the disparity. Sometimes reparation is achieved through white lies subtly reminding family members that everyone remains the same, that we are not different from each other. "When you go back, tell them the refrigerator is not ours, it is on loan from the landlord, and the turkey was a gift from a friend, and we were wishing they would have been there with us to share it."

When the disparity is not repaired and the ties of love and duty are overstrained, the mental intactness of those with the material advantage is put at risk. Maxine Hong Kingston sees this risk as particularly high for the mother-son relationship:

> Before a letter in a white envelope reached us saying that Sao Brother's mother had died, she appeared to him in America. She flew across the ocean and found her way to him. Just when he was about to fall asleep one night, he saw her and sat up with a start, definitely not dreaming. "You have turned me into a hungry ghost," she said. "You did this to me. You enjoyed yourself. You fed your wife and useless daughters, who are not even family, and you left me to starve. What you see before you is the inordinate hunger I had to suffer in my life." She opened her mouth wide, and he turned his face

away not to see the depths within. "Mother," he said,
"Mother, how did you find your way across the ocean and
here." "I am so cold. I followed the heat of your body like a
light and fire. I was drawn to the well-fed." "Here, take this,
Mother," he cried, handing her his wallet from the nightstand.
"Too late," she said. "Too late." With her chasing him he
ran to the kitchen. He opened the refrigerator. He shoved food
at her. "Too late." Curiously enough, other people did not
see her. (Kingston, 1977, p. 175)

CONTEXT EXPLAINS THE MEANING OF BEHAVIOR

Visiting the after work activities of the uprooted Chinese in the
California railroad camps at the turn of the century, an outsider to
the culture would have found it difficult not to grow prejudices
against the *cruel* and *barbarous* orientals. He would have seen them
lift a screaming man, one of their own, and pass him over fire. To
avoid misunderstanding, the outsider would have required an interpreter, an insider like M. H. Kingston. She writes in *China Men* of
her people's belief in "passing fear over fire" (Kingston, 1977, p.
90).

This phrase refers to the custom of lifting one who had been
badly frightened and passing him over a fire. This experience pro-
duced a larger fear in the person suffering from a significant fear,
hoping that the larger fear would inhibit the lesser one. We have no
account of the casualties of this aversive training technique, but it
was clearly a cultural means of last resort. It was something the
culture tried on its severe anxiety and panic cases, because it had
few options and no access to medical help. These people were virtually enslaved within these labor camps for making the Western rail-
roads. Passing "fear over fire" was a compassionate act, performed among peers in the context of helping each other at the end
of a long working day. In that context of helpfulness and concern,
the ordinary meaning of the act of passing someone over fire was
changed.

The therapist's viewpoint similarly can change by shifts in context. For a long time, a colleague cherished the notion that what is
wrong with most tense people is their attitude towards errors. When

this therapist made a mistake, all he needed to do was go over the mistake and accept it as part of his vulnerability and his humanity. He had elevated this notion into a kind of relaxed, "that too is all right" philosophy, and was becoming very laid-back about human errors. He was trivializing the meaning of self-forgiveness in his practice, until he saw a cartoon that allowed him to look at his working context differently (see Figure 1). The caricature showed a man in a stretcher, about to be wheeled by a nurse into a surgery room. He is looking up wide-eyed at an inscription right above the operating room's door. Under the door stand two doctors in surgical masks eagerly waiting for him. The inscription above them reads, "To err is human." Suddenly, his convenient philosophy felt far too relaxed, and the gap between the mental health professional and the patient was closed. Sharing a perception of the world from the viewpoint of the concerned patient upon whom a possible error was to be performed, the world looked differently. He let go of the "that's O.K. too" philosophy, and his concept of guilt began to change. Guilt, which for him was mostly a nuisance, and nothing but an obstacle in therapy, was now reconsidered. Guilt was the nagging voice of responsibility, the standard which steers the self and prevents great blunders (Montalvo, 1985).

VIEW OF THE WORLD: USE OR MISUSE OF BELIEFS

To share a certain way of viewing the world is often the first step in inventing appropriate therapeutic interventions. Consider the grief work done in the following case.

Mrs. Rodriguez was extremely sad after the loss of her infant son. A month after the burial, she was still complaining of always seeing a little light over her child's bureau. The preoccupation with the light, which she watched until late at night, became her main engulfing relationship. Concerned about her praying, complaining, and despairing, her maid of many years offered an opinion. "Of course the little light is over his bureau. You have not gotten rid of his clothes. You must do your part." Mrs. Rodriguez proceeded to remove lovingly every little piece of clothing in that bureau, and as the light disappeared, she was filled with peace. By shedding the

FIGURE 1. Joaquin Salvador Lavado (Quino) is the creator of this brilliant cartoon. The authors of the article, "Nine Assumptions for Work with Ethnic Minority Families," Montalvo and Jutierre, used it in Buenos Aires, Argentina. The cartoon is one of many gems in the book Quinoterapia.

child's clothing, she had loosened a vital link of her attachment of the child to her, and of her to him.

This upper middle-class Puerto Rican woman shared with her lower working-class maid a quasimystical perception of the world. Her maid, however, maintained a more direct access to the means of coping with problems associated with that way of viewing the world. For her, the light clearly represented the soul of the child who cannot leave because the mother is not ready to let him go. The therapy she offered was classic in its simplicity. She focused on a concrete belonging, a possession that once belonged to that child, and showed the grieving woman how, by letting go of the object she could permit his soul to go on as well. Thus she gave the woman a concrete way to release her deeply held attachment.

One learns, however, that regardless of the advantages of this particular way of viewing the world, if people misuse it, trouble ensues. Misuse entails failing to do your part or wanting to manipulate hidden forces through varieties of stubborn passivity rather than shared activity.

Consider the case of Mr. and Mrs. P. They have made a modest fortune with their grocery store in New York City. Now the children are gone, and they are alone wondering what to do with their lives. "Should we sell the house?" "Would it be wise to sell the business and move back to Puerto Rico?" With these uncertainties, they sink into obsessive depression and stagnation.

An increasing number of couples like this one, in the midst of a mid-life crisis, seek professional help. When the therapist sees them they are usually neglecting their business, as well as their social and sexual life, and are passively waiting for direction—sometimes even waiting for mystical or supernatural guidance. They misunderstand and resist the therapist's lack of empathy with their passivity. Therapists who look around for whatever culturally syntonic materials could lighten and support their work do better with these families. They use whatever in the culture may help those couples come closer to seeing that they have to make their own decisions, not just wait for the spirits to make them for them. To nudge them away from mystical determinism and allow a place for their own choice-making in the larger providential design, popular stories are useful.

Certain stories help summarize the culture's best reality testing and elicit no-nonsense reactions from the patients using their culture's emotional and cognitive resources. Alvarez Guedes' repertoire offers this one:

> One night Mrs. B. wakes up her husband, "Do you hear it?" "Hear what?" he asked. "A soft voice asking me to pay attention." Indifferent her husband goes back to sleep. Shortly afterwards she wakes him up again. "I heard it again, did you hear it this time?" By now he is curious. "No, I did not hear it. What did it say?" "It just said: 'pay attention.'" This goes on for a few nights. To her surprise, one night the husband clearly hears the voice. "Pack up," the voice said. "Sell the store, get all your money and go back to the island." Anxiously they do as the voice said. Once back on the island they still feel adrift, lost. They do not know what to do with this new stage in their life. They listen avidly for guidance, and the voice tells them, "Go to the casino. Take all your money." So they do. After much uncertainty they approach the roulette. They hear the same voice distinctly saying, "45." Realizing this is the moment they have been waiting for, they put all their money on 45. The roulette goes around and around. It comes to a stop . . . NUMBER 44 . . . and the voice says . . . "SHIT!" (Guedes, 1983)

Through stories we can even tell ourselves that the spirits, like us, are fallible and capable of misguiding us. Guedes emphasizes that the spiritualism inherent in a culture is misused when it is summoned at the expense of the self.

ALERTNESS TO CULTURALLY ENDORSED COERCION

The human relationship to the cosmic or supernatural scheme seems to be, in most cultures, notoriously vulnerable to misuse and difficult to work with therapeutically. Such relationships are easily placed at the service of those who need to control coercively, to rob choice, from the other. The enormous credentializing and legitimizing power given to "religious conversions" by the family's culture often facilitates that negative process. It is a process of cultural endorsement that must be carefully watched since it can trap the most alert therapist into serious misunderstanding.

The mother of an adolescent girl abused by her father goes into therapy. She has lots of difficulty in mobilizing protectiveness towards the girl. Because of her rigid patriarchal outlook, she often felt the girl was to blame. To protect the girl's well-being, the authorities put the father in jail, and soon after, the girl too was removed to a foster home. After a few months, the mother more or less complied with the view of the therapist. She painfully admitted that her husband was dangerous. He could do the same to her other children. She did not want him back. In the meantime, the foster home reported that the girl was beginning to act defiant and strange. She was resistive and rebellious with her foster parents, breaking curfews, using tons of lipstick, and generally trying to look older, sending erotic signals to older youngsters in school.

The therapist soon discovered that sometimes the girl even thought she was her father's girlfriend. All these behavior changes emerged during a period in which the mother talked with the therapist as if she was indeed distancing from her abusive husband. However, she was actually misleading the therapist and fostering the relationship of the girl with the father. The mother had visited him and had come back to tell the girl that he had received the Lord now. He had undergone a religious conversion and was a different man. The mother wanted her daughter to reconcile with him and write to him. The girl began writing letters, and the father answered with pornographic responses attempting to reinvolve her. During this process the girl started acting psychotic.

The mother had dropped her guard and sacrificed her daughter. Herself a victim of subordination in her own tyrannical patriarchal family of origin, she was unable to resist being deceived once more by her husband's story. That story skillfully framed the man's behavior as part of a transcendent scheme. She was convinced, not just by him, but by the irresistible authenticating power that her culture grants those experiences. This authentication makes possible further coercion.

CONSENT PREVENTS AND CORRECTS
MISUNDERSTANDINGS

What a therapist sees as coercive or non-coercive between a husband and wife from a different culture often leads to basic lessons for the therapist. The most basic one is on the significance of the therapist requesting permission before intervening. Such a move will tend to prevent misunderstanding.

At the end of a session with a couple, a therapist met a request from a wife. "Would you just tell him [husband] that in this country he should stop bossing me around in front of people." Apparently, she would not mind putting up with being ordered around by her husband in the tight patriarchal context of her country. Here, in the States, already influenced by the liberated stance of women, she was beginning to object to such treatment. The therapist turned to the man. "I think she wants to ask you something. Can she?" Then, quickly, back to the woman, "You tell him." The wife went ahead and expressed her request in no uncertain terms as the session ended.

Professionals from Central America, watching this therapy through a one-way mirror, were upset. For most of them, the therapist had "overstepped" the lines of the culture. They jumped on the therapist. The therapist defended himself. "By returning the question to her, I was facilitating her own revolt against the practices of her culture." They did not let him get away with this. "You were disrespectful of the culture. You pitted yourself against what these people have decided the relationship between a man and a woman should be. You invited her to fight him just by the act of allocating as much concern to her as to him all throughout the session." The therapist replied, "This woman felt it was no longer her role to accept coercion from her husband. She would have been able to put up with him had he been more considerate of her in other life areas."

To guide the therapist's understanding of the culture, the couple was consulted. The man was asked, "How did you feel about how I handled her request?" He answered, "I was glad that you asked first for my permission for her to talk against me. It is the custom for the woman to go through the man . . . She embarrassed me in front of you, just like I embarrassed her in front of her American friends. You wanted her to attack me, but you still treated me as the head of this family." The woman, too, was debriefed. She smiled, "Thank you. He is still doing it, but he is doing it less."

GUIDANCE FROM THE FAMILY
FOR THERAPIST MODIFICATION

The importance of such efforts to let the participants guide the therapist through the culture cannot be overrated as a way of preventing misunderstanding and expanding the therapist (Montalvo & Gutierrez, 1983).

A pediatrician visiting Puerto Rico in the early 1950s was invited to attend a baby's wake. A "baquine" was going on. He saw family and relatives of the baby not crying, but drinking and laughing, while the infant lay on top of the table with ice around him. He was shaken by this image, which has all but disappeared from the experience of poor Black families in certain coastal areas of the island. Trying not to misunderstand these Puerto Rican families and judge them as being unfeeling to a child's death, he searched for the underlying view of the world organizing their experience. He turned for guidance to the infant's grandfather, who explained, "We don't cry because our tears would wet the little angel's wings. If the angel's wings get wet, the soul of the baby can't fly to heaven. What's there to cry about, anyway? By having an early death, he didn't have to go through this valley of tears." Through the "baquine," the family was upholding a coping stance that helped to face its dismal existence, strengthening itself to deal with more hardships to come. "Though in grief, let us be happy that at least one of us was saved from pain." By seeing the family's wish to relate to the good fortune within the misfortune, the doctor not only avoided a misunderstanding of the culture, but gained an appreciation of its strength by grasping its priorities.

Any misunderstanding about the priorities organizing and justifying the persons in their culture provides an opportunity to learn not only about that culture but also about our own prejudices. This revelation of prejudice can happen in therapy or outside of therapy.

Right after the first anti-AIDS TV commercials hit the streets, the following racist story emerged in New York. Five Puerto Rican addicts are in an alleyway passing their needle around getting ready to shoot up into their veins. Right in the middle of this process, they are interrupted by one who arrives late. "What are you guys doing? Don't you watch TV? The stuff gives you AIDS man." One of them looks up reassuringly, "There's nothing to worry about. We're all wearing condoms."

This is an ignorant attack against the underprivileged. These Puerto Ricans are dumb. They do not understand what is going on in the world. The story laughs at Puerto Ricans instead of with them, but it also manages to criticize the gap between the poor's subculture and the ruling middle-class establishment. That establishment spent large sums of money to educate the community to lessen the chances of AIDS but failed to target the use of needles, the main source of contamination among the large populations of lower-class Blacks and Hispanics. Those first self-serving commercials, emphasizing only the middle-class worry about "safe sex," have given way to more culturally encompassing materials avoiding intercultural misunderstanding.[1]

Cultural misunderstandings happen all the time. They are caused by our "knowledge" or wrong expectations about who or what is included in a culture and what that culture means by this or that behavior. Such wrong expectations are often corrected by openness to experiences that promote modification of the therapist's prejudices.

In a shopping mall a therapist saw an ex-patient coming towards him. This woman had become a single parent through divorce, slipping, as do many, from a fairly comfortable working-class status into poverty. She was finally emerging from eight years of being trapped as a member of the permanent underclass and was now a computer programming student. As she approached him, he reflected on how he had helped her years ago. He would not put up with her feeling sorry for herself. He had told her that. When she complained bitterly, he had confronted her, pushing her to work seriously on her recovery. He was glad he did not indulge her needs for dependence. To have done so would have been a disservice to her. She looked good now.

She interrupted his thoughts curtly, "Do you remember me?" "Yes, I do," he answered expecting a friendlier greeting. "You know, I always wanted to tell you something. You never gave me a break, you know that? You never understood what I was going through with the kids and no job. You thought it was me, not what I was going through." "Well, I'm sorry, but maybe my lack of pity did help you. I wanted you to take charge of your life," said the therapist. She replied, "But you wanted me to do it when I couldn't, and it would have helped if you would have understood that. I'm glad I moved on and found another therapist." She turned and walked away, leaving the therapist with a disturbing vision.

Defeated, the therapist thought perhaps he had misunderstood the priority needs of this ingrate. Next, he saw one of his poor clients, a jobless man, and was surprised to hear himself commiserating more and fearing less the effects of his sympathy. He listened to the man holding himself together by externalizing, blaming the system, and this time, he challenged nothing. He found himself reassessing even his campaign against those whom he thought were patronizing and condescending to the poor. Perhaps he was against those do-gooders who display compassion not just because they robbed the poor's autonomy, but because they made him feel unkind or uncaring. Overly conscious of how often throughout history people have coopted and exploited others in the name of compassion, he had too effectively concealed his own empathy.

UNCOVERING STEREOTYPES

Catching our moments of misunderstanding remains a time-honored way of discovering preconceptions and stereotypes, a first step to improving our interventions.

Dr. A. faced a hyperanxious Rastafarian man who appeared under enormous pressure to get across his problem. His accent made him hard to understand. To get within this man's culture and grasp his complaint, Dr. A. rushed in, "You mean pills?" What the man said he thought, must have been "pills." Some Rastafarians in the big city push pot and pills. The man shouted back, "No man, I mean bills, bills!" The man was under pressure to pay bills, not to pay for pills. The embarrassed feeling arising in this therapist, who quickly corrected himself, was no different from the one of the lawyer in the next story.

A Puerto Rican lawyer attended a meeting called by the City Hall for all the town's minorities. Koreans, Vietnamese, Blacks, and Hispanics were represented. The discussion centered on their difficulty as minorities in obtaining small business loans from the local banks. Angered by a perceived unfairness, the lawyer complained, "The city must be making it easier for banks to give loans to the most recent arrivals, the 'boat people.' Yet we Hispanics have been here forever, but cannot get loans!" The Vietnamese man jumped in, "We have our own banking system, we don't get no loans from no city." The embarrassed lawyer learned that this new minority had arrived with a well-developed tradition for sharing in banking co-ops, which evolved long ago in fishing villages of Vietnam.

A Navajo mother and her son, who had several DWI arrests, were asked, "Why does he keep doing it?" Rubbing his shirt sleeve, the mother replied, "See this? His father and friends are like that too. Thirty five degrees, and they go outside in light cotton shirts and no coats." As if on cue, the young man started bragging about drinking from nine to four while driving his pick-up truck with friends. By following the content of their English, the therapist misunderstood this mother and son as tangential and enigmatic (following the stereotype that Indians are enigmatic). Reconsidering the sequence of the discussion, not just its content, the therapist dropped his preconception and recovered a message. To withstand excessive cold is the equivalent of withstanding excessive drinking. The mother was conveying that the males had conned themselves into believing that by binging on liquor without complaining they were being "good Indians," stoic Indians. They had twisted a wonderful ancestral value, stoicism, which helped their people bounce back from personal loss and adversity, into one more rationalization for alcohol abuse.

By establishing contrasts between our stereotypes and the real world, we get some of the most revealing lessons about a culture. Take the situation of Mercedes, a South American woman who in her seventies visited the prosperous United States for the first time. Observing in amazement everything around lower Manhattan, she turned to her daughter and whispered, "See that man there? He sells newspapers, yet look how well dressed he is!'' The man, a Wall Street broker in a three piece suit, was carrying the Sunday New York Times under his arm. Therapists are not far from Mercedes when it comes to how they get into misunderstandings.

NOTE

1. To supplement interculturally encompassing materials, the development of subculture-specific products has emerged. See "Ojos Que No Ven" (Eyes That Fail to See), an educational video available from the Latino AIDS Project (415) 647-4141.

REFERENCES

Guedes, A. (1983). *El de la ruleta*. Santurce, PR: Gema Records.
Kingston, M. H. (1977). *China men*. New York: Ballantine Books.
Montalvo, B. (1985). On blunder avoidance. *Family Therapy Networker, 9* (1), 51.
Montalvo, B., & Gutierrez, M. (1983). A perspective for the use of the cultural dimension in family therapy. In C. J. Falicov (Ed.), *Cultural perspectives in family therapy* (pp. 15-32). Rockville, MD: Aspen Systems Corporation.

Five Key Factors in the Treatment of Black Families

Nancy Boyd-Franklin

Over the past two decades, the prevalent "deficit" theories have continued to guide clinicians in the treatment of Black populations. For family therapists, this theoretical framework has created a skewed perspective of the familial patterns of many Black individuals. The terms "disorganized, chaotic, depressed and deprived" were employed to describe the lives of Black families in America (Moynihan, 1965). More recent literature has begun to combat this deficiency theory by highlighting the fundamental strengths that are inherent in Black families (Hill, 1972; Billingsley, 1968; McAdoo, 1981; McAdoo & McAdoo, 1985; Lewis & Looney, 1983; Hines & Boyd-Franklin, 1982). Based on this research, five key areas of strength can be delineated: (1) the bond of the extended family, (2) the adaptability of family roles, (3) strong religious orientation, (4) an integral belief in the value of education and the work ethic, and (5) the ability to develop and utilize effective coping skills in the face of socioeconomic hardship.

It is important to note that these strengths are not presented in a comparative sense with other ethnic groups, nor are they intended to show that these are necessarily greater in Black families than in other groups. They are intended to illustrate the strengths inherent

Nancy Boyd-Franklin, PhD, is on the faculty of the Department of Psychiatry, University of Medicine and Dentistry of New Jersey, New Jersey Medical School, Newark, NJ.

The author would like to express her appreciation to Ms. Beverly Martin for her assistance in the preparation of this manuscript.

Requests for reprints should be sent to Dr. Nancy Boyd-Franklin, Community Mental Health Center, University of Medicine and Dentistry of New Jersey, Department of Psychiatry, 215 So. Orange Avenue, Newark, NJ 07103.

in Black families which can and should be utilized in treatment. The incorporation of these strengths into therapeutic strategies for working with these families is the primary purpose of this article. Each key strength will be briefly elucidated and followed by clinical implications and examples of how they can be integrated into a comprehensive treatment approach for this clinical population. Before we begin our exploration of the strengths, however, it is important to discuss the diversity which exists among Black families.

CULTURAL DIVERSITY AMONG BLACK FAMILIES

Black families in this country are definitely not a monolithic group. There is no entity which can be defined as *the* Black family. There is a tremendous amount of cultural and socioeconomic diversity among these families. Black families from the North and those living in the South have many shared traditions, but there are also many differences. There are also important differences between urban versus rural families (Boyd-Franklin, 1989). There are many Black families who were not brought to this country as slaves but who came as immigrants from the West Indies (Brice, 1982) or from Africa and who brought their own unique cultural issues and diversity. This paper will focus primarily on Black, Afro-American families whose ancestors were brought to this country as slaves. The case examples reported herein were drawn primarily from a Northern, urban, inner-city sample. In a number of instances, examples will also be drawn from Black middle-class families. An in-depth discussion of all of these diverse elements is beyond the scope of this paper. However, the recognition of this diversity is an important safeguard which must be built into any of the literature on ethnicity. We must be ever vigilant about the dangers of stereotyping. In this context, it is important that the material presented in this paper be utilized by the reader, not as a set of cultural absolutes, but as a flexible set of hypotheses which can be tested with each new Black family in treatment (Boyd-Franklin, 1989).

THE BOND OF THE EXTENDED FAMILY

Black Americans have a heritage of shared loyalty and strong kinship bonds that date back to their historical origins in Africa. In our contemporary society, reliance on a kinship network, not necessarily restricted to linear genealogical patterns or "blood lines," remains a primary mode of "familial" interaction. Stack (1974) noted that many Black families evolved patterns of "co-residence, kinship-based exchange networks linking multiple domestic units, elastic household boundaries, and lifelong bonds to three generation households." According to Stack, this elasticity of familial boundaries "proves to be an organized, tenacious, active, lifelong network" (p. 124). Thus, family therapists must be willing to operate within a treatment plan that may include, as White (1972) pointed out, a number of "uncles, aunts, big mamas, boyfriends, older brothers and sisters, deacons, preachers" (p. 45) who may be important to a particular Black family. White also makes the observation that a variety of adults and older children participate in the rearing of any one Black child. This creates a situation in which various persons interchange roles, jobs, and familial functions. As a result, many Black children are not bound by an externally imposed demarcation between male and female roles, e.g., only women should cook or do household chores.

More recent scholars and researchers have further clarified the roles of extended family members. McAdoo (1981), for example, has demonstrated through her research that many Black families are able to maintain extended family ties as they move toward upward mobility and middle-class status. Bagarozzi (1980) and Boyd-Franklin (1989) have discussed the struggles of middle-class families in this process. Lindblad-Goldberg and Dukes (1985) have shown that the most functional Black single-parent families maintain these ties.

Sager and Brayboy (1970) have demonstrated that the traditional definition of family must be expanded, and they noted that therapists must reevaluate and, in the case of many Black families, abandon limiting notions of a nuclear family structure. The "system approach" to therapy with families has become inextricably linked to family therapy. Traditionally, this approach has been confined to a system that is defined as the nuclear family. However, treatment that went beyond the structure of the traditional family began when a social network approach was employed. Pattison (1976), in a review of the literature described the work of family therapists who included relatives, friends and neighbors in the family sessions when the extra-familial person played a role in the dynamics of the family seeking treatment. Minuchin and associates (1967, 1974) began to apply such a model of family therapy with low-income Black families. As a result of their work with subgroups within these families, they started to investigate the impact of extended family members and members of the family's social network. They concluded that to be effective, the therapist must first build a strong alliance with the immediate family members so as to elicit their cooperation in encouraging the involvement of significant others in the network. This is considered crucial since those individuals outside the family may provide emotional support or act as catalysts to challenge the maladaptive modes of interaction among family members and pull them toward change. Although this approach incorporates some aspects of social network system treatment, there is a difference in the way the therapist utilizes the strengths offered by the extended family. In these cases, they stress the importance for the clinician to (1) explore the kinship network with the family, and (2) select only those individuals relevant to immediate or emerging therapeutic goals. Thus, unlike network therapists, these authors advocate the treatment-oriented selection of the significant others rather than inclusion of large segments of the family's social system.

Genograms and Their Use in Therapy
with Black Families

As an aid to clinicians in exploring such kinship networks, as well as clarifying treatment goals, the genogram has been found to be most effective (Hines & Boyd-Franklin, 1982). Guerin and Pendagast (1976) contend that genograms can be used to introduce important structural questions about the roles of the different family members, their relationships and conflicts. Until recently, the literature on how genograms can be employed in the treatment of Black families has been sparse. McGoldrick and Gerson (1985) provide a comprehensive overview of the use of genograms in family therapy.

One of the most frequent mistakes made by clinicians has been to gather the genogram in the initial interview with the family. These can be counterproductive and in some instances, destructive to the therapeutic alliance. Many Black families are suspicious of professionals "prying" into their lives. Some issues, e.g., illegitimate births, the marital status of the parents or the paternity of the children may be "family secrets" which members may not want to reveal or discuss with an outsider until a relationship of trust has been created. Therefore, it is best to delay gathering information for a genogram until the therapist has established a bond of trust with the family.

Construction of an accurate genogram can be very effective in drawing together an overview of family dynamics that can be translated into treatment strategies and interventions. The following case history illustrates the effectiveness of this tool.

> The G. family, a large Black family, entered treatment after their daughter Janine (age nine) had been briefly removed from the family by a local child welfare agency. Her caseworker felt that the living conditions and housing were so poor that she was not being well cared for. Janine and all of her siblings presented behavior problems at home and in school. The family consisted of the mother, age thirty, and three siblings, ages fifteen, thirteen, ten. The family had been living in an apartment which was literally "falling apart." In the first session, the mother expressed a sense of being overwhelmed. She was unable to find an adequate living arrangement on the stipend allowed by her monthly welfare check. The family needed help but reported that they had no one from whom they could seek help. In their first session, the therapist supported the mother's executive, parental role in the family and was able to mobilize the family around their desire to stay together.
>
> In the third session, after gaining the family's trust, the therapist began to inquire about their support system and to help them search for sources of help. Within this context, she sug-

gested that they draw a genogram together. Although the mother had stated that she had "no one," the genogram and carefully asked questions uncovered many sources of help. For example, she had a sister in the same city whom she rarely called. After encouragement, Ms. G. contacted her and the sister offered to supply the security deposit on a new apartment. Ms. G. also identified a close friend of the family who, although not a "blood relative," was very close to Ms. G. and her children. This person offered to go out with her to search for an apartment. The genogram exercise also helped to highlight how isolated the family was and Ms. G. was able to discuss how this had come about. It also focused attention on the need for this nuclear family to come together and support each other. Ms. G. was helped to begin to restructure and delegate tasks at home. For example, the fifteen-year-old daughter was asked to support the apartment search by caring for Janine and the other children while her mother went out to look. As structures and supports were built, the children's acting out began to diminish.

This case illustrates the role which the genogram exercise can serve with a Black family if it is properly introduced. It also demonstrates the role which family therapists who work with Black families must often provide, i.e., helping them to cope with pressing survival issues such as poor housing, financial burdens and sometimes a sense of isolation.

ADAPTABILITY OF FAMILY ROLES

It is essential that clinicians who treat Black families recognize that a system may be functional even though it deviates from the traditional concept of family which is most familiar to the therapist. Role flexibility can be a vital force that can be mobilized in times of crisis. On the other hand, the boundaries in a family can become so blurred that there is no clear division of responsibility or source of authority. The parental child system and the three-generational system containing a grandmother or other maternal figure are perfect examples of this type of nebulous familial pattern.

Parental Child System

In many Black families, it is common for parental power to be allocated to a child, male or female, particularly if there are many children, or if both parents work. Minuchin (1974) reported that "the system can function well. The other children are cared for, and the parental child can develop responsibility, competence and autonomy beyond his years." However a family with such a structure may run into problems if the delegation of authority is not explicit. According to Minuchin, this frequently occurs when the child lacks the power to carry out the responsibilities he or she attempts to assume. Difficulties also arise when the parents abdicate their responsibilities, and the child is forced to become the main source of guidance. Thus, the child is confronted with decision making at a period in life where developmentally he or she is unprepared (Minuchin, 1974). Behavioral problems in school often emerge among parental children in late adolescence. These adolescents act out their feelings of being stressed through delinquency, sexual impulsiveness or inappropriate handling of younger siblings when the demands of the household impinge on their own needs to be with peers.

According to Minuchin (1974), the best strategy for working with parental child families is to "realign the family in such a way that the parental child can still help the mother" (p. 98). Thus, the goal of therapy is not the elimination of the child's parental role which may be essential to the family's survival. Instead, the clinician needs to facilitate redistribution of the child's responsibilities or, in some cases, assist the family to make better use of external resources available to them. The therapeutic guideline, according to Minuchin, is to clarify the boundary between mother and child so that the existing familial structure can be more functional. "The boundary between mother and the other children has to be modified to allow them direct access to her. The parental child has to be returned to the sibling subgroup though he maintains his position of leadership and junior executive power" (Minuchin, 1974). It is imperative that the family therapist find out if this type of system exists early in the treatment process. Foley (1975) points out that "In an initial family interview it is always wise to check out the amount of responsibility given to this child, and if the child is over-burdened to suggest a more equitable division of labor'' (p. 33).

Three-Generational System

Generally, the grandmother plays a central role in many Black families, and the boundary problems presented by such three-generational systems must be handled sensitively. The clinician's role is not to evict her from her position in the family nor to radically alter the structure of the family. The goal here is to build upon the fundamental strength of such a system by facilitating a working alliance among the executive members of the family. Thus, their roles and responsibilities can be clarified and each member can become more supportive of the others. Minuchin (1974) has given clear examples of the steps toward restructuring this type of family in which a grandmother is central. In many Black families, however, many extended family members play a major role in decision making and child rearing. In Black families where this extended family structure works well, lines of authority are clear, generational boundaries are maintained and tasks are clearly delegated. In many of the families who come into treatment, however, these structures and boundaries have never existed or have deteriorated over the year. In these situations, the adults may give input to a child or children in a chaotic way. Rules and boundaries are not clear and there is acting out. In these situations, the family therapist's task is to help the family restructure itself so that boundaries and lines of authority are clear. The following family illustrates this process.

> The K. family was a Black family consisting of Alice, a fourteen-year-old girl, and her paternal grandmother (age sixty-five). Mrs. K., Alice's mother, had died ten years earlier of a drug overdose. Her father was a drifter who came in and out of her life. Her maternal aunt was her only remaining tie to her mother's family. Mrs. K. reported that she could not handle Alice's behavior. She was rude toward her and would "talk back." At times she would "run away from home." As the therapist began to work with this family, it became increasingly clear that Alice's father and maternal aunt played a very key role. Whenever her grandmother attempted to set

limits or discipline her, she would contact her father or "run away" to her aunt's house. Because none of the adults in this executive system were in contact regularly, they often contradicted each other and undermined the grandmother. The therapist supported the grandmother in calling a meeting of all of the adults with Alice. They were able to clarify the ways in which Alice was manipulating their involvement. With the therapist's help, they were able to put aside their differences and come together as an executive, parental group for Alice. They decided that the grandmother, who lived with Alice, must be clearly "in charge" and that no one else was to intervene with her without first consulting with her grandmother. Both her father and her aunt were clear with Alice that she could not "run to them" when she had a disagreement with her grandmother. Alice was helped to share with her father and her aunt her need for their involvement at times other than "crises." The therapist helped them to work out a regular system and schedule of contacts. Alice's angry arguments and running away episodes stopped within a few weeks.

Subgroup meetings are very valuable when working with underorganized families (Aponte, 1976), since extended family members may be an essential part of the executive system of the family. However, the therapist must be very problem focused when making decisions about subgroup composition and its importance to the facilitation of the treatment process. This decision should be based on a careful analysis of who is crucial to the resolution of the delineated problem.

STRONG RELIGIOUS ORIENTATION

It is important for therapists working with Black families to acknowledge and in some cases utilize the pervasive role religion can play in the lives of family members. The research of Lewis and Looney (1983) with Black working-class families demonstrates the very central role which religion has played in their lives. Griffith et al. (1980), Knox (1985), Mitchell and Lewter (1986), have all explored the role of spirituality and religion in the lives of many Black families and in treatment interventions. Much more research is required on the role of religion in the mental health of this population. It is quite apparent, however, that the church has provided a forum for expression with regard to leadership, creative talents, and emotional catharsis. For example, the father of a family might be a janitor during the week but hold a position of responsibility as a deacon or trustee in his church. A mother who feels burdened and depressed due to the obligations of raising a family along may find an emotional outlet by singing in the church choir and renew her sense of hope through the spirituals and gospels.

In the initial stages of family therapy, inquiries about church activities and family member participation can reinforce self-esteem and be an effective joining strategy in working with Black families. Larsen (1976) suggests that therapists who are acquainted with Biblical passages can utilize this knowledge to support therapeutic recommendations. This can be helpful when trying to break through the tendency of some religious individuals to attribute their current problems as God's will, and relinquishing any personal control over their lives. At times, the very fact that one member of the family is devout may be directly related to the family's presenting complaint, i.e., being overly strict in terms of behavior at home, inhibiting expression due to religious beliefs. In such cases, a therapist's greatest resource may be the minister or friends from the church group. When a family's minister has been actively involved in family crises, it might very well be most beneficial if the minister was called upon to act as a co-therapist. It is fascinating how family therapists routinely contact a prior therapist of a patient, but will not call a minister who has been involved in counseling the family members. This type of resource can be very important in the overall therapeutic process and should not be underestimated or neglected when devising a treatment plan. The following example illustrates these points:

> Mary, an eighteen-year-old Black woman initially requested individual treatment. She was very depressed and was totally unable to differentiate from her family or her (Apostolic) Church. Her minister, and his wife who were also her godparents, had a very powerful role in her family. Her mother was a

woman of thirty-six who had "raised her children in the Church." Mary and her brother (age seventeen) had been active in Church activities from an early age. Mary's issues came to a head when she had a very angry confrontation with her mother because she was late for Church on Sunday.

As the animosity between them began to escalate, Mary found it difficult to be in the same room with her mother and there were constant arguments between them. Because of the intensity of the conflict, the therapist suggested a family session. Because of their central role, Mary was asked to invite her minister and his wife as well as her mother and brother.

It became very clear in the session that Mary and her mother had a very enmeshed relationship. Mary shared with her mother that she had become very restrictive and would not allow her to breathe. Mary's minister was able to help her mother see that she was so frightened that Mary would repeat her history of having a child out of wedlock, that she was "holding on too tight." The minister was able to help Mary's mother see that Mary was a "good girl" and did not need these constant restrictions. The therapist then encouraged the mother to talk with Mary about her own life and her fears for her daughter. Both cried a number of times in the session and were able to make the first step toward differentiation. The minister, because of his history with the family, was able to open up areas which would have been closed to the therapist. He was also privy to "family secrets" which had not been shared with the therapist. In addition, his intervention helped to refocus the attention on the mother-daughter relationship and allowed them to work directly on issues of separation and differentiation.

Many Black Churches are very enmeshed in families. Often individuals must struggle with the task of maintaining their own differentiation of self (Bowen, 1976) and remaining connected to their "Church family." Mary's experience of having a "family" connection to her minister is not unusual.

Often the minister and his family, because they often live in the same community for generations, will have many members of the "church family" who have become part of their extended family lives.

THE VALUE OF EDUCATION AND WORK ETHIC

Many Black families place a very high value on education and on achievement orientation. Black parents generally expect their children to surpass them in achieving the comforts of life. These are very basic values which Black families share with many other ethnic groups. They are stressed here because many clinicians are often confused by the presentation of these beliefs in some Black families and have difficulty recognizing them as a strength. It is often easier for clinicians to recognize these strengths in upwardly mobile Black working-class or middle-class families. Lewis and Looney (1983) in their study of well-functioning working-class Black families show that many of these families gave their children a clear message that they could "make it" in spite of discrimination. Boyd-Franklin (1989) clarifies this further.

> Education is seen as the way out of poverty for many Black families as it is for many other ethnic groups. For some Black families, however, although the value and the belief in education are very strong, the ability to operationalize this in terms of the schooling of their children has not been accomplished. This is particularly true of some inner-city Black families who feel powerless to change their schools and who have been made to feel unwelcome in these institutions. (Boyd-Franklin, 1989)

Boyd-Franklin describes ways in which therapeutic interventions can be used to empower these families to make a difference in their children's lives. Thus, this strong belief in the value of education can be utilized to engage Black families in treatment. For example, many Black families are referred for family therapy and become engaged because of their concern about the consequences of poor school adjustment that may jeopardize their children's opportunities to advance educationally and their ability to get jobs later. In conjunction with the typical stress associated with adolescence, low-income Black youth are often faced with the need to make decisions about their work and educational goals at younger ages than their more economically advantaged counterparts. They have fewer ways of acting out their anxieties and frustrations. Concern for their children's future as well as the reactivation of their own sense of powerlessness, rage, and limited resources to assist their offspring in starting out in life, may lead parents to react to their children in ways that exacerbate the problems. Thus, the goal of therapy is, on the one hand, to support the strong belief and positive expectations of the family and on the other to assist parents in distinguishing between their own personal issues and goals and those of their children. Reinforcement of a sense of mastery is crucial in these cases; helping family members focus on their resources that can be employed to support and assist their children toward a better lifestyle is a primary therapeutic goal when working with Black families with adolescents.

Sometimes educational advancement can create further assistance and strain. This has been true for many immigrant groups in this country. Many middle-class Black family members who do succeed in the professions are also often confronted by a sense of alienation from the origin kinship network. This can lead to familial conflicts and dysfunction as the successful family member continues to achieve financial security and professional status in the realm of the middle class. Emotional pressure to maintain ties with the kinship network while simultaneously climbing the ladder of success, all too often puts a strain on the entire familial structure. Again the family therapist may be called upon to help the stressed family member find a balance between their own responsibilities and stressors of the White-dominated world of work and their sense of obligations and bonds to the kinship system. This requires that the therapist acknowledge the socioeconomic realities and racist attitudes that often confront middle-income Black families, and help them build and create their own unique model of coping strategies to establish an equilibrium within the family system.

COPING SKILLS

If there is any one strength which is constantly demonstrated by Black families, it is the ability to survive and cope in the face of economic and social adversity. As previously discussed, the flexibility of familial roles, and the bond of the extended family which provides a viable support network in times of crisis are two of the coping strategies Black families have effectively utilized to perpetuate and maintain a familial structure. Unfortunately, these coping skills and strategies have been seen as liabilities by some family therapists. Such practices as "child-keeping," i.e., a relative raising a child rather than the biological parent, and the parental child system are usually labeled dysfunctional or maladaptive. Therefore, when Black families come into treatment, they may pick up cues that are interpreted as criticisms or a sense that their familial patterns are not "conducive to mental health."

Other therapists are particularly concerned about the "resistance" issues with Black families. In a survey of family therapists, clinicians were asked to cite the most common problems found in the treatment of Black families (Boyd, 1977). Forty-three percent of those queried considered resistance to therapy a major obstacle in the treatment of this population. Perhaps this resistance can be seen as a reaction to the perception on the part of Black families that their strengths and abilities to successfully cope in the face of adversity, e.g., low income, racism, and the vagaries of the ecostructure (schools, courts, social agencies), are not acknowledged. When they do come for treatment, frequently the emphasis is on how they "deviate" from the norm, i.e., the nuclear family. Thus, an effective strategy to help build a sense of trust and a therapeutic alliance can be overt acknowledgment of positive regard and recognition of the Black family's coping strategies. This type of joining with the family will encourage the family to open up and be more receptive to the acquisition of the new skills and recommendations on how to enhance the familial system. The next section will discuss the multisystems model of treatment which can help to facilitate this treatment process.

MULTISYSTEMS MODELS

The multisystems model (Boyd-Franklin, 1989) is a non-traditional treatment approach which allows the therapist a great deal of flexibility in working with Black families. Its treatment strategies can be incorporated very effectively with other cultural groups as well, particularly those which tend to have extended family systems. It allows the therapist to conceptualize interventions with any family at many different levels including the individual, the subsystem, the family household, the extended family, the Church and other networks, and the social service systems.

This model builds upon many of the problem-solving techniques of the structural family therapy model (Haley, 1976; Minuchin, 1974). It stresses the importance of joining first with Black families and establishing trust. It then helps to acquaint the family with the therapeutic process by focusing on the problems which the family wants to address and change.

The therapist can then choose to intervene at any or all of the multisystems levels. By targeting particular problems, the therapist is able to keep the family problem focused and empower them to intervene at the appropriate system levels to produce change.

This model is applicable to all Black families, but it is particularly useful when working with poor, inner-city Black families. It builds upon the work of Aponte (1976), and Hartman and Laird (1983). For poor Black families, many other, outside systems intrude on the family and exert tremendous power in their lives. These systems might include schools, courts, child welfare agencies, housing offices, welfare departments, police, hospitals, other health and mental health providers. The multisystems model provides principles which are very useful to the family therapist in helping Black families to "navigate these systems." Often the therapist will find that meeting with representatives from these various agencies with the family will help them to assess the boundary, alignment and power issues involved. Often the family therapist may find it necessary to restructure or help the family renegotiate and clarify its relationship with a particular agency. This model reinforces family strength and competency, and contributes to the empowerment of Black families in family therapy.

SUMMARY

The strengths and vibrancy of Black families have been the primary focus of this article. Frequently these positive attributes are not acknowledged within the more traditional treatment approaches. All too often the Black families seeking help are confronted by therapist behaviors implying that their familial patterns are dysfunctional in comparison to the "norm," i.e., the nuclear family. These strengths can be mobilized by the therapist to enhance the therapeutic process, restructure the family system and promote significant changes in behavior.

REFERENCES

Aponte, H. J. (1976). The family-school interview. *Family Process*, *15*, 303-310.

Bagarozzi, D. A. (1980). Family therapy and the Black middle class: A neglected area of study. *Journal of Marital and Family Therapy, 6*(12), 159-166.

Billingsley, A. (1968). *Black families in White America*. Englewood Cliffs, NJ: Prentice-Hall.

Bowen, M. (1976). Theory in the practice of psychotherapy. In P. Guerin (Ed.), *Family therapy*: Theory and practice. New York: Gardner Press.

Boyd, N. (1976-77). Clinician's Perceptions of Black Families in Therapy. Ph.D. dissertation, Teachers College, Columbia University, 1976-77.

Boyd-Franklin (1989). *Black families in therapy: A multisystems approach*. New York: Guilford Publications.

Brice, J. (1982). West Indian families. In M. McGoldrick, J. K. Pearce, & J. Giordano (Eds.), *Ethnicity and family therapy*. New York: The Guilford Press, 123-133.

Foley, V. (1975). Family therapy with Black disadvantaged families: Some observers on roles, communications, and technique. *Journal of Marriage and Family Counseling, 1*, 29-38.

Griffith, E. H., English, T., & Mayfield, V. (1980). Possession, prayer and testimony: Therapeutic aspects of the Wednesday night meeting in a Black church. *Psychiatry, 43*, 120-128.

Guerin, P., & Pendagast, M. A. (1976). Evaluation of family system and genogram. In P. Guerin (Ed.), *Family therapy: Theory and practice*. New York: Gardner Press.

Haley, J. (1976). *Problem-solving therapy*. San Francisco: Jossey-Bass.

Hartman, A., & Laird, J. (1983). *Family centered social work practice*. New York: The Free Press (Division of Macmillan, Inc.).

Hill, R. (1972). *The strengths of Black families*. New York: Emerson Hall.

Hines, P., & Boyd-Franklin, N. (1982). Black families. In M. McGoldrick, J. K. Pearce, & J. Giordano (Eds.), *Ethnicity and family therapy*. New York: Guilford Press.

Knox, D. H. (1985). Spirituality: A tool in the assessment and treatment of Black alcoholics and their families. *Alcoholism Treatment Quarterly, 2*(3/4), 31-44.

Larsen, J. (1976). Dysfunction in the Evangelical Family: Treatment Considerations. Paper presented at the meeting of the American Association of Marriage and Family Counselors, Philadelphia, October.

Lewis, J., & Looney, J. (1983). *The long struggle: Well-functioning working-class Black families*. New York: Brunner/Mazel, Inc.

Lindblad-Goldberg, M., & Dukes, J. (1985). Social support in Black, low-income, single-parent families: Normative and dysfunctional patterns. *American Journal of Orthopsychiatry, 55*, 42-58.

McAdoo, H. P. (Ed.). (1981). *Black families*. Beverly Hills, CA: Sage Publications, Inc.

McAdoo, H. P., & McAdoo, J. L. (Eds.). (1985). *Black children: Social, educational and parental environments*. Beverly Hills, CA: Sage Publications.

McGoldrick, M., & Gerson, R. (1985). *Genograms in family assessment*. New York: W. W. Norton & Co.

Minuchin, S., Montalvo, B., Guerney, B., Rosman, B., & Schumer, F. (1967). *Families of the slums*. New York: Basic Books.

Minuchin, S. (1974). *Families and family therapy*. Cambridge: Harvard University Press.

Mitchell, H., & Lewter, N. (1986). *Soul theology: The heart of American Black culture*. San Francisco: Harper & Row, Publishers.

Moynihan, D. (1965). *The Negro family: The case for national action*. Washington, DC: Office of Policy Planning and Research, U.S. Department of Labor.

Pattison, E. (1976). A Theoretical-Empirical Base for Social Systems Therapy. Presented at the 33rd Annual Conference of the American Group Psychotherapy Association. Boston, February 1976.

Sager, C., & Brayboy, T. (1970). *Black ghetto family in therapy: A laboratory experience*. New York: Grove Press.

Stack, C. (1974). *All our kin: Strategies for survival in a Black community*. New York: Harper & Row.

Circles and Cedar:
Native Americans and Family Therapy

Terry Tafoya

Long ago, there was a young woman whom we would call in our language "aiyaiyesh" meaning "stupid" or "retarded." While all the other young people of her age helped their elders, the aiyaiyesh girl would sit beneath the Cedar tree, day after day and all day long, watching the world go by. Finally, the Cedar Tree could not stand it any longer, and spoke to her.

"You're so aiyaiyesh" the Tree said "now watch and I will show you how to do something." The Tree showed her how to take its roots, coiling their cool moist paleness into circle upon circle, fashioning the first hard-root cedar basket in the Pacific Northwest. Circles are very sacred to Native people . . . the wind moves in its strongest power in a circle . . . the circle represents the world, which turns in a circle. When she completed this first basket, the Cedar Tree approved of it but pointed out that it was naked and that a basket to be really finished required patterns—designs.

The aiyaiyesh girl began crying for she knew no patterns. The Cedar Tree told her to start walking, keeping her eyes, her ears, and her heart open, and she would discover all sorts of patterns for her basket. And so it was she traveled, and different beings would speak to her . . . the rattlesnake showed her its diamond-shaped designs; the mountains showed her the shape of triangles; the salmon showed its gills . . . all around her were the designs of shadows and leaves and colors. And

Terry Tafoya, PhD, is Professor in Residence, Department of Psychology, Evergreen State College, Olympia, WA 98505.

when she had learned to put all of these designs into her baskets, she returned to the village where she taught her relatives
and her friends how to make these baskets. And she wasn't
aiyaiyesh anymore. Ana cush nai.

— Traditional Sahaptin Legend

This story can be understood as a central paradigm for the way in
which many Native Americans conceptualize relationships, responsibilities, learning, and teaching, in short, the core elements of
Family Therapy.

It is an erroneous assumption on the part of many mental health
professionals that Native Americans are "just like everyone else"
and that if there ever were relevant differences, they disappeared
along with the buffalo; any problems in therapy arise from socioeconomic deprivation, i.e., the "culture of poverty." In fact, research overwhelmingly supports the continuation of Native cultural
differences that can enhance or impede treatment (Axelson, 1985;
Manson, 1982; Sue, 1981; Tafoya, 1989).

It should also be emphasized that there are over 300 tribes in the
United States, as well as over 50 in Canada (Deloria, 1977; Tafoya,
in press a; U.S. Congress, 1987). The Indian population has consistently been on the increase since the late 1800s, and a significant
number of the Native population is under the age of 18 (Tafoya,
1989; U.S. Congress, 1987; U.S. Indian Health Services, 1978).
There are over 2,500 laws and regulations which affect American
Indians and Alaskan Natives and yet do not apply to the general
American public (Sanders, 1973). The complications of Native history in connection with federal and state governments is mind-bog-
gling.

American Indians, Alaskan Natives, and Native Hawaiians (all
considered to be Native Americans) are unique among American
minorities in that they possess a political/legal relationship with the
federal government. Identity for American Indians, if not, in fact,
in spirit, is often associated with blood quantum, with federal recognition typically associated with being a quarter blood of a federally recognized tribe. Even this is massively confusing in defining
one's identity. At least nine different legal definitions of American
Indian have been offered (Sanders, 1973). Among some tribal

groups or communities, identity as a Native may be more closely tied to the ability to use one's traditional language, involvement in ceremonies and clan activities, and the prestige and status of one's family. As discussed later, identity is also an issue with both the many younger people of Native ancestry who "adopted out" prior to the late 1970s and to Native people who attended Federal Boarding Schools, which curtailed their traditional and language usage.

There is tremendous variation among tribes regarding gender roles, language, religion, acculturation, and relationship with non-Indians. Any attempt to generalize results in an unfortunate substitution of one stereotype for another (Sue, 1981; Tafoya 1982, 1989). There are, however, some commonalities, as well as some potential problems, which can be discussed in regard to concerns of Family Therapy.

TRADITIONAL HEALING APPROACHES

In many tribes, healing ceremonies were (and are) frequently done within an extended family setting (Tafoya, 1989). Rather than therapy being done behind the closed door of an office, healing "work" is often done in people's homes or in ceremonial places like Longhouses (which in some cases, actually evolved into separate specialized structures following the non-Indian insistence that Native people move into "conventional" style housing). A common feature of some rituals is a public disclosure, such that one's repressed emotions are brought before the extended family by either the patient or by the healer (Indian Doctor is the term most used in English, as well as Medicine Man or Woman, whereas the term shaman is sometimes used by a few California tribes and by others heavily influenced by anthropological jargon; tribes have their own terminologies that can be quite specific).

This "public confession" which is frequently found in traditional healing can be compared to the relevance of Network Therapy. In fact, one of the pioneers in Networking, Carolyn Attneave, is a Delaware/Cherokee Indian, who has worked with creating what are fundamentally artificial clan systems for non-Indians. Thus, a public statement of the problem allows the Network to mobilize its members to maximize its resources (Speck & Attneave, 1973).

Storytelling is often an integral part of therapy, providing a non-threatening and indirect way of structuring the problem in a way that has been adapted by Milton H. Erickson (Erickson was also of Native ancestry) and by his followers in terms of therapeutic metaphor (Haley, 1985; Watzlawick & Weakland, 1977; Zeig, 1982, 1985). The stories, either legends or "case histories" of other patients (especially of older relatives of the person being treated) serve to "triangulate" the problem of the patient, providing a comfortable distance if he or she becomes too fearful of dealing with the issue directly. Depending on his or her nonverbal responses, the skilled Indian Doctor or the therapist can then increase the parallels between the characters in the story and the patient's life, or back off a bit (increasing the angle of the triangle) by emphasizing "this is, of course, somewhat different from your situation" until finally, as rapport is achieved, solutions and resolutions can be offered in the story form (Gilligan, 1987).

In the case of the aiyaiyesh girl of the legend, she can be understood as partaking in a type of Network Therapy, of establishing her relationships with those beings around her (since many Indian languages do not distinguish between "animal" and "human" one must refer to "salmon people," "snake people," — "human people" (Tafoya, 1982, 1989).

Characteristics of much of Native American traditional therapy can be seen as systemic interventions that would eventually become part of the standard repertoire of Family Therapy, especially as associated with the MRI "school" as it was influenced by Erickson:

1. *Ordeal Therapy*: The aiyaiyesh girl is required to undergo a strenuous journey for her education, thereby investing her energy in her own "cure" (cf. Erickson's classic technique of sending patients to climb Squaw Mountain in Arizona (Haley, 1985; Zeig, 1982, 1985).

2. *Humor*: The full story, told aloud, is one that evokes a great deal of laughter. I have never been to a Native healing ceremony in which moments of great solemnity were not balanced by humorous remarks and insights. While this reflects the old maxim that "the reason why angels can fly is because they take themselves lightly," it also very much ties into many tribal traditions of sacred clowns in which clowns are constantly reframing one's perception of a situa-

tion (usually in a far more energetic manner than an average Family Therapist).

3. *Rituals*: Rituals are very much a part of Native healing. Although not dealt with in this version of the legend, it is understood that one doesn't just "make a basket" or "weave" or "bead" or "hunt", rather, one must have the appropriate attitude in one's actions. Rituals allow one to enter this creative frame of mind, and also, as Onna van der Hart (1982) has suggested, they permit a context and a container for powerful emotions. It should be stressed that a Native healer will not prescribe the same ceremony or ritual for every patient, even when patients present with the same symptoms, any more than a physician would prescribe penicillin to all patients with upper respiratory infections. Obviously, while rituals also help people to reach altered states of consciousness (q.v.) (Jilek, 1982; van der Hart, 1982), less attention has been paid to how rituals influence emotional arousal, a cross-cultural component Torrey and others have suggested as a sien qua non of healing (e.g., Torrey, 1983.)

4. *Altered States of Consciousness*: Altered states can be seen as breaking down the barriers of "everyday" consciousness that may serve to maintain the problem. An altered state is part of the aiyaiyesh girl's experience as she expands her awareness to communicate with nonhuman entities—or else, depending on one's paradigm, externally objectifies her awareness to gain new insight. The aiyaiyesh girl is undergoing an archetypal vision quest, an action associated with fasting, and its concomitant impact on her biochemistry and consciousness. Jilek has suggested the drumming of many Native ceremonies can also induce trance, especially when it occurs at a rate of 5-7 counts per second (Jilek, 1982). More research is being applied to informal induction of trance states that go on as a normal part of Family Therapy (Zeig, 1982, 1985). For example, microanalysis done in taking family history actually serves as age regression; asking the patient to imagine a different outcome, or work with goal setting can be a hypnotically induced form of positive hallucination; circular questioning can result in confusion of context markers, etc.

5. *Paradoxical Intervention*: Paradoxical intervention can clearly be seen in this story, where as Watzlawick and colleagues would

suggest that a level II change, rather than a level I change, is occurring (Watzlawick, Weakland, & Fisch, 1974). Thus her solution is contained within the problem. She is isolated from her human community. The intervention? She must increase her isolation and leave her community entirely, until she can return as an integrated and productive member.

6. *Directive Therapy*: The aiyaiyesh girl's Therapist (the Cedar Tree) is very specific in altering her behavior. As will be discussed later, this is a critical factor in the expectations of many Native clients regarding adherence to treatment. Traditional healing often involves "homework" assignments that the patient or family is expected to follow. This emphasizes the strong authoritarian role of the healer in many traditional cultures. The Cedar Tree's technique (to be later used in Ericksonian approaches) is to be open-ended in its injunctions — thus the girl is directed to discover her patterns, but *not* told what they would be, or where to find them — she is simply instructed to "be aware."

7. *Insight*: Again, with an emphasis on the MRI School and its Ericksonian influence, it should be understood that traditional healing rarely will stress insight. The concentration is on altering present actions which then impact emotional states, rather than expecting a therapist to alter the emotional state and then achieve behavioral change. Just so, the girl is never asked "how do you feel about this? — Why do you think you're so different? — What would happen if you change?"

CROSS-CULTURAL CONCERNS

The preceding brief overview of some concerns in traditional healing concentrated on the parallels between Family Therapy and Native American approaches and did not touch on some of the differences in worldviews that can impede or enhance service delivery. Many have stressed the importance of what has been termed the interaction or primary worldview (i.e., biomedical explanations of illness) and secondary worldview (i.e., culturally specific explanations of illness such as taboo breaking, witchcraft, out of harmony, spirit intervention, etc.) in connection with health-seeking behavior. The implication is that if the biomedical treatment is in conflict with the culturally specific explanation of illness, the patient will not comply with instructions or medication. A diabetic Yaqui tribal member with a diabetes-related ulceration may feel that she has been "witched" with a "viva" spitfire that burned her. Assuming the ulceration can even be treated, if her concern about being "witched" is not addressed, she may not care about a new hygienic routine as a preventive method to forestall gangrene. This can be thought of almost as a spiritual modification of Maslow's hierarchy of needs.

In many tribes, anger is conceptualized as a form of psychic energy that is "thrown" at another person. This emotion (envy, greed, and hate also fall into this interactional category) then "sticks" to the spirit body of the recipient to form what the Indians term "Tschitaimuch," a type of spiritual pollution that will eventually "dim" the radiance and health of the spirit body until, eventually, the person becomes ill. Thus, many purification ceremonies deal with the ritualistic cleansing of the spirit body that is believed to extend approximately 1 1/2 inches beyond the physical body. As a result, many Native people are taught to very carefully monitor their anger, and not express it openly, in order to avoid harming others. This is obviously in conflict with a primary worldview approach by most Anger-management clinics. This also offers an explanatory model of why expression of anger is so often a part of Native alcoholism, since it is so repressed when one is sober.

Another culturally specific problem, which some Native clients experience in working with therapists, is tied to a concept that Lakota people call "wacunza" (Albers & Medicine, 1983; Medicine, 1982). This translates as "to cause to happen" and refers to a nonlinear causation of illness. From a western viewpoint, it is logical that if one breaks a taboo, one can be punished. The wacunza concept teaches that the one breaking the taboo may not be the one to suffer the consequences in a direct way. Rather, someone in the extended family will become ill, such as an innocent child or elder. Fetal Alcohol Syndrome would be an excellent example of how a mother can wacunza her child while not being injured by the alcohol herself. Thus a Family Therapist might incorrectly diagnose a client taking responsibility of harming a loved one as being a form of western "projection" when, in fact, it is an accepted part of the culture.

Not all Native families will experience the same types of cultural interference problems. Historically, many tribes practiced "fostering" where children freely moved (often by their own choice) from extended household to extended household. If there were stress in living with a grandparent or parent, an adolescent might simply move in with an aunt for a few months or longer. As more and more Native people become urbanized (a little more than half the Native American population now resides in urban areas) and are separated from their families, this option is no longer a viable one. Consequently, families may not have the skills necessary for resolving conflicts that were once handled by separation.

Carolyn Attneave and I have earlier described some differences between "typical" Anglo-American families and "typical" Native American families, with illustrated Native genograms (Tafoya, 1982). Traditionally, many tribes would not consider people to be fully functional adults until they were in their mid-fifties or a grandparent. Thus, child-rearing responsibilities effectively skipped generations such that the young parent would actually "parent" his or her grandchildren. The idea was that younger people of an extended family should be wage-earners and providers while the retired generation "parented." This is not to say that some nurturing skills were not expected of mother or fathers, but rather that the majority of responsibility would often fall outside of the biological parents. The Native genogram also shows the close association between first cousins, considered to have a relationship to that of siblings. Grandparents and their siblings (thus also the first cousins of the grandparents) form the first sphere of influence on the children. Also included as in the in first sphere, would be clan relatives and godparents, nonbiological relatives that would not even appear on the Anglo-American genogram. The biological parents (as well as aunts and uncles) of the children are located on a secondary sphere of influence.

While traditional Native Family structures provided a healthy and variable form of childrearing and better distributed loss (Speck & Attneave, 1973; Tafoya, 1982), a number of relevant factors impact upon contemporary Indians and Family Therapy issues. Federal

Boarding Schools, for example, have had an immense effect on families. Treaties made between American Indian nations and the U.S. federal government included a provision for Native Education. The 19th century attitude that Christianity was synonymous with civilization meant that Federal Boarding Schools maintained a missionary bent which emphasized the separation of Native children from the "savage" influence of their families (Deloria, 1977, 1985; Kelso & Attneave, 1981; Nichols, 1986; U.S. Senate, 1987). Students were sent as far away as possible when school officials discovered that they would escape. Thus, Pacific Northwest children would frequently be sent to Oklahoma and California while Navajo and Eskimo students found themselves in Oregon. Many children were removed from their families at the age of five and could not return, even during the summers, for many years.

Public schools, funded by property taxes, excluded Native children. This was based on the fact that reservations are federal land (like military bases) and the Native parents living on them were paying no property taxes. In the 1930s, the Johnson-O'Malley Act allowed Native children to attend public schools by paying districts a per capita allocation for serving Native children living on or near a reservation.

Boarding schools are still active today, and often service not only children who would otherwise not be able to attend a public school, because of geographical isolation, but also a combination of students who may not have "fit in" to a public school (at this point many school counselors automatically recommend an Indian Boarding School so the public school no longer has a "problem" student): students from poverty level families, who feel the school can offer more resources than they can; children with severe emotional and adjustment problems who have no other alternative within compulsory systems; and finally, some Native students with a strong desire to simply be in an all Indian school.

While today's schools are more tolerant of the cultural needs of students, historically, Native students were physically beaten for speaking their own language. In addition, church attendance was mandatory and students were instructed to think of their traditional ways as dangerously pagan and shameful.

For the Family Therapist, this means that very few Native people have had pleasant educational experiences. While some elders can serve as cultural resources, a particular family's elders may have "had the Indian beat out of them." Subsequently, they may give little to no support to grandchildren seeking information on their Indian identity, and indeed, may have been among those Indian people reared with the message that the only way to succeed was to turn their back on anything Indian and to marry non-Indian spouses.

Boarding School students, even contemporary ones, are isolated from their families during critical learning experiences. For example, Alaska Native youth don't have an opportunity to learn bush survival skills because they are attending schools when such skills would normally be taught. Thus many students suffer low self-esteem from having very limited knowledge of what someone much younger should know. These older students may never have the chance to learn these skills since it would be inappropriate for an adult to try to find out what a child should know.

Finally, there are some families that have no living memory of how to parent children of Boarding School age, since these children were always away. Thus, parenting classes may be quite critical in working with such families who have literally no parenting backgrounds in certain areas.

Adoption also plays a critical role in many Native families. With the advent of birth control, the number of white children available for adoption declined while the need for adoptable children continued to increase, resulting in more and more "minority" children being in "demand."

Prior to the passage of the Indian Child Welfare Act of 1978, it was estimated that up to 25% of American Indian children were being reared in non-Indian homes (Kelso & Attneave, 1981; Manson, 1982; Tafoya, 1989). These children were overwhelmingly (over 90%) removed for "neglect" as opposed to "abuse." Neglect basically meant whatever non-Indian judges and social workers decided it meant, based on the standards of white communities. Before the revision of the Washington State Activity Codes, being reared by the nonbiological parents, for example, could justify the removal of children for "neglect" even though parenting by grandparents is a typical Native American Family style.

John Joseph Westermyer, a psychiatrist doing research in Minnesota in the 1970s, found that these adopted children generally fared well in their white homes until adolescence. At that point, their academic achievement and attendance, which had not been statistically different from their white neighbors, suddenly plummeted. Their suicide rate jumped up to five times the national average for their general American counterparts (Kelso & Attneave, 1981; Tafoya, 1989).

It is suggested that these children psychologically identify with being white and that they do well up to the point at which that they undergo ego separation from their adoptive families and are identified as being non-white by those outside of the families. Thus, an adolescent trying to date or get a first job is not perceived as a Caucasian, and is treated accordingly. A minority child growing up in a minority family has modeled how a minority adult deals with racism and discrimination appropriately. A minority child growing up in a white home had modeled how a *white* adult deals with such problems, thus learning inappropriate behaviors.

Indeed, such children are frequently in a double bind of being unacceptable in Indian communities because they "act white" (i.e., their nonverbal communications and values reflect those of their adoptive parents) and unacceptable to a white community because they are visibly different.

When I used to write a regular column for a major Seattle newspaper, the article which generated the most reader feedback was one on this topic. It ended with the statement that Indian (and other minority) children had special needs which white parents could not meet in isolation from minority communities and the claim that such adoptive parents would need to make an extra effort to provide appropriate exposure to culturally specific role models. The response was completely negative, with scathing letters accusing me of stating that white parents should not be allowed to adopt minority children (although this was never mentioned in the column).

In the fall of 1986, our clinic got a phone call from a white parent asking for assistance in working with his adopted adolescent Indian son. Because of a long waiting list, we referred them to a Native American female therapist in private practice. During the intake, she stated that she felt this was a family issue and wanted to deal with it through co-therapy with a male Family Therapist who was Indian. When she mentioned my name, the adoptive father became upset, saying "Not Terry Tafoya! We're afraid of him. Twelve years ago he wrote an article saying that white parents shouldn't adopt Indian children" (C. Couch, personal communication, Sept. 15, 1987).

Within the space of eight weeks, I received five referrals of adopted Native American adolescents with suicidal and behavioral problems. This is obviously an issue of concern not only for the followers of Bowen, but for any Therapist dealing with Family of Origin. Due to stereotyping, many non-Indian families do polarity flips between perceiving Indians as romantic mystics and as drunken savages. On the extreme negative side, some adoptive parents emphasize separation from biological relatives, fearing that their adopted children will become alcoholics.

For Native adolescents, this may become a self-fulfilling prophecy, wherein they feel rejected by their non-Indian community and, finding mystics and buffalo in short supply, opt for drinking binges (since this is what the media teaches about what "Indians do").

For a people with such a strong emphasis on tribalism and on belonging, these adopted children find that they do not know what tribe they are but only that they are Indian. Because of legal restrictions, adoption records may be sealed, making it impossible to trace ancestry.

The problems which Native Americans have faced have been so severe that some therapists see similarities to survivors of the Holocaust, in terms of a pervasive sense of loss and devastation and the aftermath of survival guilt for those who "made it." For Therapists pursuing this topic, it is critical to determine the Native client's perception of what "being Indian" may mean. If adopted, what were the injunctions or the "script" which the family gave to the child? There may be bereavement issues that the adult Native client may need to deal with around childhood removal from the biological family and any unresolved anger of abandonment by that family.

SPOUSE INTERACTIONAL CONCERNS

In the urban clinical setting in which I work, I have yet to see a Native American couple in my eight years of practice. About 5% of our clients are Native American and I assume that Native couples are more frequently seen by the Seattle Indian Health Board. This raises intermarriage issues for these mixed couples, whose communication styles, values, and expectations may differ considerably. For example, gender roles are of prime importance. A Native male from a strong matrilineal background may experience problems in a relationship with a wife accustomed to male authority. Child discipline, employment, and birth control, may take on added confusing significance.

An incident accorded relatively minor importance in general American culture (e.g., a death outside of the immediate family, or a daughter's first period) may be of paramount concern among many Natives. A need to hold certain ceremonies at a specific time (weddings, funerals, memorial services, naming ceremonies) may result in bitter fighting among spouses and extended families, the point of which may also appear bizarre to the Therapist.

Many Native events dealing with change in status (e.g., funerals, namings, marriages, etc.) are accompanied by "giveaways" (sometimes referred to in the literature as a "potlatch," a term delivered from the Nootkan "potlatch" meaning "giveaway") (Tafoya, 1989). Food, money, and gifts are given away at this time and not to the "hosts" (as in white weddings or funerals) but to the "guests," since in a culture based on oral tradition, witnesses validate an event. A guest receiving a gift would therefore be expected to testify that this event did take place and that it was handled appropriately. There is also the concept that sorrow shared is halved; joy shared is doubled.

Traditionally, the family network supported these giveaways so that there was not a solitary economic drain on an individual. For Native people isolated in cities or estranged because of marriage or religion, there may be a strong sense of guilt for not behaving in an acceptable manner at one of these status change points. One can also imagine the confusion of a non-Indian spouse upon being told that his or her in-laws will be giving away all the furniture, dishes, utensils, and even the carpet, when a household member dies. For many tribes, especially in the Pacific Northwest, a secondary giveaway during a memorial service is then held within a year or so, sometimes in conjunction with raising a headstone.

Additional concerns might revolve around the actual disposal of the body (some tribes abhor cremation or dismemberment, such as an autopsy, since the body is conceptualized as a seed that is planted whole into the ground at death) or the significance of the death of someone not even considered to be a relative by white standards. For those tribal members who believe in keeping the body whole, amputation is a terrible thing. It is not unusual for the amputee to keep the part frozen to be buried with the rest of the body (one hopes) at a much later date. Some tribes save hair over a lifetime to be buried with the body. These are obviously potentially important issues for therapeutic exploration. A Native client may be unable to articulate why something is important, but simply knows that it is.

For some tribes, there are incredibly complex rules as to who can do what, and when. A client might therefore feel that something can be done, but that he or she is not the right one to do it. Some actions might require elaborate initiation and years of training, or even birthright, to grant one the opportunity to do a specific action, like healing or naming a child.

ISSUES OF FAMILY THERAPY

In an initial contact with Native American clients, non-Native therapists are often able to successfully alienate them with the handshake that may occur in the waiting room. While a "strong, firm" handshake may signal confidence and warmth to white people, for many Indians it is perceived as a quintessential competition of whites to prove how domineering they can be. Not all tribes traditionally shook hands. For those Native people who have adapted the handshake, it is usually expressed as a very light grasp, sometimes only a brushing of fingers. This interaction may leave the non-Indian therapist erroneously feeling that the Native client is a "cold fish," withdrawn and nonassertive.

To show respect, the Native client may not initially seek eye contact (a well documented phenomenon) which may encourage counter-transference by the Therapist of insecurity and dishonesty (Tafoya, 1989). Sociolinguists Ron and Suzanne Scallon have further suggested that Native American rules of dominance may be the mirror image of Americans in general. While Native concepts of power are associated with displaying (i.e., an elder demonstrating how to do something to a passively observing youth), white concepts of power are associated with passively observing (i.e., "Show me you need help, tell me your problem, and then I'll decide what to do for you"). When Native clients enact their subordinate position by passively observing, waiting for the dominant positioned Therapist to start, the Therapist may judge the client as having low affect and being withdrawn or hostile (Tafoya, 1982).

Further research in sociolinguistics indicates a difference in "pause time response" between native English speakers (i.e., most whites) and many Natives. This is the unconsciously controlled signaling of when one person finishes and another can speak—turn taking. For native English speakers, this is a one-second pause; for Native Athabaskan speakers (e.g., Canadian Dine Alaskan Athabaskans, Navajo and Apache) this may be 1.5 seconds (Tafoya, 1982). This is enough of a difference such that an English speaking therapist (or spouse) may constantly interrupt the Native client before he or she can begin, never providing a long enough pause to signal the Native client that it is his or her turn. The Native client is thus again in danger of being diagnosed as resistant and passive-aggressive. In my own research with the Tiwa language of the northern Pueblos of New Mexico, this pause time may be 4-5 seconds long.

Although a Native client may only have English as his or her means of oral expression, research by linguists such as William Leap clearly shows a three-generational influence on English of these Native American patterns. In other words, if a Native client's grandparent spoke an Indian language, the client will not necessarily process English in the manner of a native English speaker. This has led Leap to making a formal distinction between an English Speaker (most whites) and an English User (most Natives) (W. Leap, personal communication, 1986). Because the client is using English, the Therapist (and a non-Native spouse) may erroneously assume that they are all meaning the same thing while discussing issues when, in fact, they are not.

Most Native languages, for example, have no original words or concept to measure time in the manner of English and, in fact, do not usually have terms of standardized units of measure (foot, meter, minute, gram, etc.). Indeed, the Lakota word for time translates "to strike" from the Boarding School clocks that "struck" the hour (Hall, 1983). Native measurements are based on comparisons or, what Leap has called, "guesstimates." This may result in the well-known term "Indian time" that is being erroneously mistaken as meaning always being late for appointments when, in reality, it refers to doing something "when the time is right."

In the same way, few tribes have Native concepts for verbally expressing "I'm sorry" or for making excuses. With a philosophy that one is responsible for one's own actions, there is little need to apologize or to call in to cancel an appointment . . . if one is not there, this is obvious, and it is understood that if one could have been there, one would have, so why call? Obviously, many Native people working in urban areas have learned to adjust to the alien mores of whites regarding these issues. Traditionally, however, one will "pay off shame" through public ceremony and gift-giving rather than a vocal apology.

The policy of gift-giving is one that may come up periodically in treatment since Native beliefs emphasize a circularity — if one has been given something, there is a sense that the recipient will respond in some manner. In traditional healing, the patient will give the Indian Doctor food, or blankets, money, tobacco, etc., and the circle is complete. With the advent of third-party payment, through insurance of Indian Health Services, a Native client may not be involved in completing this circle. It is therefore not at all unusual for Native clients to provide some gift to the Therapist either upon initiation or closure of treatment. To refuse such a gift (the tendency of analytically-trained therapists) would be contraindicated.

It should also be stressed that the Native American population suffers from a remarkably high incidence of otitis media, an inner ear disorder that can lead to severe hearing impairment (Manson, 1982). A soft-spoken Therapist may find that a particular Native client is not ignoring questions, but is simply unable to hear and considers it impolite to ask the Therapist to repeat the question. When a hearing loss is not initially identified, a student may do poorly in school, especially if he or she follows the earlier described model of passively observing . . . to ask a question is implying the Teacher (or therapist) is not acting appropriately. Rather, it is assumed that when a student is ready for more complete information, the "elder" will provide it. In other words, knowledge is a privilege one earns, not a right one expects. Elders will monitor progress and provide information based on one's assessed readiness.

This tendency on the part of some Native people to neither ask direct questions nor challenge treatment can lead to a number of problems. For example, I was asked to do a client-centered consultation for a young Chippewa man who was undergoing a series of reconstructive facial surgeries, following an unsuccessful suicide attempt with a shotgun. The chief social worker told me that the young man had been very uncooperative with the auto mechanics training program which had been set up for him as part of his outpatient therapy. He had been working as an auto mechanic in the midwest before coming to Seattle. Upon discussion, it turned out that he had indeed worked in a garage but had been able to advance to the position of assistant manager. He desired vocational training but in business management, rather than auto mechanics.

In a more severe situation, a coastal Indian woman was admitted to the "locked ward" of the hospital, where her examining psychiatrist had entered into her chart suicidal ideation based on her cutting her hair (self-image/ego destructive) and her description of "knives around the doorway." Upon my review, I found out that the woman was an active member of the Shaker Indian Church, a Northwest coast religion that is a syncretic blend of traditional beliefs and Christianity. Her uncle had died and her extended family (members of a fundamentalist sect) did not want to participate in what were considered the appropriate mourning ceremonies of the Shakes (the Uncle had been of the Shaker faith). The cutting of her hair was an accustomed practice intended to show the loss of a loved one (for many tribes, loss of a spouse or child may result in braids being cut off).

In much of the federally built Reservation housing, the construction is very poor and locks fail to work after a few years. It is, therefore, a common practice to place butterknives around the doorframes to serve as a type of wedge lock to keep out undesirables (e.g., nocturnal drunks). This is what she was referring to by the "knives around the doorway." Needless to say, the real issue here

revolved around the need for Family Therapy to deal with accom-
modation concerns within her social network.

Native Americans are diagnosed as having depression at a rate 4-
6 times the national average. Current research in this field indicates
that there is frequently an initial affective disorder prior to alcoholic
problems and that substance abuse may actually be an attempt to
self-medicate (Manson, Walker, & Kivlahan, 1987). If this is, in
fact, the case, it would explain the high rate of failure for Indians
involved in alcohol treatment programs. If the underlying affective
disorder is not dealt with, it is only logical that the "detoxed" client
would go back to drinking. One of my clients, for example, had
been diagnosed as alcoholic but was also suffering Post-Traumatic
Stress Syndrome related to his Viet Nam war experience. Further
examination disclosed unresolved bereavement and abandonment
issues stemming from his father's death and his mother's leaving
him prior to his eighth birthday.

In my own work with Native American alcoholics, I find a consistent pattern of response to the question "What would happen if
you didn't drink?" to be "I wouldn't be able to talk to people." If a
native client has poor communication skills (or perhaps more accurately, "inappropriate" skills), it would be reasonable to assume
that such a client might have difficulty with an AA model requiring
him or her to talk about personal problems and history in a public
setting. For this reason, when referring to AA, I also recommend a
communications and assertiveness training program prior to the alcoholism treatment.

Further research in Native American depression indicates a difference in "threshold" time for diagnosis. By cultural standards,
Native individuals might be classified as depressed, prior to the
standard two weeks' duration suggested for DSM-III-R.

CASE EXAMPLES

There are times when I feel that it will be therapeutically appropriate to incorporate Native American rituals into my work, regardless of the ethnicity of the client. It should be stressed, however,
that I do so only if such actions will be in keeping with the worldview of the clients. For example, I would not have considered doing

a more traditional style healing ceremony with the Indian Shaker woman discussed earlier because her religion historically associates such actions with paganism and condemns them. The Shakers have their own interventions, however, and these can instead by utilized. I was asked to do a healing ceremony for an older Native man by the in-patient staff but declined when I interviewed him and discovered that he was a Pentecostal minister.

A 37-year-old woman of Native American ancestry of a Plains Indian tribe was self-referred to me following her psychiatric hospitalization for depression and suicidal ideation. Her mother had died shortly after her birth, cutting her off from her Native American extended family, while her non-Indian father had incestuously abused her. She was married with two children, and overly involved with a number of activities, which included serving as youth director for a protestant church, attempting to complete her graduate degree, and working as a liaison person for a national Indian concerns program for her church.

I instructed her to bring in people who were significant to her to take part in a Naming Ceremony. I specifically invited her individual therapist (who declined) and made certain that at least one of her Indian friends came. Typical of how I work in our clinic, I also asked several mental health professionals to take part, including asking one of the psychiatrists to drum. I did a cleansing ceremony on her to stress the idea of removing the "tschitamuch" described earlier and then induced a light trance state through storytelling. I told the story of how Chipmunk got her stripes (the result of her being scratched on the back by the Owl Woman) in a version that stressed how, through betrayal, Chipmunk was motivated to grow into a Warrior Woman, thereby providing a framework for her. I then asked the Director of our clinic, and then a non-Indian, to escort the patient into the room with the patient's Indian friend on her other side. This escorting is typical of Coastal Salish namings and was structured to emphasize the balance of the patient's mixed heritage. Blankets were placed over the three women, in the traditional manner, with an explanation that the blankets they wore were symbolic of the love and respect that was also covering them. They were sung in with an entry song and directed to take the patient to a blanket on the floor (traditionally, Namings take place in a Longhouse, in the same area a funeral would take place, and the blanket thus separates the one being named [considered in some ways to be "reborn"] from ground touched by the dead). She was told a second legend about the Origin of the Silver Salmon, in which a culture hero married a Salmon women, resulting in the Salmon's return each year to feed the tribe. It was explained to her, in her trance state, that the Salmon can be reborn, that salmon ceremonies return the bones of the fish to the water so it can be renewed. The name given to her translated as "Silver Salmon Woman," with the additional explanation that the name meant "She who gives, yet is renewed." This was to place her own background of being very active at providing for others, while at the same time creating an association of renewal by doing so, rather than one of exhaustion.

Those present who had been called as "witnesses" (as is becoming more common on the Coast, the ceremony was also videotaped, a high-tech form of validation) were given small gifts (two quarters wrapped in cloth, again, typically done in the calling of witnesses in Coastal ceremonies) and instructed to "Indian Preach," i.e., give words of wisdom based on their own experience to the one being named. This provided the opportunity for her friends and relatives to openly express, in a public setting, their feelings of love and acceptance for her while allowing mental health workers, who did not know her, to share in a very personal manner some of their own feelings about names and gift-giving in association with identity.

By the next day, she had been discharged from the hospital. She resumed working within two weeks on a more reasonable schedule. The ceremony was done in July and she was told that, while this was the actual ceremony, she would need to reaffirm the new name in a Longhouse within the Indian community, at which point she would be responsible for a giveaway. This was done to future-orient her for a January activity and to reinforce her responsible work, in order to afford a giveaway. In January, this was successfully completed to emphasize her acceptance within the Indian community that she did not earlier feel. This also led to her returning to South Dakota to seek out her maternal relatives.

Interestingly, I got a phone call from the patient a few weeks after the initial ceremony, relating her recurring nightmares of abusive experience. I began by telling her that it was possible to regain the memories without re-experiencing the pain but then hesitated since I did not know the approach of her primary therapist. For that reason, I concluded by telling her that this was something she needed to bring up with her own counselor.

A friend who was with her during the phone conversation reported that the patient immediately went into a trance state while speaking on the phone and after hanging up, still in a trance, stated, "I just realized I don't have to have those dreams anymore." The nightmares then ceased.

White concepts of introspection and insight-oriented therapies may have little or no relevance to many Native American clients. Remember that traditional ceremonies and healing practices emphasize activity and observation, often in the context of the extended family or network system. For this reason many Native clients become impatient and will terminate therapy that is primarily client-centered and reflective, since the expectation is that the Therapist/ healer is a person of wisdom capable of providing concrete suggestions for action. Strategic and directive interventions may therefore be a preferred choice. It is also important to clearly outline in the initial session what the Therapist can and can't do because if clients are anticipating a social worker-like involvement with their affairs, they will obviously be disappointed with the behavior of many Family Therapists.

In describing the various Katsina ceremonies of the Hopi, Native linguist Michael Lomatuwayma stated:

> The Katsinas bring rain by carrying the message of the Hopi to the deities who affect the rain. The deities are more abstract than the Katsinas.
>
> The Katsinas make it more real . . . you don't know the meaning behind it — all you know is that it will work for you.
>
> It brings rain, it carries messages back to whoever is making it rain. (Heard Museum, The "Rainbow Touches Down" Display, 1986)

Dreams and symbolic visions were often traditionally "acted out" — manifested by members of one's community (Albers &

Medicine, 1983; Deloria, 1977). As I have suggested elsewhere (Tafoya, 1989), concrete symbols serve as touchstones for increasingly abstract conceptualizations. These symbolizations may be connected with physical objects that function as meditative devices to re-access emotional states associated with wellness/harmony. I have used this idea in a modified therapeutic intervention with a number of both Native and non-Native clients and patients.

A 34-year-old Alaskan Native man, married to a non-Indian woman, was having problems with binge drinking, primarily related to his not being able to adequately deal with anger and frustration. The drinking binges were periodic "explosions" of retaliation against his wife and non-Indian step-children. Part of the problem was a distinct communication difference in expressing anger. Like many Natives, the client became more withdrawn as a way of communicating irritation and disapproval. The other family members expressed their anger in a vocal and physical manner. As a result, the step-children could not tell when they were "crossing the line" of acceptable behavior on the client's response. In clearing up these communication confusions (in the process, the client stated a wonderful paradox, yelling at this wife "I *can't* tell you no"), the client had an evening drinking episode, at which point his wife called asking for help.

They were told to come in the next afternoon, and upon entering the office, were instructed not to say anything. They were told that it had been emphasized in their Family Therapy sessions that if something wasn't working then it made sense to try something different. Since the client had been drinking, a conventional psychotherapy approach was obviously not working, and we were going to try something different, thereby modeling for them what we had discussed earlier.

My co-therapist and the client's spouse were handed drums and a cleansing ceremony was done on the client — a brushing off of his spirit body, following an explanation of what was being done and why. After the cleansing he was given a small deerskin "medicine bag" and then instructed to take out the objects contained in it. He removed a piece of cedar and was told that it represented the plant people. He was to touch it and realize that he had a relationship with the green things of the earth. At that point, he took over the verbal descriptions of the other objects: a small eagle feather, representing the people of the air; an abalone shell, representing the people of the waters; and, finally, an amethyst crystal, to represent earth herself. He had entered a light trance state during the cleansing, which he maintained. He was instructed to place the crystal between his wrists, with the explanation that northwest coast Native concepts of power locates energy centers at one's joints, obvious in the depiction of northwest coast art, where these centers are shown as circles or "eyes." He was then directed to access feelings of competence, of security and strength, and to let those feelings travel down his arms and enter into the crystal where they could be stored. A feedback loop was provided and associated with the crystal holding, typical of hypnotherapeutic work (Gilligan, 1987; Zeig, 1982, 1985). Thus, he was told that as he could feel a heat growing in the crystal (obviously, it would warm up upon continued contact with his skin), this would help him in placing the feelings of strength into this crystal. Typical of clients doing this exercise, a single tear fell from his eye as he achieved peak intensity. He was told that he could draw this feeling of strength from the crystal when he needed to do so. Therefore, the next time he felt a need to drink, he would be able to place the crystal between his wrists and regain the ability to resist drinking.

This can be explained in a number of ways. From an Ericksonian perspective, the medicine bag works to expand his awareness of connectiveness to counter his earlier feelings of isolation, while the crystal assists in a self-hypnotic induction that allows a more useful emotional response. In the language of neurolinguistic programming, the ceremony combines the "4-tupile" approach (visual; auditory [drumming and the cleansing song]; kinesthetic [contact with the bag and its contents—pressure of the crystal]; and olfactory [deerskin is smoked, and retains a distinct fragrance]) to provide an anchoring of the competence response to provide ready access in the future. From perhaps a more conventional explanation, this also involves an interaction of the spouse in a significantly different manner. Systemically, the intention of the crystal is a pattern disruption. If he utilized it, he could not automatically go through his established stages of frustration, anger, and drinking.

With respect to Western tradition, it should be pointed out that, historically, the amethyst is associated with protection against drunkenness, the mythological result of Bacchus, the God of Wine, protecting a young woman from attack by turning her into a stone and splashing wine on her, staining her purple.

This intervention, combined with more conventional Family Therapy treatment, gave the client both a sense of self-mastery and a specific behavior which he could utilize at his own discretion. It also provided the other family members with an undeniable signal that he was upset, allowing them to appropriately alter their own behavior. Following the ceremony, the family was seen for another two months, at which point the couple enrolled in vocational courses at a community college. Contact was limited to quarterly telephone calls for follow-up. For nearly two years, there have been no further alcohol-related problems.

SUMMARY

For many Native Americans, there is an old joke about "yes" always being a better answer than "no" since white officials tend to stop asking one questions if one says "yes" but will ask *more* questions if one says "no." With the epistemological concern of how a question can determine an answer, it is suggested that a Therapist consider, for a few moments, how his or her regular form of soliciting information requires a client to respond in an expected way.

For most Native tribal peoples, the circle is a sacred symbol and a model for relationships. This fundamental concept of reciprocity is very important in establishing rapport. Most therapists have been trained to disclose little personal information about their own backgrounds and may accuse clients who desire such information of avoiding their own psychological problems with a glib statement of "I'm not in therapy here, you are." From a systems approach, this separation of client/Therapist is an incorrect attitude in the first place.

Native Americans, upon first meeting each other, are usually less interested in what the other "does" (a white orientation of identity) and are much more concerned with what the other "is." Thus, the question "Where are you from?" is really asking the tribal origin of the other person, attempting to determine the existing relation-

ship — could we possibly belong to the same tribe? The same cl[a
Extended family? Could we belong to tribes that are traditional ene-
mies?

Incidentally, unless the Therapist primarily identifies as being
Native American him or herself, it will be counterproductive to
attempt rapport with a statement of having a "great-great-grand-
mother who was an Indian princess." This is felt to be patronizing,
at best. Native clients, coming from a culture that associates age
with wisdom and dominance, may ask the Therapist's age and question the Therapist's competence if he or she is significantly younger
than the clients.

Indirect forms of questioning, such as stating that the Therapist is
one of three children, and then waiting for the client to talk about
his or her own family, may solicit a more cooperative response
from a Native client than direct questioning, which does not model
a circle of interaction. As rapport is established, more attention can
be appropriately placed on the client's history and feelings.

Therapists should also be aware of clients whose Native background is a romantic fantasy, based solely on reading anthropology
texts. This is an altogether different treatment issue. The fact that a
client claims Native ancestry is not proof that such ancestry is there.
Such a client may feel alienated from his or her own actual heritage
and may have concluded that life's unhappiness is related to cultural
difficulties, which are nonexistent.

American Indians and other Native Americans have had so much
outside interference by federal and state governments that there is a
strong sense of respecting an individual's choice, even to the point
of accepting self-destructive behavior. This will frustrate many
Therapists working with tribal governments and mental health programs, such that they will often hesitate in initiating or supporting
battered wives projects, suicide prevention, or substance abuse activities since to do so would place the tribal government in the same
hated role of interference as their federal or state equivalents.

It is my contention that a great deal of the frustrations that many
Therapists experience in working with Native Americans is directly
related to their assumption that Native Americans are "just like
everyone else," especially when they speak English and come from
economically deprived environments. In reality, many central val-

ues and informally learned sociolinguistic behaviors remain intact, regardless of Indians leaving the reservation for urban life (Medicine, 1982; Sue, 1981, Tafoya, 1982, 1989), and these orientations are significantly different from those of white middle-class populations (Manson et al., 1987; Tafoya, 1982).

In most cases, Native American clients and patients behave in internally consistent ways, reflecting a perfectly logical worldview that frequently overlaps with, but does not encompass, western thought (cf. Tafoya, 1982). Native American clients and patients will range across the full spectrum of response in terms of cultural diversity and attitude, with some people being indistinguishable from Anglo families and others requiring an interpreter for the sake of an English speaking Therapist. With the history of those Native people "adopted out" prior to the late 1970s and the tribal histories of intermarriage, the physical appearance of a client will provide little information regarding his or her cultural orientation. Remember that it is preferable for a Therapist to directly ask the ethnicity of a client, rather than incorrectly "guess" a Native American to be Asian, Hispanic, black, or white.

Ultimately, the best advice to Family Therapists dealing with Native Americans may be the words of the Cedar Tree to the Aiyaiyesh girl: "Keep your eyes, and your ears, and your heart open," working with the people actually in front of you, and not with your expectations of what they should or should not be. Rapport is not achieved by wearing Indian jewelry and having a Navajo rug in your office, but by modeling being open, warm, and genuine, being aware that you may make mistakes by your cultural ignorance, and by stating so before the mistakes happen. Clients and patients are not coming to you for you to be a native person, but for you to be a Therapist. In fact, like other minority members, Native Americans may deliberately choose a non-Indian referral to avoid knowledge of personal issues made public to other people of their own community.

If you can successfully combine Native and non-Native approaches, you will tend to strengthen both. For example, in the case of the Yaqui diabetic mentioned in the beginning of the chapter, she might respond better to treatment by explaining that the new hygiene pattern is a form of mental and physical discipline designed to help restore harmony and, that before and after she initiates her cleansing, she needs to say a prayer to help her protect herself against witchcraft. This again emphasizes self-mastery and a sense of control in addressing her secondary worldview.

Patients requiring specialized medical attention but who hesitate to ask assistance of the extended family for transportation because they feel it to be selfish, can be chided for selfishness based on their denying young people the opportunity to show respect for their elders (by driving them to treatment) and by forcing more inconvenience to the extended family in the future as the condition worsens.

Like the Cedar Tree, how can you as a Therapist find the solution contained within the problem? How can you help your clients and patients to discover additional ways of relating to either world? How can you assist your clients and patients to creatively complete their circles?

REFERENCES

Albers, P., & Medicine, B. (1983). *The hidden half.* Washington, DC: University Press of America.

Axleson, J.A. (1985). *Counseling and development in a multicultural society.* Monterey, CA: Cole Publishers.

Bureau of Indian Affairs. (1986). *American Indians today: Answer to your questions* (Doc.#E 77 A 431). Washington, DC: Department of the Interior.

Deloria, V., Jr. (1977). *Indians of the Pacific Northwest.* New York: Doubleday.

Deloria, V., Jr. (1985). *American Indian policy in the twentieth century.* Norman, OK: University of Oklahoma Press.

Gilligan, S. (1987). *Therapeutic trance: The cooperation principle in Ericksonian Hypnotherapy.* New York: Brunner/Mazel.

Haley, J. (Ed.). (1985). *Conversations with Milton Erickson, M.D.* New York: Triangle Press.

Hall, E.T. (1983). *The dance of life: The other dimension of time.* Garden City, NY: Anchor Press.

Jilek, W. (1982). *Indian healing: Shamanic ceremonialism in the Pacific NW today.* Surrey, BC: Hancock House.

Kelso, D.R., & Attneave, C. (1981). *Bibliography of Native American Indian mental health.* Westport, CT: Greenwood Press.

Manson, S. (Ed.). (1982). *New directions in prevention among American Indian and Alaskan Native communities.* Portland, OR: Oregon Health Services University.

Manson, S., Walker, R.D., & Kivlahan, D.R. (1987). Psychiatric assessment and treatment of American Indians and Alaskan Natives. *Hospital and Community Psychiatry*, 38, (2), 165-173.

Medicine, B. (1982). New roads for coping: Siouxian sobriety. In S. Manson (Ed.), *New Directions in Prevention among American Indian and Alaskan Native Communities* (pp. 189-212). Portland, OR: Oregon Health Services University.

Nichols, R.L. (Ed.). (1986). *The American Indian: Past and present*. New York: Knopf.

Sanders, T.E. (1973). *Literature of the American Indian*. New York: Glencoe Press.

Speck, R.V., & Attneave, C. (1973). *Family networks*. New York: Pantheon Books.

Sue, D.W. (1981). *Counseling the culturally different*. New York: Wiley.

Tafoya, T. (1981). Dancing with Dash-Kayah: The mask of the cannibal woman. *Parabola*, VI (3), 6-11.

Tafoya, T. (1982). Native cognitive styles. *Journal of American Indian Education*, Jan. 24-36.

Tafoya, T. (1989). *Circles and cedar: Native American epistemology and clinical issues*. Durdrich, Holland: Kluwer Academic Publisher.

Tafoya, T., & Rowell, R. (1989). Counseling gay and lesbian Native Americans. In M. Schernof (Ed.) *A Resource Guide for Gay and Lesbian Health Professionals*. New York: The Gay and Lesbian Health Professionals Association.

Torrey, E.F. (1983). *The mind game: Witchdoctors and psychiatrists*. New York: Jason Aronson.

U.S. Congress Senate Select Committee on Indian Affairs. (1987). *Indian child welfare act: Hearing before the select committee on Indian affairs* (100th Congress). Washington, D.C.

U.S. Indian Health Services Office of Program Statistics. (1978). *Indian health trends and service* (DHEW Pub No. 78-12009). Washington, DC: U.S. Department of Health, Education, and Welfare, Public Health Services Administration.

Van der Hart, O. (1982). *Rituals in psychotherapy: Transitions and continuity*. New York: Irvington Press.

Watzlawick, P., & Weakland, J.H. (Eds). (1977). *The interactional view: Studies at the Mental Health Research Institute, Palo Alto, 1965-1975*. New York: Norton.

Watzlawick, P., Weakland, J.H., & Fisch, R. (1974). *Change: Principles of problem formation and problem resolution*. New York: Norton.

Zeig, J.K. (Ed.). (1982). *Ericksonian approaches for hypnosis and psychotherapy*. New York: Brunner/Mazel.

Zeig, J.K. (Ed.). (1985). *Ericksonian psychotherapy*. New York: Brunner/Mazel.

Assessment and Treatment
of Chinese-American Immigrant Families

Evelyn Lee

INTRODUCTION

In the last two decades, there has been a tremendous influx of Chinese immigrants and refugees in the United States. They differ in country of origin, dialect, political background, migration pattern, socioeconomic level, and familiarity with Western Culture. In order to treat Chinese-American families successfully, the therapist needs to understand the unique world view and life experiences of each group and to develop culturally appropriate interventions at various phases of the treatment process. The purpose of this paper is to sensitize therapists to the complexities and diversity of different major Chinese subcultures and to present an alternative family therapy model which is more compatible with Chinese value orientation, family structure and communication patterns.

This paper is divided into two parts. Part I attempts to identify the major characteristics and different types of Chinese-American families. Previous literature has presented Chinese-Americans or Asians as a homogeneous group and has failed to recognize the importance of differing client value orientation resulting from the impact of social changes during the past few decades. This paper will explore the impact of political changes, the force of industrialization, and the effect of cultural transition in the contemporary Chinese family system. Part II attempts to translate our understand-

Evelyn Lee, EdD, is Assistant Clinical Professor, Department of Psychiatry, School of Medicine, University of California, San Francisco; and Chief Program Director, Department of Psychiatry, San Francisco General Hospital.

Her mailing address is: Department of Psychiatry, San Francisco General Hospital, 1001 Potrero Avenue, 7G 22, San Francisco, CA 94110.

ing of the Chinese experiences into effective clinical strategies in the assessment and treatment of the immigrant families. The proposed approaches are drawn from three major conceptual frameworks: Chinese philosophy as influenced by Confucianism and Buddhism; holistic concept of health and illness; and social system theory and its application to family therapy (Madanes and Haley, 1977).

PART I: THE CHARACTERISTICS OF CHINESE-AMERICAN FAMILIES

Background

Three major national immigration policies helped create the sudden influx of Chinese-American immigrants and refugees. In 1965, a new U.S. Immigration law which eliminated exclusion quotas brought a surge of largely middle-class Chinese from Hong Kong, Taiwan and other Asian countries. After the end of the Vietnam war in 1975, around 800,000 Southeast Asian refugees arrived in the United States (Office of Refugee Resettlement, 1985). The majority of the second wave of "boat people" were Chinese from Vietnam. Since 1979, after four decades of "closed-door policy," the U.S. started to admit immigrants from mainland China. The emergence of the new Chinese immigrants has brought significant changes in the social, political and economic structures in Chinese communities and many major cities in the United States. For example, a decade before the revision of the Immigration Act, there were only 25,000 people of Chinese descent residing in the city of San Francisco. In 1986, there were an estimated 150,000. In the past decade, the overall number of Asians in San Francisco increased at a rate of close to 100 percent (Viviano and Silva, 1986).

The majority of newly arrived Chinese immigrants came from China, Taiwan, Hong Kong and Vietnam. Since 1949, important changes have taken place in the political, social and economic structures in those countries. It is very important to understand the impact of political unrest and societal modernization on Chinese personality and family structure.

In mainland China, a dramatic change has taken place in both the political system as well as in social ideology. Family relationships which were previously rooted in Confucian ethic were changed drastically by the ten years of the Cultural Revolution. Many families experienced forced separation. A total of seventeen million urban youths were sent to the countryside for "reeducation" (Butterfield, 1982). Many youths lashed out at parents in public meetings. The actions of the Red Guards in torturing and challenging their school authority figures transgressed thousands of years of ethics to respect teachers. Consequently, the traditional patterns of social relations that espoused filial piety and respect for elders no longer dominate life in contemporary China (Chu, 1985).

In the decades after World War II, both Hong Kong and Taiwan have undergone rapid growth in light industry and expanded export-oriented international trade. The force of industrialization, Westernization, urbanization and economic affluence resulted in a rapid change in Chinese social and family structure. While the older and middle generational Chinese still embody some traditional culture, the younger generation Chinese who are born and raised in Hong Kong and Taiwan have shown some evidence of their rejection of conservatism and traditionalism. Relevant studies in Taiwan indicated that the younger Taiwanese tend to have a high need for autonomy, self-expression, self-assertion, and individual-oriented achievement (Yang, 1986). Studies in Hong Kong also showed the fading of traditional Chinese values. The younger generation is found to be less traditionally oriented, better educated, and not sharing the habits and attitudes of their parents (Lee, 1985).

The majority of the Chinese refugee population came from Vietnam, Laos and Cambodia. Many came from the second "waves" of Southeast Asian refugee settlement. A significant number of them are survivors of hunger, rape, incarceration, forced migration and torture. Between 1977 and 1980, an estimated half-million "boat people" left Vietnam, and 200,000 of them died at sea. Many of them were Chinese (Knoll, 1982).

Cultural Differences of Chinese-American Families

Chinese-American family structures and subcultures are in transition. There are individual differences among Chinese-Americans.

They represent a wide range of cultural values from very traditional (such as the newly arrived elderly from the rural area of China) to very "Americanized" (such as a third-generation American-born Chinese professional). Each person differs in age, familiarity with Western culture, educational background, and can fall into any one point of the continuum. This paper will attempt to summarize the cultural differences and classify Chinese-American families into four major types. Figure 1 shows the spectrum of modern Chinese families in the United States. The therapist should be flexible and use treatment modalities which are compatible with the specific cultural orientation of the family.

Type 1: The Traditional Families

Such families usually consist of all family members who were born and raised in Asian countries. These include families from agricultural backgrounds, families who are recent arrivals with limited contacts with Western culture, immigrants who are older at time of immigration, and families who live in Chinatowns with little or no contact with American society. Family members speak their native Chinese dialects and practice traditional Chinese teachings in their daily lives.

Traditional Chinese culture is influenced by its agricultural background and dominant moral and religious thoughts such as Confucianism, Taoism and Buddhism. In summary, Chinese philosophy emphasizes harmonious interpersonal relationships, interdependence, and mutual obligation or loyalty for achieving a state of psychosocial homeostasis or peaceful coexistence with family or other fellow beings (Hsu, 1971). Confucius believed that the family was society's most important institution. If there was order in each family, there would be order in society. Family socialization practices are marked by a particular emphasis on the cultivation of collective consciousness and responsibilities of the members. "Face-losing" or "face-gaining" concerns not only the person directly involved, but also the family. Family interactions are determined more by prescribed roles defined by the family hierarchy, obligation, and duties than by a person-oriented process. Often, family harmony was achieved at the cost of individual interests.

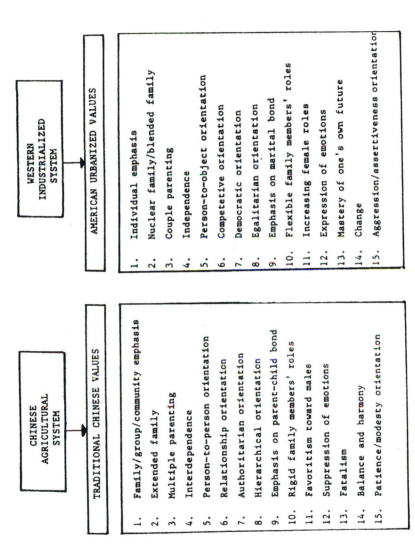

CHINESE AGRICULTURAL SYSTEM	WESTERN INDUSTRIALIZED SYSTEM
TRADITIONAL CHINESE VALUES	AMERICAN URBANIZED VALUES
1. Family/group/community emphasis	1. Individual emphasis
2. Extended family	2. Nuclear family/blended family
3. Multiple parenting	3. Couple parenting
4. Interdependence	4. Independence
5. Person-to-person orientation	5. Person-to-object orientation
6. Relationship orientation	6. Competetive orientation
7. Authoritarian orientation	7. Democratic orientation
8. Hierarchical orientation	8. Egalitarian orientation
9. Emphasis on parent-child bond	9. Emphasis on marital bond
10. Rigid family members' roles	10. Flexible family members' roles
11. Favoritism toward males	11. Increasing female roles
12. Suppression of emotions	12. Expression of emotions
13. Fatalism	13. Mastery of one's own future
14. Balance and harmony	14. Change
15. Patience/modesty orientation	15. Aggression/assertiveness orientation

FIGURE 1. Spectrum of Modern Chinese-American Families

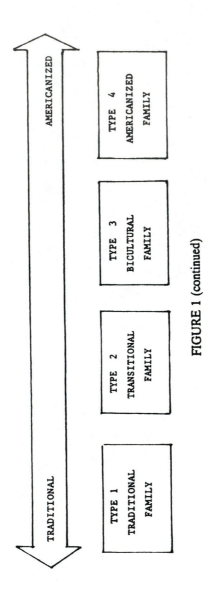

FIGURE 1 (continued)

In most traditional families, marriage is arranged to ensure the family prosperity and continue the man's family life rather than on a basis of romantic love. In marital relationships, couples do not express love overtly. The spousal relationship is deemed secondary to the parent-child relationship. Marital conflicts are usually resolved by other adult mediators or confidants. Divorce is rare and brings family shame.

Since the parent-child bond is considered to be more important than the husband-wife dyad, the strongest emotional attachment for a woman is usually not to her husband, but to her children, especially the sons. Parents are expected to play the role of "a stern father" and "an affectionate mother" in child rearing. Most parents demand filial piety, respect and obedience from their children. Sons are more valued than daughters. In most of the extended Chinese families, affective ties for children are not focused solely on their parents, but spread over a wide range of adult figures. Traditionally, siblings play important roles for each other throughout life. Parents expect to be taken care of in their old age. The most common way for children to show their affection and devotion toward their parents is through taking care of the parents' physical needs instead of expressing emotions in words.

Type 2: The Transitional Families

Such families usually consist of parents and grandparents with strong traditional beliefs living with the younger generation who are Westernized. Such families usually arrived about a decade ago when their children were young, or are families with American-born children. The family system usually experiences a great degree of cultural conflict between the acculturated children and the traditional parents. In such families, the parents usually do not speak good English, while the children speak little or some "broken" Chinese.

Type 3: The Bicultural Families

Such families usually consist of parents who are professional, English-speaking, and quite "Westernized" like their children. Such families usually came from middle- or upper-class family backgrounds and grew up in urban cities such as Hong Kong, Taipei or Saigon. Family members are well acculturated, bilingual and bicultural. They have the ability to take advantage of the strengths of both Eastern and Western cultures. They are able to integrate the two contradictory value systems, without much confusion. In such families, the power structure has moved from a patriarchal to an egalitarian relationship between parents, similar to American families. Decision making is not solely the father's; "discussions" are allowed between parents and children. Such families typically do not live in Chinatown, but live in the suburbs. The "nuclear" family members usually visit their "extended" family members on weekends and during holidays.

Type 4: The "Americanized" Families

Such families consist of parents and children who are born and raised in the United States. As generations pass, the roots of Chinese culture begin to slowly disappear, and individual members do not express their interest or make any effort to maintain their Chinese identity. Interracial marriages in such families are very common. Family members communicate in English only, and adopt a much more individualistic, competitive and egalitarian orientation.

The above-mentioned four types of Chinese-American families may have different help-seeking patterns. The traditional families generally consist of new immigrants and refugees who come to agencies with many specific concrete problems that require assistance and language interpretation. Most of them suffer from adjustment disorder, depression and psychosomatic complaints. Some war victims suffer from PTSD (Post-Traumatic Stress Disorder). The transitional families usually need help in resolving parent-child conflicts, role confusion, and marital difficulties (Lee, 1982). The bicultural families require little help from counseling agencies and appear to be quite adaptable. The presenting problems of the "Americanized" families are commonly associated with intrapsychic turmoil (low self-concept, marital or other significant relationship, identity conflict, and depression). They are likely treated with the psychodynamic modalities which focus on self-exploration, while the traditional and transitional families are likely treated with cognitive/behavioral modality (Murase, 1982). It should be noted that not all Chinese-American families fall into these four types as described. The groupings are meant to be a general framework which can be used to approach families in the clinical situation. Chinese-American families differ in many respects. Effective therapy requires the therapist to see each family as unique and individual rather than in terms of ethnocentric stereotypes.

PART II: ASSESSMENT AND TREATMENT OF CHINESE IMMIGRANT FAMILIES

Family Assessment and Evaluation

Part II of this paper will present some major evaluation criteria and treatment strategies in working with the Chinese immigrant families. This model may not be applicable to the "Americanized" families. Assessing the Chinese who are still highly influenced by Eastern culture requires taking a holistic view of health and an interactive and contextual perspective on behavior. The therapist must focus not only on the medical or intrapsychic features of the clients, but also on the integration of the physical, social, political and cultural factors. The assessment must include information beyond traditional intake data (Lee, in press). The following section summarizes the kind of information needed in each of the key areas (see Figure 2).

1. Family Migration and Relocation History

In taking a thorough history, the therapist should not concentrate solely on recent symptoms and events which happened in the United States. Exploration of the following family migration history is extremely important (Lee, 1986). The use of a genogram with family members is found to be very useful.

   a. Premigration experience (life in the homeland): country of origin, family composition, education and employment status, support systems, political background, and war experience.
   b. Migration experience: why did the family decide to leave, who

FIGURE 2. Suggested Guidelines for Family Assessment of Chinese-American Families

AREA OF ASSESSMENT	ASSESSMENT CONTENT
1. Family migration and relocation history	1. • Premigration experience • Migration experience • Impact of migration on individual and family life cycle.
2. Degree of loss and traumatic experience	2. Losses: • significant family members, relatives and friends • material losses • loss of community support • spiritual loss Trauma: • physical trauma • psychological trauma
3. "Cultural shock" and adjustment problems	3. • Language, housing, transportation, employment, child care, racism....
4. Differences in rates of acculturation of family members	4. • Years in U.S. • age at time of migration, exposure to Western culture • professional affiliation • contacts with American peers • English-speaking ability • work or school environment
5. Work and financial stress	5. • Downward mobility • Status inconsistency • Long working hours • Language difficulty • Racism at work place
6. The family's place of residence and community influences	6. • Type of neighborhood • Availability of support system • Community stigma

7. Physical health and medication history

- Degree of somatization
- Medical history of patients and family members
- Western and herbal medicines
- Consultation with physician and indegenous healers.

8. Assessment of family problems

- Inter-generational conflicts
- In-law conflict
- Marital difficulty
- Sibling rivalries
- Hostile dependent relationship with sponsor
- Special issues: role reversal, inadequate communication and split loyalties

9. Assessment of family strengths

- Functional coping strategies
- Support from individual and family group
- Support from the Chinese community and service providers

10. Family's concept of mental illness, help-seeking behavior and treatment expectation

- Symptoms and problems as perceived by family
- Causes of the problems as perceived by family
- Relationship with post-traumatic events
- Family help-seeking behavior
- Family treatment expectation

stayed behind and why, who sponsored the trip, what was the means of escape, and what were some of the traumatic events?

c. Impact of migration on individual and family life cycle: The readjustment to a new culture is a prolonged developmental process of adjustment, which will affect family members differently, depending on the individual and family life cycle phase they are in at the time of transition. For example, refugees who migrate during adolescent years are confronted by not only migration and acculturation stresses, but also the special developmental tasks such as identity and sexual role formation, separation and individuation (Lee, 1988). Families that migrate with young children are perhaps strengthened by having each other, but they are vulnerable to the parental reversal of hierarchies. Families migrating when their children are adolescents may have more difficulty because they will have less time together as a unit before the children move out on their own. Thus the family must struggle with multiple transitions and generational conflicts at once (McGoldrick, 1982).

2. Degree of Loss and Traumatic Experiences

This area is particularly important in working with Chinese who experienced World War II, the Civil War in China, the Cultural Revolution and the Vietnam War. There are four types of losses associated with immigration and refugee status: (a) loss of significant family members, relatives and friends; (b) material losses: business, career, properties; (c) loss of community support and cultural milieu; (d) spiritual loss: freedom to practice religion. The therapist needs to assess two types of trauma: (a) physical trauma: torture, rape, starvation, imprisonment; (b) psychological consequences of trauma: rage, depression, grief, survival guilt, PTSD. It is important for the therapist to encourage the family members to discuss their war experiences and to assess the degree of losses and trauma. However, the therapist needs to pay special attention to the *readiness* of the family members in order to determine when and how much to probe.

3. "Cultural Shock" and Adjustment Problems

Many new immigrants are placed in a strange and unpredictable environment. As minority members, they have to learn and get used to the behavioral and value orientation of American culture. Problems encountered such as language, housing, transportation, employment, child care, racism, etc., can be overwhelming. The therapist's concerns over such problems and ability to offer some solutions are usually highly appreciated by family members.

4. Differences in Rates of Acculturation of Family Members

Chinese families differ greatly in their adaptive abilities and motivation to deal with the cultural conflicts inherent in the process of immigration. Individual family members within one household likewise differ greatly in their rates of adaptation and acculturation. In general, the degree of acculturation of each family member depends upon the following variables: (a) years in United States; (b) age at time of immigration; (c) exposure to Western culture in the country of origin and in U.S.; (d) professional affiliation; (e) contacts with American peers; (f) English-speaking ability; (g) work or school environment. It is important for the therapist to assess the acculturation rate of all family members. Many family problems are caused by intergenerational conflicts and value differences (Lee, 1988).

5. Work and Financial Stress

From a high occupational and social status in their home country, many Chinese are "demoted" in the new country from professional to menial, from elite to an impoverished minority. "Downward mobility" or "status inconsistency" leads to low self-esteem, insecurity, and depression. Many who have jobs tend to work long hours and face language difficulty and racism in their work place. Taking a detailed work history and showing empathy towards work and financial stress, especially at the beginning phase of treatment, can foster therapeutic alliance with the clients.

6. The Family's Place of Residence and Community Influence

Whether or not the family lives in an ethnic neighborhood will influence the impact of the family cultural heritage on their lives (McGoldrick, 1982). For those Chinese who live in Chinatown, the Chinese community support systems provide a temporary cushion against the stresses of migration that usually surface in the next generation. On the other hand, members also have to cope with the community pressure caused by shame of losing face due to the stigma of emotional problems. Those who live in areas with relatively small Chinese populations, such as the Midwest or the South, generally have had more trouble adjusting and were pressured to assimilate more rapidly. The therapist needs to have a good understanding of the sociocultural influences of the community where the family resides.

7. Physical Health and Medication History

A culturally appropriate psychotherapeutic modality for Chinese must be able to address and respond to the holistic modes of thinking. Chinese health beliefs and practice center on balancing "yin" and "yang" elements of the body to maintain health and treat illness. The well-documented tendency of Chinese to "somatize" their emotional problems has to be recognized as part of their holistic conception of man as an indivisible, somatic-psychic entity. It is important for the therapist to routinely request information on the patient's physical condition and family medical history. Close consultation with physicians or indigenous healers, wherever possible, are highly recommended. In addition, the therapist needs to take a detailed medication history (including herbal medicine).

8. Assessment of Family Problems

Migration stress, acculturation stress and many environmental stresses can cause psychological problems in contemporary Chinese-American families. The therapist needs to assess the following interpersonal conflicts:

a. intergenerational conflicts (generation gap, cultural gap, language gap, education gap);
b. in-law conflict;
c. marital difficulty;
d. sibling rivalries;
e. hostile dependent relationship with sponsor.

Special attention should be paid to the issues of (a) role reversal between parents and children, (b) inadequate communication, (c) split loyalty, and (d) biological parenting vs. emotional parenting.

9. Assessment of Family Strengths

In addition to the assessment of family problems, careful assessment needs to be made with respect to the following family strengths: (a) functional coping strategies such as the Buddhist teaching of karma, and "yuan," the Confucian teaching of the "middle way" and interpersonal harmony; (b) support available from family, school, friends, relatives, sponsors, teachers; (c) support available from the Chinese community and service providers.

10. Family's Concept of Mental Illness, Help-Seeking Behavior and Treatment Expectation

In working with new Chinese immigrant and refugee families, there are some unique diagnostic issues that may surface with this population. Due to the vast difference between the Eastern culture and the Western culture, there are many culturally-derived beliefs or behaviors that might be misinterpreted as deviant within mainstream American culture. Alternatively, there is the possibility of erring in the opposite direction and misattributing important clinical signs to culture. This may lead to overdiagnosis or underdiagnosis. Therefore, in the assessment process, it is essential for the therapist to encourage the client and his or her family members to discuss openly their cultural viewpoints on the causes of the problem, their past efforts in coping with the problem, and their treatment expectations. The discussion can be based on the following questions:

a. What are the symptoms and problems as perceived by family members?
b. What do family members think are the causes of the problem?
c. Are the presenting problems related to the past traumatic events?
d. Where does the family go to get help?
e. What are the family's treatment expectations?

Treatment Strategies

*1. Forming a Social and Cultural Alliance
with the Family*

During the first session, the therapist should address the family in a friendly, warm, and formal manner, using last interest in the person involved rather than focusing on procedures is helpful, given the culture emphasis on interpersonal relationships. Asking non-threatening personal questions at the beginning phase of conversation can put the family at ease ("Did you have a hard time finding the agency?" "Have you had lunch yet?" "Is today your day off?" "When did you come to the United States?"). During the initial state of relationship, the family may expect the therapist to do a certain amount of self-disclosure concerning his personal, academic and professional background. Self-disclosure allows the family to better assess the therapist as a person and enables the development of a necessary level of trust and confidence. It is helpful for the therapist to share some of his own cultural background and his familiarity with the Chinese culture to establish his credibility. With respect to the traditional age/sex hierarchies, it is advisable to address questions to the father first, then the mother, then to other adults and finally to the older and younger children. Directing the opening to the parents helps establish culturally-consonant generational boundaries (Lee, in press).

2. Structuring the Initial Sessions

Chinese-Americans, in general, enter treatment with much apprehension, suspicion and ambivalence. To receive help from professional counselors is to publicize the family's disgrace. In addition, lower verbal facility and reluctance to express feelings and talk about family problems to a stranger and in front of other family members may make them uncomfortable and anxious. In the initial phase of treatment, the interview sessions should be more structured. The therapist needs to educate the family members about their roles, the function of the agency, the diagnostic procedure, and an estimate of number of sessions, and whom should be seen in family sessions.

The therapist preferably should see the whole family, at least for the first time, in order to observe the family members interact. However, there are many situations when this would not be possible or clinically appropriate. Depending on the presenting problem, the family communication style, and the readiness for therapy of the family members, the therapist may see the whole family, subsystems, or significant others at different stages of therapy. A *"flexible sub-family system approach"* in the establishment of therapeutic alliances with family members at times can be helpful. Allowing an extended period of time for the initial sessions and increasing the frequency of therapy sessions in the beginning phase of therapy may be necessary in order to capitalize the heightened energy induced by crisis (Lee, in press).

3. Defining the Problem and Setting Treatment Goals

Family therapy approach with Chinese families should be "problem-focused," "goal-oriented," and "symptom-relieving." The initial concerns and problems brought by the family should be accepted graciously and taken seriously, with the recognition that such concern may be the family's way of entering treatment. Family members ask for professional help because of the difficulties they encounter with one particular family member, usually the child. Parents are either unaware of their roles in contributing to the problem, or unwilling to discuss it openly in front of their children. In order to engage the family in therapy, it is important for the therapist to: (a) acknowledge the identified patient as the problem; (b) assist the family to shift from "person-focused" to "problem-focused"; (c) focus on the effect on each family member due to the problem; (d) verbalize the family pain caused by the difficulties; and (e) reinforce the sense of family obligation and the significant role of the family member in solving the problem together. At times, it may be helpful to encourage family members to elaborate their previous attempts in dealing with the problem. The realization of their coping failures, and the unpleasant consequences if the problem is uncorrected, may motivate the family to continue in treatment. The therapist should take on an un-blaming attitude toward the family and the identified patient. The approaches such as generalization and normalization can be used to reduce shame and guilt. The therapist makes general statements relevant to the migration or traumatic experiences, and helps the family to make personal connection with the universal problem. For example, the therapist may ask, "Most new Chinese immigrants have difficulties in finding good jobs or suitable housing. Did you have the same problems?" or, "Many Chinese who experienced the Cultural Revolution had a difficult time. What were some of your experiences?" However, in some situations, the therapist may use the family sense of guilt and obligation to participate in treatment for the sake of the "family name."

In working with traditional Chinese, the treatment goal should be oriented to the present and the conscious rather than the past and the unconscious, based on relational and interpersonal rather than interaction and intrapersonal. Rather than defining goals in abstract, emotional terms, goals may be best stated in terms of external resolution, or symptom reduction. Long-term goals may best be broken down into a series of easy-to-understand, achievable, measurable, short-term goals. Once the family is engaged in the therapeutic relationship, the therapist can gradually introduce other more "insight-oriented" goals and renegotiate with the family members (Lee, in press).

4. Employing a Benevolent but Authoritative Attitude

Because Chinese families view relationships in terms of a vertical hierarchy, extreme caution is advised against adopting a democratic attitude in the therapeutic relationship. The therapist will need to take a much more authoritative attitude to build his or her credibility (Lee, 1982). The following are some possible means to acquire therapeutic power: (a) to obtain sufficient information about the patient and the family prior to seeing the family; (b) to offer some possible explanation for the cause of the problem; (c) to show familiarity with the family's cultural background and make necessary "cultural connection"; (d) to provide a set of cues that help the family to judge the therapist's expertise, i.e., professional degree, years of experience etc.; (e) to offer the family some immediate solution to the problems.

Among immigrant and refugee patients with a history of long years of separation from their loved ones, there is a yearning for an actively empathic parental figure. A giving, benevolent therapist who exhibits warmth and empathy is more able to gain the trust of his or her clients (Lee, 1982). This requires not only careful listening to the clients, but also trying to do something that will be helpful in relieving symptoms. Due to the strong sense of obligation in the culture, clients may view keeping appointments or taking medication as doing something for the therapist in return for the therapist's concern (Lee, 1987).

5. Building Alliance with Members with Power

An accurate assessment of the power structure of the family is essential. Generally speaking, there are two types of power in the family system: "role prescribed power" (usually given to the grandfather, father, eldest son or the sponsor); "psychological power" (usually maintained by the grandmother or the mother). Treatment will not be effective without permission of the leader(s) in the vertical, hierarchical structure. Therapists should acknowledge their power in decision making, avoid competition, and engage them in therapy with all possible means (Lee, in press).

6. Using Directive Therapy

"Talk therapy" is not common in most Asian countries. Many come to see an "expert" with the cultural expectation of receiving directives. Nonjudgmental listening and neutrality in the therapist's responses may be viewed as a lack of interest or incompetence. Since verbal expression of feelings is not encouraged in traditional Chinese families, the client's dissatisfaction may not be made known to the therapist (Lee, 1982).

7. Assuming Multiple Helping Roles

Flexibility and willingness to assume multiple helping roles enhance the therapeutic relationship, especially in working with multiproblem families. In addition to being the counselor, the therapist should be comfortable to play the role as teacher, advocate, intermediary, and interpreter etc. (Lee, 1982).

8. Applying a Psychoeducational Approach in Family Treatment

Education is highly valued in Chinese culture. The psychoeducational approach based on social learning principles may be compatible with many Chinese values and beliefs. Such intervention focuses on four major areas: (a) education about the illness (or problem); (b) communication training; (c) problem-solving training; (d) behavioral management strategies (McGill and Lee, 1986).

9. Reinforcing Culturally Sanctioned Coping Mechanisms and Cultural Strength

In many circumstances, especially during the time when family members are coping with death, losses, and unpredictable changes, one of the functions of therapy is to reinforce socioculturally sanctioned behavior. For example, based on the philosophy of Buddhism, the therapist may discuss concepts such as karma and fate with family members during their mourning. Through discussion, they learn to take reality as it is, accept it, and live with it. If appropriate, the use of familiar Chinese philosophical and religious sayings and Chinese folk songs and stories can be very effective as means to reinforce social/cultural sanctioned behavior.

Chinese families often possess many cultural strengths. Strengths such as support from extended family members and siblings, support from their religious community, the strong sense of obligation, the strong focus on educational achievement, the work ethic, the high tolerance for loneliness and separation, and the loyalties of friends or between employer and employee should be respected and used creatively in the therapeutic process (Lee, 1982). The most important strength the Chinese family possesses is its survival spirit. The ability of family members to cope with the war, immigration, and acculturation stress should be respected and praised (Lee, in press).

10. Overcoming Language and Cultural Barriers

There are marked subgroup differences of dialect and communication style among the various Chinese refugee groups. (The majority of the immigrants from China and Taiwan speak Mandarin. The primary dialect for Chinese from Hong Kong, Vietnam and Canton, China, is Cantonese. However, many different dialects are spoken by Chinese from different villages, cities or regions such as Toisanese, Fukienese, Hakka, Chungsan, Swatow, Shanghaiese, Taiwanese etc.) It is important for the therapist to work with interpreters who can provide both correct language and cultural translation. In order to minimize misdiagnosis and inappropriate treatment, both interpreter and clinician need to be trained in cross-cultural communication skills. A training videotape recently developed by Lee (1987) on working with interpreters in mental health can be used for such training. The therapist needs to pay special attention to the non-verbal communication style of the family and his or her own. Clinicians should also pay attention to their own racial and cultural background in working with Chinese-American families. Forming a social and cultural alliance with the family is a much easier task for the bilingual/bicultural Chinese clinician who is also an immigrant or refugee. Selective sharing of the therapist's own immigration or refugee experiences can be very facilitative to the therapeutic process. However, Chinese-American clinicians should be sensitive to countertransference issues. For example, the clinician who is also still dealing with unresolved trauma-related dynamics may respond by projecting anger or other negative feelings onto the clients, or feel the need to take care of his or her own issues rather than focus on the client. Or, an American-born Chinese clinician who is struggling with his or her own unresolved cultural identity conflict may not be in the best position to offer assistance to Chinese clients who need help around the same issue. Many foreign-born Chinese immigrants and refugees, especially those who live in Chinatown, have very little contact with other non-Chinese populations. The clinician needs to be sensitive to the negative stereotypes the Chinese families may have towards his or her own racial background. Inviting the clients to discuss racial differences may be therapeutic at times. However, Chinese clients may feel uncomfortable in discussing such issues at the beginning phase of the treatment. They may be more willing to give their honest opinion after some degree of trust has been established (Lee, in press).

CONCLUSION

Most Western family therapy approaches have been limited in their application to families with Eastern value orientations (Kim, 1985). Traditional Western approaches predicated on the assumptions of horizontal relationship, individualism, independence, expression of emotions, and change may go counter to the traditional Chinese values of vertical relationship, interdependence, self-control, and acceptance of fate. This paper offers an alternative assessment and treatment model that takes into account the political, social and cultural background of Chinese-American families. The proposed framework is intended to be a stimulus for future development of a systematic approach which is more compatible with Chinese-Americans' world view and family characteristics.

Effective cross-cultural family therapy requires not only the knowledge of cultural differences but also professional skill to promote positive changes which are congruent with cultural norms. The establishment of therapeutic alliance is not only based on mutual trust, but also the therapist's ability to empathize with compassion. Many recent Chinese-American immigrants are survivors of war, political turmoil, socioeconomic changes, and cultural transition. They deserve our respect, and the best we can offer as mental health professionals.

BIBLIOGRAPHY

Butterfield, F. (1982). *China: Alive in the bitter sea*. New York: Times Press.

Chu, G. (1985). The emergence of the new Chinese culture. In W.S. Tseng & D.Y.H. Wu (Eds.), *Chinese culture and mental health* (pp. 15-27). Florida: Academic Press.

Hsu, F.L.K. (1971). *Under the ancestor's shadow: Kinship, personality and social mobility in China*. Stanford: Stanford University Press.

Kim, S. (1985). Family therapy for Asian Americans: A strategic-structural framework. *Psychotherapy, 22*(2), 342-348.

Knoll, T. (1982). *Becoming Americans*. Portland: Coast to Coast Books.

Landau, J. (1982). Therapy with families in cultural transition. In M. McGoldrick, J. Pearce, & J. Giordano (Eds.), *Ethnicity and family therapy* (pp. 552-572). New York: Guilford Press.

Lee, E. (1982). A social systems approach to assessment and treatment for Chinese American families. In M. McGoldrick, J. Pearce, & J. Giordano (Eds.), *Ethnicity and family therapy* (pp. 527-551). New York: Guilford Press.

Lee, E. (1988). Cultural factors in working with Southeast Asian refugee adolescents. *Journal of Adolescence, 11*, 167-179.

Lee, E. (in press). Family therapy with Southeast Asian refugees. In Marsha Mirkin (Ed.), *Social and political contexts of family therapy*. New York: Gardner Press.

Lee, E. (Executive Producer). (1987). *Working with interpreters: The therapeutic triad*. (Video Tape). San Francisco: Calman Video Productions.

Lee, R. (1985). Social stress and coping behavior in Hong Kong. In W.S. Tseng & D.Y.H. Wu (Eds.), *Chinese culture and mental health* (pp. 193-211). Florida: Academic Press.

Madanes, C. & Haley, J. (1977). Dimensions of family therapy. *Journal of Nervous and Mental Disease, 55*, 88-89.

McGill, C. & Lee, E. (1986). Family psychoeducational intervention in the treatment of schizophrenia. *Bulletin of the Menninger Clinic, 50*(3), 269-286.

McGoldrick, M. (1982). Ethnicity and family therapy: An overview. In M. McGoldrick, J. Pearce, & J. Giordano (Eds.), *Ethnicity and family therapy* (pp. 3-30). New York: Guilford Press.

McGoldrick, M. (1985). *Genograms in family assessment*. New York: W.W. Norton & Company, Inc.

Murase, K. (1982). *Mental Health Treatment Modalities of Pacific/Asian American Practitioners*. San Francisco: Pacific Asian Mental Health Research Project.

Office of Refugee Resettlement. (1985). *Refugee resettlement program*; *Report to the Congress*. Washington, D.C.: U.S. Government Printing Office.

Viviano, F. & Silva, D. (1986). The new San Francisco. *San Francisco Focus*, *9*, 65-75.

Yang, K.S. (1986). Chinese personality and its change. In W.H. Bond (Ed.), *The psychology of the Chinese people* (pp. 106-160). New York: Oxford University Press.

Contextual Family Therapy
of Addiction with Latinos

Yvette Flores-Ortiz
Guillermo Bernal

The last fifteen years have seen an increase in the empirical and clinical investigation of drug abuse in the United States. However, for the most part, the literature has not addressed the extent of the problem among Latinos* nor the specific treatment needs of this population. This article proposes to: Examine the problem of drug abuse and addiction among Latinos; review the role of the family among Latinos substance abusers, and present ongoing work toward the development of a framework of therapy that integrates cultural and social processes in its approach to drug abuse.

For the last seven years, the authors have been involved in the development of culturally sensitive treatment approaches for the diverse Latino populations of the San Francisco Bay Area of California (Bernal & Alvarez, 1983; Bernal & Flores-Ortiz, 1983, 1984; Bernal & Rodriguez-Dragin, 1985; Bernal, Flores-Ortiz & Rodriguez-Dragin, 1986). Our work with Latino clients affected by a

---

Yvette Flores-Ortiz, PhD, is on the faculty, California School of Professional Psychology, Berkeley, CA.

Guillermo Bernal, PhD, is on the faculty, Department of Psychology, University of Puerto Rico, Rio Piedras, PR.

Work on this article was supported by a grant from the National Institute of Drug Abuse (No. 5 RO1 DA03543) awarded to Guillermo Bernal, Principal Investigator and to James L. Sorensen and Yvette Flores-Ortiz, co-investigators, while the authors were at the University of California, San Francisco.

---

*The term Latino is used here to refer to individuals of Indo-Hispanic roots, whose national origins are in countries of South America, Central America, Mexico, the Caribbean or the United States.

123

variety of psychological disorders has led us to utilize an intergenerational family therapy approach almost exclusively. The theoretical basis of our clinical work is based on the Contextual Intergenerational family therapy model (Boszormenyi-Nagy & Spark, 1973; Boszormenyi-Nagy & Krasner, 1986). The contextual framework and treatment applications that will be presented here have been evaluated empirically in a clinical outcome study (Bernal et al., 1987) of Contextual family therapy with methadone maintenance patients and their families. In the following sections, we will discuss briefly the scope of the problem of addiction among Latinos, describe key concepts of the Contextual approach, and provide a clinical case example.

SCOPE OF THE PROBLEM OF LATINO DRUG ADDICTION

The view of drug abuse as a major social problem, rather than a sign of individual pathology, has gained considerable support over the last two decades. The pioneering work of Coleman and Stanton (1975, 1978), Kaufman and Kaufman (1979), and Stanton (1977, 1981) among others, underscored the relation of family variables, socioeconomic indicators, and larger societal issues to patterns of drug abuse. Until recently, differential rates of drug abuse for Latinos were difficult to determine since some indicators included all Latino groups as "white," and did not differentiate among the various Latino groups (e.g. Puerto Ricans, Mexicans, Chicanos, etc.).

The findings of the 1985 national survey showed that drug use in this country is still "unacceptably high" (Rouse, 1986, p. 2). While drug abuse in general has remained stable or declined since 1982, the rates of cocaine abuse increased from 4.2 million in 1982 to 5.8 million in 1985. Latinos ages 12 to 17, had the highest rate of cocaine abuse (as compared to white and Black youth).

All drug abuse indicators find that Latinos are overrepresented in drug related arrests, and underrepresented in treatment programs (Mandel & Biernacki, 1986). Specifically, Latinos of Mexican origin (Chicanos) are found to be overrepresented in treatment for inhalants, heroin and phencyclidine (PCP), and underrepresented for all other drugs.

Perez, Padilla, Ramirez, Ramirez, and Rodriguez (1979) study of Chicano youth in East Los Angeles found high rates of marijuana and alcohol use across all ages and sex cohorts studied. The authors conclude that drug use generally increased as a function of age and sex, with males abusing more drugs (in particular alcohol, marijuana, and PCP).

A recent needs assessment study of drug abuse problems in the Mission district of San Francisco (Flores-Ortiz, 1986) found a pattern of self-reported poly-drug abuse among a sample of Latinos. Specifically, alcohol, PCP, marijuana, cocaine, and crack were commonly used by youths 5-12. For 12-18-year olds, alcohol, heroin, marijuana, cocaine and PCP were significant problems. Over half of the young adult population (19-25-year olds) utilized all drugs but abused mainly alcohol, heroin, cocaine, and marijuana. This pattern was similar for 26-35-year olds. Those between 36-50 years abused mainly alcohol and marijuana, although abuse of heroin and cocaine was not unusual. Individuals older than 50 primarily continued to abuse alcohol, and to a lesser extent barbiturates and marijuana.

In addition, Flores-Ortiz (1986) surveyed 16 drug and mental health programs. Fifty-seven percent of the clients in these agencies were Latino or Chicano. The primary reasons for admission were related to alcohol, heroin or PCP abuse. Latino men were overrepresented in the drug arrest data for the Mission district, where drug offenses were primarily for heroin and PCP.

Drug abuse is clearly a major problem in this country. For Latinos, primary drug problems include alcohol, heroin, marijuana, cocaine, inhalants, and PCP. The drug problem can be assessed in economic, social, and health terms. Most recently the AIDS epidemic has once again underscored the health implications of intravenous drug use. As of May of 1988, the overwhelming majority of new AIDS cases were Black and Latino individuals (24.8% and 14% respectively) a significant proportion of whom are IV drug users (Morales, 1988).

EXPLANATIONS OF DRUG ABUSE AMONG LATINOS

A number of theoretical conceptualizations have been offered to explain the disproportionate rates of drug use by Latinos (e.g. Casavantes, 1976, Perez et al., 1979). These conceptualizations have focused on intrapsychic, cultural or sociological explanations. Casavantes (1974) for example, hypothesizes that Chicano heroin addicts are influenced by unique cultural factors such as *machismo*, *carnalismo*, and *personalismo*. Generally, *machismo* refers on the one hand to "excessive" maleness, characterized by an emphasis on virility, aggressiveness, and sexual conquest, and on the other hand to chivalry, loyalty and protection of women. *Carnalismo* refers to a primarily Chicano friendship style which emphasizes loyalty and brotherhood. Carnal (friend) comes from the Spanish word "carne," flesh. Thus a carnal is someone of one's own flesh. *Personalismo* is characterized by a value of interdependence, mutual respect and giving. Casavantes (1974) proposes that these cultural factors, in addition to the impact of poverty, the effect of Catholicism (primarily fatalism) and "Chicano family dynamics" must be considered both in terms of conceptualization and treatment of Latino drug abuse. Most authors agree that a combination of "ecological factors" such as language and migration, "structural factors" of family and peer group, and economic factors (drug cost, supply, etc.) will determine the individual's likely pattern of drug use and abuse.

While most authors underscore the importance of familial, cultural, economic, and social correlates of drug abuse, to date few empirical investigations have been conducted to determine the specific correlates of drug abuse among Latinos. With the exception of Bernal et al.'s (1987) and Szapocznik, Scopetta, Aranalde and Kurtines' (1978) drug treatment programs, few culturally based drug services are described in the literature. In fact, most treatment methods generally support individual treatment and rehabilitation (e.g. detox, maintenance, AA, etc.) which tend to view addiction as incurable and the problem primarily of the addict. Such treatments historically have attempted to treat the addiction by fostering separation of the addict from his or her family context, or by treating the individual separate from the family (i.e., Alanon, Alateen). However, the view of addiction as a family problem has gained considerable support in the literature over the past decade.

THE ROLE OF THE FAMILY IN SUBSTANCE ABUSE AMONG LATINOS

As systems theory and the field of family therapy developed, interest in the family systems of drug abusers grew (Harbin & Maziar, 1975; Coleman & Stanton, 1978; Reilly, 1975). In order to understand the high relapse rate among addicts, researchers began to emphasize the need to better understand the family context of substance abusers. Clinical and empirical investigations began a systematic evaluation of the structure, roles, rules and transactions of families with an addicted member. These studies generally excluded Latino addicts.

In general, the clinical literature has described the families of drug addicts, particulary those abusing opiates, as enmeshed systems, with little differentiation between the addict (usually a young man) and his mother. Mothers most often are described as indulgent and overprotective (Harbin & Mazier, 1975). Fathers generally are characterized as weak, ineffectual, distant or absent (Coleman & Stanton, 1978). Addiction is viewed as serving a homeostatic function for the family, a classic triangulation in which marital tensions are diverted by focusing on a problem child. Drug problems are seen to develop most often during adolescence, a time when the family as a system must deal with the impending separation and eventual individuation of the children. The more enmeshed the family, and the greater the spousal difficulties, the more likely the family is to have trouble letting a child go. Thus addiction has been seen as an attempt by the identified patient (addict) to pseudo-individuate yet remain dependent on the parents.

Kaufman's work (1979) pointed out the role of siblings and the cross-cultural differences he found in his studies of Jewish and Italian addicts. Kaufman noted that while certain patterns appeared in most addicted families, the extent of enmeshment varied, as did the overall "need" for the symptom of addiction in a given family.

As with earlier propositions about the role of the family in schizophrenia, certain family structures, roles and rules were viewed as
addictogenic (Coleman & Stanton, 1978). While the family generally was not "blamed" for the problem of addiction, it generally
was held responsible for the maintenance of the problem. Consequently, many interventions called for "parentectomies" (Cotroneo
& Krasner, 1976), in order to facilitate the individuation of the
addict (Haley, 1980).

The resultant ascription of blame on the family may be attributed
in part to the almost exclusive focus on early writings on *nuclear*
family relationships and patterns (Bernal & Ysern, 1986). However, while studying and treating addicted individuals Coleman and
Stanton (1978) noted a pattern of multiple early losses in the families of origin of heroin addicts. With this work, intergenerational
family patterns began to be considered in the study of addiction.
These authors proposed that in addition to serving homeostatic
functions, the heroin addiction provided an opportunity for resolution of unresolved mourning. Stanton (1977) viewed the addict as a
savior, the one who willingly assumes the role of victim in order for
the family to continually mourn the previous death(s). In their view,
families of heroin addicts attach special significance to death, with
the addict being substituted for the deceased member. Based on this
conceptualization of drug abuse, treatment interventions were developed which focused on resolving unmourned losses and promoting systemic change to "free" the addict from his/her role in the
family.

The work of Coleman, Stanton, and Kaufman, among others,
pointed to the limitations of focusing solely on the nuclear families
of heroin and other drug addicts. Indeed, while acknowledging the
importance of intergenerational family patterns, most research and
treatment endeavors continued to focus on structural change in the
nuclear families of addicts. The extent to which Latino families
with an addiction problem are similar to non-Latino families has
remained an empirical question until recently. Elsewhere we have
proposed (e.g., Bernal and associates, 1983, 1985, 1987) that Latino families might appear enmeshed, overinvolved, and addictogenic in self-report measures of family functioning or clinician's
ratings, given the absence of cross-cultural norms for these scales,

and the tendency among clinicians to pathologize what may be in fact cultural differences. Specifically, the Latinos' emphasis on *familismo*, reliance on the family, and de-emphasis on individuation of children may be viewed as pathogenic within a purely structural or systemic analysis of a Latino family.

TOWARD A CULTURAL AND SOCIAL-CONTEXT SENSITIVE FAMILY THERAPY

Based on the findings of our clinical outcome study, we underscore the importance of understanding both nuclear and extended family dynamics, as well as the socioeconomic and political context of addiction. Specifically, we found a number of important differences between the 16 Latino families who participated, and the remaining Black and Anglo sample. The sixteen Latino families who received treatment were of lower middle class background, mostly of Catholic affiliation, although only 2 could be considered practicing Catholics. Only two of the families did not have extended family relations available in the San Francisco Bay area. About half of the families consisted of an unmarried addict living with his family of origin, while the rest were couples. The couples, however, all remained in very close contact or lived with one of the members of the spouse's family or origin (usually the male's). Of the couples, only 2 were marriages of Latinos with Latinas. All the Latina addicts were married to men who were also heroin addicts. Fourteen of the 16 Latino clients also had significant alcohol, marijuana, and to a lesser extent, barbiturate addictions.

Two of the addicts were third generation, and two were born in Central America but migrated to the United States as children. The remaining participants in our study were second generation (i.e. the children of immigrants to this country). Given the recency of the migration, it was essential to assess the stage of the family migration process (Sluzki, 1979), and the degree of intergenerational conflict present. In 12 of the 16 families, the parent (usually mother) spoke primarily Spanish, while the addict was mostly English speaking. As a result, communication problems between the addict and his or her parents were frequent and severe. In addition, the treatment needed to be conducted in a bilingual format.

In addition to creating a context of intergenerational conflict, the migration experience of all of these families had contributed to the break up of the parents' marriage. All of the Latina mothers were either divorced or had been separated for years. Thus, no Latino fathers participated in the treatment of the addict. In several cases, the mothers had migrated alone to seek work in the United States, leaving their husbands and children in their native country. The ensuing separation of the spouses had resulted in an eventual estrangement and divorce. In other cases, the couple had separated after arrival in the United States. In both instances, the children had minimal, if any contact with their father. Thus, in addition to the normative losses associated with a migration, these families had experienced the loss of a cultural ideal of an intact interdependent unit. While the pattern of the absent father and a potentially overinvolved addict-mother dyad was also present in Black and Anglo addicts, the reasons for this situation among Latinos were clearly associated with the migration experiences of these families.

As most Latino addicts lived with their families of origin, the households tended to include extended family relations as well (i.e., grandparents, separated or divorced siblings and their offspring, aunts, etc.). Of particular relevance for treatment was the fact all of the relatives were quite involved with the problems of the addict, either serving as a resource (emotional or financial support), or as a source of conflict. Many siblings of addicts continuously attempted to hold the addict accountable for his or her addiction by efforts to instill guilt for the suffering caused to the family, and the shame that the addiction brought. While family members within the household attempted to cope with the addiction, Latino families often tried to keep the problem a secret from relatives "back home" and the larger community.

None of the 16 families had ever sought family or individual therapy before, perhaps in part because few bilingual family services were available that also could address substance abuse issues. An additional factor in the lack of service utilization might be the tendency in Latino families to rely on familial sources of support and to feel stigmatized by mental health services (Bernal & Flores-Ortiz, 1983). Moreover, our clinical team developed and implemented culturally specific and congruent recruitment and interviewing methods which included home visits and contacts with all family members (nuclear and extended).

An important evaluation tool with Latino families was the genogram. Each family was asked to develop their own genealogy. Data generated were then used to plan specific interventions within our contextual approach. The genogram also was used to identify intrafamilial and contextual resources.

In summary, many of the patterns identified in the literature were present in these Latino families: absent father, a seemingly overinvolved mother-child dyad, and an "enmeshed" family system. Multigenerational patterns of drug abuse, abandonment of women by men, and parent-child separations due to economic and familial reasons were obvious legacies in the families of Latino addicts in treatment. Finally, the genograms of these families indicated multiple losses and major intergenerational conflicts related to the migration. Our work with Latino addicts suggests that while family patterns may seem on the surface to be quite similar to those of Anglo addicts, the genesis and maintenance of addiction may be related to both cultural and historical realities with very different roots from other groups. Thus, to better understand the dynamics of addiction among Latinos, both a systemic and an intergenerational-contextual analysis are essential.

CONTEXTUAL APPROACH TO THE TREATMENT OF ADDICTION

Contextual family therapy is an intergenerational approach that aims at including all available individuals into its preventive strategy (Boszormenyi-Nagy & Ulrich, 1981) for the benefit of current and future generations. A modality that is focused on both past, and future generations may have more face validity for the treatment of problems such as drug abuse, that in part have been shown to be rooted in generational conflicts.

A fundamental goal of Contextual therapy is supporting trust in relationships. We have found that trust is a central issue with families and couples with a drug abusing member. A framework of therapy that incorporates at the level of theory the language and concept of trust may be able to achieve more permanent and preventive results than other approaches. However, due to the limitations of space, a complete presentation of the foundations of Contextual theory and therapy is not possible. Elsewhere Boszormenyi-Nagy and colleagues have written extensively on this topic (Boszormenyi-Nagy, 1987; Boszormenyi-Nagy & Krasner, 1986; Boszormenyi-Nagy & Ulrich, 1981). It is not our intent, either to argue that contextual therapy is better than any other family therapy of addiction. That question can only be answered by outcome studies. Here we will limit our discussion to highlighting what we consider to be central aspects of the Contextual approach and our modifications of some of these concepts for the treatment of Latino drug abusers.

Central to the Contextual approach are the four dimensions of relational reality (Boszormenyi-Nagy & Krasner, 1986), which include: (1) the historical context of acts and legacies; (2) the individual psychological context; (3) the context of transactional systems; and (4) the context of relational justice. On the one hand, these dimensions of reality serve to order for the therapist separate yet valid realities of individuals and families. On the other hand, these dimensions may help the therapist uncover human resources in the generational web.

The Historical Context of Facts and Legacy

An examination of legacy includes the understanding of basic facts in the family history. The existential facts of the family are of concern (for example, history of migration, issues of race, class, gender, etc.) as is the ability for family members to take rejunctive actions (i.e., to reconnect with family members in order to establish a dialogue and relatedness and thus prevent future generations from sharing a legacy of disjunction). With regards to drug addiction, the family's legacy of loss (through early death, tragedy, migration) is viewed as contributing to the onset of addiction as a symptom of family dysfunction. Viewed as an intergenerational dialectic, drug addiction provides the family with an opportunity to mourn difficult and unresolved loss. The sacrifice of the addict for the family generally is not recognized as contributing to a relational balance between generations that in turn fosters a legacy of destructive entitlement.

We extend the dimension of facts and legacy to include social and historical processes that become a focus of discussion. We view legacies as intergenerational social dynamics linking past, present, and future generations of communities and groups. It is not enough to examine the balance of burdens and benefits among the generations of any one family. To remain within the constraints of the family is reductionistic and implicitly blames the family. We propose examining the family's legacy in its proper sociohistorical context not only as a means of rebalancing debts but also as a means of clarifying the family's social legacy.

As a social dynamic, legacy mandates originate from the earned entitlements of a particular social and political history. How and in what way society provides for its members will determine how and in what ways its members contribute to society. Thus exploring historical and social legacies often reveals the relation between a society and its various communities and subgroups. Such an explanation may reveal how with Latinos, issues such as: the specific origins of the family in terms of nationality, race, and class; the migration history; and the impact of discrimination, racism and other social processes on the family systems and its members must be considered.

The Individual Psychology Context

In addition to the legacies of a given family, Contextual therapy is interested in the individual psychology of each of its members. Here from the therapist's own therapeutic framework (psychodynamic, existential, behavioral) an evaluation is made of each member's psychological resources and conflicts and each member's specific contribution to symptom maintenance and problem resolution. For Latinos, a Contextual therapist must assess the level of biculturality, ethnic identification, and related conflicts. The extent to which the addict finds him or herself between cultures, or has internalized stereotyped views of his or her ethnic/cultural group may have a bearing on the maintenance of addiction as a symptom. Furthermore, the extent to which the addict feels torn with regards to cultural loyalties, familial obligations, and fulfillment of less familial and more individual goals, may impact the second or third generation Latino's ability to function biculturally, or balance competing cultural and familial obligations. In addition, birth order, gender, family role, and a history of separation from the parents during critical developmental periods must also be considered as important contributors to the addictions.

The Context of Systemic Transactions

The structure and organization of family communication, transactions, etc. are pertinent to the understanding of family homeostasis and the cyclical patterns that maintain drug abuse. The Contextual therapist works to identify these patterns and generates hypotheses concerning power dynamics, transactional processes, alliances, and hierarchies among family members, and loyalty issues in the development of such family processes.

With Latinos, notions of enmeshment, individuation and appropriate boundaries must be considered in the context of the cultural value of sacrifice and the high emphasis on "familism" (Bernal & Flores-Ortiz, 1983) since these cultural ideals may demand a different degree of loyalty from children and influence the type of family relations. In addition, systemic analysis cannot be restricted to nuclear family relations, given the cultural ideal of family extendedness and patterns of intergenerational relationships, which may be more common among Latinos than other ethnic groups.

The Context of Relational Justice

The notion of the ethics of relational justice is Boszormenyi-Nagy et al.'s (1980, 1986, 1987) unique contribution to family theory. *Relational ethics* signifies "the long-term preservation of an oscillating balance among family members, whereby the basic interests of each are taken into account by the others" (Boszormenyi-Nagy & Ulrich, 1981, p. 160). Such oscillating balance translates into an accumulation of credits that creates earned entitlement in subsequent generations. The fair distribution of benefits and burdens in relationships translates into a relational justice that builds trust. Unfair or disproportionate distributions of benefits and burdens depletes trust and erodes the resources of the next generation. Within each family an intergenerational ledger of debits and merits is recorded in the lives of each of its members. The therapist aims to foster a dialogue among the family about the balance of benefits and burden (Boszormenyi-Nagy & Krassner, 1986) as a way of supporting responsible relatedness and trust.

Understanding the dimension of relational justice helps to clarify one of the consequences of drug abuse in families. Drug abuse can be seen as an expression of invisible loyalty which keeps the identified patient in a dependent, pseudo-individuated position bound to the parents, who in turn remain as caretakers for a psychologically crippled adult. By remaining with the family the addict is loyal, and by perhaps "giving" a meaning to his/her parents' life without any acknowledgment, the addict is invisibly loyal. Another way of contributing might be by helping the family *not deal* with issues of separation which brings up the theme of loss, death, and mourning.

The Contextual therapist is concerned with examining the legacy and exploring alternative demonstrations of loyalty that are not destructive. The therapist thus supports initiatives from family members in personalizing their family history and re-owning their family legacy in efforts to find positive manifestations of loyalty. Thus, by crediting the addict with his/her specific contributions to the family, the family is helped to understand their own legacy and seek alternative ways for the addict and his/her family to express loyalty. Also, by examining the existential facts of a family, the relationship of early losses to the symptom of addiction can be made, and steps towards rejunction with distanced relatives, mourning the lost relationship, etc., can begin. In this way, the Contextual therapist works at eliciting dialogues among family members.

The Latinos' cultural emphasis on respect, trust, and interdependence often facilitates the development of such dialogues, particularly when the family connects trust-building and rebalancing of relations with preventive consequences for future generations and the overall benefit of the family. In fact, many of the addicts in treatment agreed to participate in our program only because a child or a young relative had begun to abuse drugs. Often the addicts felt responsible for this, and entered treatment in hopes of preventing their relative's continued drug involvement. It is our clinical impression, now empirically validated, that Contextual therapy is helpful for Latinos with a problem of abuse in part because it uses a language (trust, obligation, intergenerational balance) that validates and fits the culture of the family. Further, the therapist's focus on fostering respect, dialogue, and preservation of the family by rebalancing, reconnecting, and crediting sacrifices and contributions, facilitates the engagement of the family into treatment.

CASE ILLUSTRATION OF CONTEXTUAL FAMILY THERAPY AMONG LATINOS WITH DRUG ABUSE

Our work with the intergenerational family therapy program of drug abuse (Bernal et al., 1987) included the evaluation and treatment of 41 families of which 16 were Chicano/Latino families. These families originated from diverse countries in Latin America, including Mexico, Puerto Rico, El Salvador, Nicaragua, Guatemala and Costa Rica. The focus of our work with these families was an understanding of their intergenerational and cultural patterns, the social roots of drug abuse, and the specific legacy and loyalty issues of each family.

The early work with families of Latin American origins (Bernal & Flores-Ortiz, 1983; Bernal, 1982; Bernal & Alvarez, 1983; Bernal, Flores-Ortiz & Rodriguez-Dragin, 1986) revealed a high degree of disconnectedness from the extended family in the country of origin, as well as from the culture of origin. Many Latino families face the pressures of assimilation, adaptation, and acculturation to the new society. These pressures are compounded when the Latino group in question shares a legacy of having been dominated or conquered (e.g., Puerto Ricans and Mexicans). Disconnection to the legacy becomes particularly severe due to loyalty conflicts between the new and the old, the present and the past.

Initially, we approached our clinical work as limited to an examination of legacies within the family context. However, minority and Third world families have much to teach us about their histories and the broader social system. The examination of the balance of obligations and entitlements for each particular family revealed intricately linked social and historical events of extreme ramifications for the family and its individual members. Our support for the awareness and reconnection of legacies often leads to: (1) a firm rootedness in history which serves to challenge cultural cutoffs; (2)

acknowledgment of the interconnectedness between social and family legacies; (3) liberation from the revolving slate of victim and victimizer through the recognition of social processes larger than the family; and (4) developing the ability to distinguish between family and social events.

Treatment followed a 10-session format with up to four additional sessions for handling specific crises. A session by session treatment manual was used in the study (Bernal, Rodriguez-Dragin, Flores-Ortiz & Diamond, 1985) and focused on identifying legacy and loyalty issues (e.g., relational imbalances, disjunctions, and unfair burdens).

The Luna Family

The transgenerational impact of migration and family separation and its relation to addiction was evident with the Luna family. The identified patient, a Salvadoran male aged 35 lived at home with his divorced mother, divorced sister (age 38), a nephew aged 9, and a great aunt (aged 88). The extended family available included a brother aged 40 who was a law enforcement officer, and his wife and children. Victor, the IP, began abusing drugs as an adolescent and had a 19 year history of heroin abuse. At the time of treatment he was enrolled in a methadone maintenance program, but continued occasionally to use heroin. Victor had not been employed for more than a few weeks since he dropped out of high school. The sister supported the family economically; mother received social security and with her money helped support Victor, including his heroin use. Mother argued that unless she gave Victor money for his drug use, he would have to resort to a life of crime. This was an undesirable situation since it would lead eventually to Victor's arrest, which would be embarrassing to his brother in the police force.

In the context of evaluating the family, a number of legacy factors became clear. As with many women from her country and social class, Mrs. Luna had left El Salvador for the United States with hopes of improving the economic situation of her family. She migrated alone, leaving her children with her own mother. At the time of her migration, Victor was 5 years old. Mrs. Luna began to send for her children, first the eldest, then her daughter, and eventually

Victor. It was 9 years after her migration before Victor rejoined the family. From the perspective of individual psychology, it could be suggested that Victor had been left by his mother at a critical developmental stage, and that the subsequent reunification would be fraught with conflict. However, an analysis of Victor's addiction and its role in the family required an assessment of the entire sociopolitical and historical context of his family. A study of the genogram revealed a three generational pattern of women leaving children with their mothers, major problems with the males (including alcoholism and abandonment of women), and overinvolvement of women with their children.

The examination of intergenerational process with the genogram served to contextualize the problem of addiction. Both addict and family members were able to view their current problems as patterns that were parallel to those in prior generations. While this certainly involves a reframing of the problem, the relational implications are both deeper and broader. As family members expanded their context to include prior generations, they began to own and understand aspects of their history. Thus the issue of "blame" became increasingly irrelevant. The family's dialogues were now centered on the consequences of continuing on a transgenerational path or altering that path. The therapist worked to foster a dialogue in which the family members could reflect on the meaning of the problem beyond the nuclear family to involve the family's particular social context as well. Once this step was made, family members began to discover or reaffirm social aspects of the problem with the reaffirmation that the family was not the cause of the problem. Rather, the family and its various generations are all victims of social conditions such as poverty, war, exploitation, and colonialism which probably warped the family in the first place.

A systemic analysis of the patterns of symptom maintenance in this family pointed to mother's support of the addiction by essentially paying for the drugs. From an ethical relational perspective, however, her "support" of his drug habit was a means of giving by compensating for her earlier "abandonment" of the addict; this also served to settle accounts with her own father who also had left the family. Moreover, the historical facts that forced her to leave her country and her children, created an ethical contradiction: In order for her to "make up" for her abandonment, her son would need to remain a dependent child — an addict.

The contextual treatment of this family focused on rebalancing the intergenerational indebtedness of children to mother. How could mother give to her son in ways that was not paying for drugs? How could son give to mother in ways that did not keep him eternally dependent? Acknowledging and crediting Victor's contribution to the family (i.e., discussing openly how he was sacrificing his adult life in the effort to help mother) was a first step in building that trust. His contributions to the family were acknowledged and his addiction was viewed as a means of helping the family avoid the mourning of past losses. The son's disconnection from his own father, his culture, and his own personal goals were also a focus of therapy. At the same time the women of the family were challenged to help Victor in non-destructive ways. Their own invisible loyalties to a family legacy of destructive entitlement became the center of the treatment. By identifying legacies, both mother and son were exonerated and the treatment shifted to identifying resources and solutions to the problem.

SUMMARY AND CONCLUSIONS

The complex set of factors in the development and maintenance of drug addiction among Latinos were examined from the perspective of Contextual intergenerational therapy. A case example was used to highlight the role of legacy and loyalty, as well as the importance of understanding the cultural context of addiction.

Our clinical outcome study of addiction (Bernal et al., 1987) obtained significant results. Specifically, improvement was found for conflict in intergenerational relationships; both families of origin and the addict described a new pattern of relating in which no one needed to sacrifice his or her individual concerns in order to remain a loyal family member. For the Latino sample, interventions which focused on family connectedness, improvement of family relations, and took the blame away from the parents were particularly welcomed. Our work with Latino addicts and their families emphasizes the importance of identifying and utilizing resources, including AA, NA, and other self-help groups. Moreover, we view family therapy as an essential aspect of the treatment of drug addiction, particularly for Latinos, given the cultural ideal of *familismo*. The findings of the outcome study and the clinical findings observed may have relevance for other practitioners who work with Latino addicts. Brief family therapy, as described in this chapter can ameliorate the problem of addiction. By fostering a genuine dialogue in and about relationships and bringing to light destructive legacies, future generations of addicts can be prevented. It is our hope that our work serves to improve the treatment for Latino substance abusers.

REFERENCES

Bernal, G. (1982). Cuban families. In M. McGoldrick, J. Giordano, & J. Pierce (Eds.), *Ethnicity and family therapy*. New York: Guilford Press.

Bernal, G., & Flores-Ortiz, Y.G. (1983). Latino families in therapy: Engagement and evaluation. *Journal of Marital and Family Therapy, 8*(3), 357-365.

Bernal, G., & Alvarez, A.I. (1983). Culture and class in the study of families. In C. Falicov (Ed.), *Cultural perspectives in family therapy*. Rockville, MD: Aspen.

Bernal, G., Flores-Ortiz, Y.G., & Rodriguez-Dragin, C. (1986). Terapia familiar intergeneracional con Chicanos y familias mejicanas immigrantes a los Estados Unidos. *Cuadernos de Psicologia, 8*(1), 81-99.

Bernal, G., Flores-Ortiz, Y.G., Miranda, J.M., Rodriguez, C., Diamond, G., & Alvarez, M. (1987). *Intergenerational family therapy with methadone maintenance patients and family members: Findings of a clinical outcome study*. Paper presented at the 18th annual meeting of the Society for Psychotherapy Research, Ulm, West-Germany, June, 1987.

Bernal, G., & Ysern, E. (1986). Family therapy and ideology. *Journal of Marital and Family Therapy, 12*, 129-136.

Bernal, G., Rodriguez-Dragin, C., Flores-Ortiz, Y., & Diamond, G. (1985). *Contextual therapy of drug abuse: A treatment manual*. San Francisco. University of California. Unpublished manuscript.

Boszormenyi-Nagy, I. (1987). *Foundations of contextual therapy*. New York: Brunner/Mazel.

Boszormenyi-Nagy, I., & Krasner, B.R. (1986). *Between give and take: A clinical guide to contextual therapy*. New York: Brunner/Mazel.

Boszormenyi-Nagy, I., & Krasner, B.R. (1980). Trust based therapy: A contextual approach. *American Journal of Psychiatry, 137*(7), 767-775.

Boszormenyi-Nagy, I., & Ulrich, D.N. (1981). Contextual family therapy. In A.S. Gurman & D.P. Kniskern (Eds.), *Handbook of family therapy*. New York: Brunner/Mazel.

Casavantes, E.J. (1974). *El Tecato: Cultural and Sociologic Factors Affecting Drug Use Among Chicanos*. Washington, DC: COSSMHO Publications.

Coleman, S.B., & Stanton, M.D. (1978). The role of death in the addict's family. *Journal of Marriage and Family Counseling, 4*, 79-91.

Cotroneo, M., & Krasner, B.R. (1976). Addiction, alienation, and parenting. *Nursing Clinics of North America, 11*(3), 517-525.

Flores-Ortiz, Y. (1986). *Substance Abuse in the Mission District of San Francisco, Ca*. Report submitted to the County Substance Abuse Services, San Francisco, Ca.

Haley, J. (1980). *Leaving home: Therapy with disturbed young people*. New York: McGraw-Hill.

Haley, J. (1978). *Problem solving therapy*. San Francisco: Jossey-Bass.

Harbin, H., & Maziar, H. (1975). The families of drug abusers: A literature review. *Family Process, 14*, 411-431.

Kaufman, E., & Kaufman, P. (1979). Multiple family therapy with drug abusers. In E. Kaufman & P. Kaufman (Eds.), *Family therapy of alcohol and drug abuse*. New York: Gardner Press.

Klagsburn, M., & Davis, D.I. (1977). Substance abuse and family interaction. *Family Process, 16*(2), 149-174.

Mandel, J., & Biernacki, P. (1986). *San Francisco County Drug Indicator Study*. San Francisco, Ca. unpublished report.

Moralez, E. (1988). H.I.V. and AIDS related cases by ethnicity patterns in San Francisco. *Multicultural Inquiry and Research on AIDS Newsletter*. San Francisco.

Perez, R., Padilla, A.M., Ramirez, A., Ramirez, R., & Rodriguez, M. (1979). *Correlates and changes over time in drug and alcohol use within a barrio population*. Los Angeles: University of California, Spanish Speaking Mental Health Research Center; Occasional paper 9.

Reilly, D.M. (1975). Factors in the etiology and treatment of youthful drug abuse. *Family Therapy, 2*, 149-171.

Rouse, B. (1986). National Household Drug Use Survey. *NIDA Notes* Washington, DC: U.S. Department of Health.

Stanton, M.D. (1977). The addict as savior: Heroin, death, and the family. *Family Process, 16*, 191-197.

Stanton, M.D. (1981). Strategic approaches to family therapy. In A.S. Gurman & D.P. Kniskern (Eds.), *Handbook of family therapy*. New York: Brunner/Mazel.

Stanton, M.D., & Todd, T.C., and associates. (1982). *The family therapy of drug abuse and addiction*. New York: Guilford.

Stanton, M.D., & Todd, T.C. (1981). Engaging "resistant" families in treatment: II Principles and techniques of recruitment. *Family Process, 20*, 261-293.

Stanton, M.D., Todd, T.C., Steier, F., Van Deusen, J.M., Marder, L.R., Rossoff, R.J., Seaman, S.F., & Skibinski, E. (1979). *Family characteristics and family therapy of heroin addicts: Final reports 1974-1978*. Philadelphia, PA: Philadelphia Child Guidance Clinic.

Sluzki, C. (1979). Migration and family conflict. *Family Process*, *19*(4), 379-392.

Szapocznik, J., Scopetta, M.A., Aranalde, M., & Kurtines, W. (1978). Cuban value structure: Clinical implications. *Journal of Consulting & Clinical Psychology*, *46*, 961-970.

Psychoeducation:
A Tool for AIDS Prevention
in Minority Communities

Mindy Fullilove
Robert Fullilove III
Edward Morales

Black and Latin citizens of the United States bear a heavy burden in the AIDS epidemic. As of fall, 1987, they represented 25% of the 60,000 cases of AIDS diagnosed from over 100 countries around the world (MIRA Research Staff, 1987). AIDS is currently contagious, incurable and fatal, and there is every indication that the epidemic will worsen. We have learned that AIDS is caused by a virus with a long incubation period and a pervasive ability to damage the immune system. Termed the Human Immunodeficiency Virus (HIV) because of its predilection for infecting and destroying cells of the immune system, this retrovirus incubates in the human

Mindy Fullilove, MD, is Assistant Clinical Professor of Psychiatry, University of California, San Francisco (UCSF); and Associate Director, Multicultural Inquiry and Research on AIDS (MIRA), a component of the UCSF Center for AIDS Prevention Studies.

Robert Fullilove III, EdD, is Director, Professional Development Program, University of California, Berkeley; and Research Associate, Multicultural Inquiry and Research on AIDS.

Edward Morales, PhD, is Director, Multicultural Inquiry and Research on AIDS.

From the Center for AIDS Prevention Studies, Departments of Medicine and Epidemiology, University of California, San Francisco. This work was supported in part by a center grant number P50MH42459 from the National Institutes of Mental Health and Drug Abuse. Please address all correspondence to: M. Fullilove, MD, MIRA, Bayview-Hunter's Point Foundation, 60625 Third Street, San Francisco, CA 94124.

143

system for years. Ostensibly healthy people can infect others for many years before becoming ill themselves. Furthermore, the majority of people infected with HIV will eventually become ill with AIDS, or with other, equally debilitating and deadly illnesses such as AIDS-related complex (ARC) or dementia. In 1987, the Center for Disease Control estimated that as many as 1,500,000 Americans may be infected with HIV, suggesting that the scope of the epidemic is probably much greater than the number of AIDS cases diagnosed at present.

The search for cures and vaccines has great urgency, but little hope of immediate success. For example, it is likely that five to ten years will be needed to develop, test and release a reliable anti-HIV vaccine. In the meantime, prevention of the transmission of the virus appears to be the only effective hope for containing and eliminating the disease. Since certain key behaviors have been identified that spread the AIDS virus—sexual contact, sharing of contaminated needles and intrauterine transmission—avoiding risk behaviors becomes a categorical imperative for everyone. The need to convince the public that it is one's behavior (and not casual contact with members of a risk group) that places one at risk of contracting AIDS has forced health officials around the world to concur: "Education is the only weapon we have against AIDS."

This paper will seek to refine that position by suggesting that *psychoeducation*—rather than *education* alone—is crucial if prevention programs are to succeed. We define psychoeducation to mean education and/or training designed to teach individuals how to manage illness (Leff et al., 1983). Psychoeducation is based on the assumption that individuals (and members of groups) can be taught to change their behavior, particularly if they are shown how. Specifically, psychoeducation interventions: (1) present technical information about disease, (2) help participants practice communication skills, (3) teach behavior management techniques, and (4) demonstrate how to accept the consequences of disease.

Psychoeducation developed from behavioral observations of families with schizophrenic members. Researchers found that schizophrenic patients were more likely to relapse if they lived with families that made frequent critical comments and/or were overinvolved (Brown, 1972). Approximately 70% of the criticisms made by family members were the result of misperceptions about the precise symptoms of the patient's illness. Most particularly, family members failed to understand that the patient's apparent laziness, hostility or defiance were not willful, deliberate acts, but were rather aspects of the disease process.

Based on these observations, an intervention "package" was developed that was designed to inform families about the nature of mental illness and to suggest strategies for coping with it. Significantly, the package focused on the family as the unit of change and sought to change the misconceptions about schizophrenia that family members typically harbor.

Although developed originally for the treatment of schizophrenic patients, psychoeducation has been applied to a wide range of disorders, including drug abuse (Wermuth and Scheidt, 1986), and childhood autism (Browning et al., 1987). Each of these adaptations of the psychoeducation model preserves these key features: (1) involving members of a social network (e.g. the family) to help promote the health of the patient; (2) assisting patients and/or members of their families to learn how to manage behavior and/or communicate needs; and (3) providing information that promotes understanding of the nature of the disease process.

If psychoeducation is to be an effective tool in containing the AIDS epidemic, it is important to understand how the people of the world are currently struggling – and in some instances, failing – to adjust to the existence of AIDS. Their ability to cope with the epidemic is complicated by a number of factors:

- AIDS is simultaneously new, incurable, fatal and contagious. It is a slow killer that subjects the afflicted to great suffering and agony.
- Because AIDS was first linked to homosexuals and later, to intravenous drug users, its image is that of a "dirty disease" (Freedman, 1987). Thus, in the minds of the non-gay, non-drug using public, fear of AIDS is coupled with revulsion and rejection.
- For minority citizens, who have long struggled to be free of

derogatory racial stereotypes, the AIDS epidemic raises twin fears: fear of the disease itself and fear of being stigmatized and ostracized by the majority as bearers of disease. In all of these arenas, psychoeducation can play a key role.

We are concerned with three issues in this paper: (1) what is the interface between health education and psychoeducation; (2) how may psychoeducation be used in AIDS prevention; and (3) what are the special problems that psychoeducation may address in minority communities? We hope to explore these issues by examining AIDS-prevention activities at the Bayview-Hunter's Point Foundation, a community-based service organization, active in the minority communities of San Francisco. Finally, in summary, the paper will explore the role of coalitions in preventing the further extension of the AIDS epidemic.

THEORETICAL ISSUES

I. Models of Health Education and Psychoeducation

Chesney (1987) has argued that as health educators attempt to intervene with new diseases they repeat an "unnecessary evolutionary cycle." Initially, they focus on "information transfer" — finding ways to give the public information about how to promote good health and/or to prevent disease. But, as our experience with cigarette smoking reveals, telling people "what's good for them" does not always produce the desired behavior change. It is at this point that the health educator begins to think about behavior modification strategies and later still, about ways in which a patient's social network(s) may be recruited to assist in changing the patient's behavior.

A recent review of national, state and local AIDS-prevention activities (Franks, 1987) suggests that this evolutionary pattern is being repeated in the AIDS epidemic. At present, for example, there is an obsession with informing the public about AIDS; less attention is being paid, however, to devising strategies for encouraging the public to undertake behavior change or for mobilizing social networks to reach those who are at risk.

II. The Uses of Psychoeducation
in AIDS Prevention

Psychoeducation can be targeted to deal with two separate "audiences" in the AIDS epidemic: the first audience is the general public; the second comprises those individuals practicing the behaviors that can spread the AIDS virus. Although the public is knowledgeable about AIDS, some widespread misconceptions exist. For example, many believe that AIDS can be spread through casual contact, such as being in a room with or playing with an infected person. A subtle, but crucial, misconception is that people with AIDS belong to easily definable — and therefore identifiable — risk groups. Thus, many people perceive AIDS to be a disease that affects only gay white men and Black drug addicts. A corollary of this belief is the assumption that these groups can and should be quarantined as a way of protecting society.

The public also both over- and underreacts in assessing its own risk for AIDS, so that, for example, health care workers are inconsistent in using gloves in health care settings while HIV-infected schoolchildren are barred from school and can become the targets of mob violence. Psychoeducation for the general public must focus on behavior change (e.g. teaching individuals how to avoid risky behavior) while correcting key misconceptions about the disease and about those who have it.

The second level of psychoeducation intervention is focused on those individuals who are already engaged in behaviors that put them at risk for AIDS. This includes those sharing needles, those having unprotected sexual intercourse and those who become pregnant while infected. These individuals often express the same misconceptions about AIDS as those expressed by the general public. However, for this group, unlike the general public, harboring misconceptions about AIDS and one's risk for infection has far more serious consequences.

Drug addiction, for example, is a chronic and relapsing illness which will continually expose the addict to risk for HIV infection. While few treatment strategies have shown much hope in addictive disorders, there are a variety of networks — those that support the addict's drug using, those that support his recovery behavior, and those that support continued non-drug use once the initial recovery phase has been completed — that must be engaged if recovery is to be permanent.

Adolescents are a representative sub-group of those whose sexual practices put them at risk. The psychoeducation "package" directed to their needs must provide contraceptive information — which is unevenly distributed in this age group — as well as a means of encouraging the use of such measures as condoms and nonoxynol 9. Here, the importance of social networks and peer groups in shaping individual attitudes and beliefs is well documented. These forces must be mobilized if AIDS awareness/prevention campaigns are to be successful (Gilbert and Bailis, 1980; Brown, 1985).

III. Special Issues of Psychoeducation in Minority Communities

Minority communities are carrying a heavy burden of infection and disease related to the AIDS epidemic. Although they constitute only 12% of the population, Blacks are 25% of the people with AIDS. Similarly, Latins, while 7% of the population, are 14% of the people with AIDS (CDC, 1987). Studies of prostitutes (MMWR, 1987), drug addicts (Lange, 1987), and military recruits (MMWR, 1986) reveal that Blacks and Latins are infected with HIV at higher rates than whites and Asians. While homosexual men are heavily represented among both Black and Latin AIDS patients, drug use accounts for the largest proportion of minority AIDS patients. Further, the drug connection is central to the transmission of AIDS to Black and Latin women who acquire HIV either through their own drug use or through sexual contact with an infected user (Bakeman et al., 1987). Significantly, Black and Latin women comprise the majority of women and children with AIDS.

These statistics present a troubling dilemma to minority communities. Drug abuse and homosexuality are stigmatized in minority communities just as they are in white and Asian communities. The anger towards minority addicts and minority gay men may be fueled further by the fear that, because of the overrepresentation of members of these groups among AIDS patients, AIDS will be blamed on all minority citizens. Moreover, the published speculations of numerous researchers that AIDS originated in Africa is viewed with horror by many in minority communities who are concerned that as fear of AIDS spreads, such ideas will spark anti-minority pogroms.

In spite of fear and anger, minority communities must respond to the epidemic which is undeniably in their homes and on their streets. In contrast to the ostensibly richer gay community, AIDS is devastating the limited resources that exist in minority communities. Funds are being diverted from already impoverished programs to respond to this new crisis.

Further, minority communities face some special needs in confronting the AIDS epidemic. For example, a significant amount of the information about AIDS is highly technical (e.g. the manner in which "relative risk" is computed, or the manner in which HIV disarms the immune system) yet must be presented to a community that is not well trained in matters related to science and technology (Fullilove, 1987). Conveying critical technical information, therefore, becomes a challenge. The language and culture of minority communities also raise special issues in developing prevention messages that are both effective and believable.

At the same time, minority communities have a long history of forming tight social networks that have been central to their survival. Although weakened by a long economic recession (Bowser, 1985), these networks carry an ethos of social responsibility and a tradition of advocacy for those who are weak and needy (Mullings, 1985). Caretaking, sharing, and accepting are essential features of these networks, sentiments that must be engaged if community-wide AIDS-prevention strategies are to succeed.

EMPIRICAL OBSERVATIONS

Psychoeducation interventions can be used to intervene in systems at a variety of levels. The following observations sketch some uses of this method in the Black and Latin communities of San Francisco.

I. Interventions with Groups and in the Community

The Bayview-Hunter's Point Foundation for Community Improvement (BVHPF) was founded in 1971 "to help residents of Bayview-Hunter's Point community in their fight against crime, alcohol, drug abuse and mental disorder" (BVHPF, 1985). The Foundation has taken an active role in AIDS prevention both on its own initiative and in coalition with other minority and non-minority organizations. Currently the Foundation has several ongoing AIDS projects: (1) Multicultural Inquiry and Research on AIDS (MIRA), an AIDS research group that is affiliated with the Center for AIDS Prevention Studies of the University of California San Francisco; and (2) Multicultural Alliance for the Prevention of AIDS (MAPA), which sponsors a variety of outreach programs for drug users and is involved in numerous short-term information dissemination campaigns aimed at reaching the larger Black community. The Foundation is typical of other community-based organizations that are beginning to become more actively involved in AIDS-prevention programs.

In this section we will describe three psychoeducation efforts undertaken by Bayview: the first directed at community leaders, the second directed at adolescents, and the third directed at intravenous drug users.

Community Leaders

Psychoeducation workshops have been developed by the MIRA research team as a means of involving Black and Latin community leaders in AIDS prevention. The objective of the program is to provide influential community figures with an opportunity to learn the facts about HIV and AIDS and to plan programs for their communities that will assist in heightening community awareness about the epidemic.

The workshop series begins with sessions on "AIDS 101," that is, basic information on HIV, HIV's effect on the immune system, antibody testing, AIDS treatment and AIDS prevention. These lectures are followed by a more informal format that allows participants to explore myths about gay men, drug users, and people with AIDS. Finally, participants plan activities that can increase AIDS-prevention activities in their own organizations. Participants reported feeling more aware of AIDS and a greater realization of the extent of the problem. Even those who were already mobilized reported they were eager to extend their activities.

These workshops demonstrate some of the key features of psychoeducation for minority community leaders. Providing information was only one component of the program's design: also included were efforts to get participants to commit themselves to design one or more AIDS-prevention activities and to describe the steps that they would take to bring these activities to fruition. This effort to educate participants while simultaneously assisting them in the creation of a plan of action should be critical to the design of similar psychoeducation programs in other communities. These workshop members will be a ready resource for community members seeking answers to questions about AIDS and for those wishing more detailed information about the epidemic and about the behaviors that place community members at risk. They will also be particularly important in reaching community members who ignore televised community service messages and who will not read posters and pamphlets carrying AIDS-prevention messages.

The workshops also confronted (and hopefully debunked) myths and misconceptions about the AIDS epidemic. Workshop members listed myths that exist in the community, such as "Addicts can't be helped" and "All gays are promiscuous." They also described important and widely held attitudes, such as "The Bible says homosexuality is a sin" and "Only people with venereal disease use condoms." Through the frank discussion of ideas, participants were able to address such concerns as, "How would I present AIDS prevention to members of my church?" One minister concluded at the end of the workshop series, "I know how to use the Bible to answer the spiritual concerns of the people in my church. Now I also have the scientific information that I need to take on these issues."

Rap Contest

As part of ongoing AIDS-prevention work with adolescents, the Foundation has had an active psychoeducation program in its youth center. Attended by local youth, the center provides an after-school meeting place, adult supervision and friendship, and health and education activities. The AIDS education of these teens began with discussion groups in which teens could talk about AIDS with knowledgeable adults. Despite some preliminary embarrassment, teens used the format to ask probing and personal questions (for example, "What are venereal warts and what can you do about them?"). Importantly, the staff's concern simultaneously communicated to the teens that AIDS was serious while providing everyone with an opportunity to explore sensitive subject matter together.

As part of the psychoeducation approach, the teens' newly acquired knowledge was put to practical use: specifically, through a "Rap Contest" in which teens wrote and performed raps on the theme "Rap'n Down Drugs, STDs and AIDS." "Rapping" is a term used to describe a rhymed message — typically in the patois of Black and Latin urban teenagers — that is accompanied with a strong rhythmic "beat." Rapping is an extremely popular indigenous art form. Professional "rappers" sell tens of millions of recordings every year, a statistic that strongly suggests that rap is a useful medium for communicating with young people. While the rhythmic and rhyming structures can be extremely simplistic (even young children can feel like they are "rappin"), both words and beat can become increasingly complex in more experienced and creative hands. Thus, this widely accessible art form creates an ideal atmosphere for a contest and a perfect opportunity for engaging the attention of teenagers.

In the "Rappin' Down Drugs, STDs and AIDS" contest, writers and performers of the winning raps were given prizes and an opportunity to record for television and radio public service announcements. More importantly, through this event, teens were given an opportunity to shape AIDS-prevention messages in an idiom that is uniquely their own. The contest itself was a social and cultural community event attended by participants, their friends and families, and local residents. The importance of the event and its theme were underscored by its presentation on a popular local television program. Winning rappers have since performed in a wide variety of civic and social settings.

In this model the act of becoming an AIDS-prevention spokesperson is part of a larger behavioral change, supporting the development of opinion-leaders in the teen peer group. In the process of performing this job, which these young poets do quite well, they develop an identification with this role, as evidenced in this excerpt from one of the raps [presented in its unedited form, as written by its author]:

> My M-I-S-S-I-O-N is to make sure you never
> use drugs again
> But thats not all that I'm gonna say, I'm gonna talk about the
> ways that you can catch A.I.D.S
> Listen up people this is not a game, I'm gonna put
> it to you straight and very plain.
> See we got a problem going on in the world and it's
> killing young boys and lots of young girls.
> It's drugs and aids, they kill everyday and to catch
> the aids virus you don't have to be gay . . .
>
> This Rapp is Fact not intuition and I'm telling you
> this because it is my mission . . .

"Mission," as used in this context, is a powerful word, which underscores the extent of identification the teens have with this process. Such identification is a first step towards creating a peer-group ethic of safe sex and "Just Say 'No' to Drugs."

Intravenous Drug Users

One of BVHPF MAPA Project's most challenging roles has involved the development of psychoeducation workshops for intravenous drug users. The program consists of sessions that provide basic information about AIDS, and emphasizes methods of prevention by encouraging participants to use condoms and clean needles. The program uses the recovery network of the addict as the social support group and encourages role-playing in which participants test their responses to social situations (e.g., being offered an opportunity to share needles) that would place them at risk.

Prior to the first workshop, participants are given an attitude survey designed to assess their knowledge and attitudes towards AIDS. The survey is re-administered at the end of the program. Pre-workshop survey responses indicate that addicts are knowledgeable about AIDS, but, as anticipated, also evidence certain misconceptions. Many do not know that Blacks and Latins make up 40% of AIDS patients, for example, nor are they clear that people who look healthy can be infected with AIDS. More serious, however, is the fact that, although participants have a useful working knowledge about AIDS and how it is transmitted, many still report engaging in risky sexual and drug behaviors.

The MAPA training is effective in clarifying misconceptions about AIDS, but has limited impact on risk behaviors. The high prevalence of these behaviors, both before and after the workshops, underscores the difficulty of designing effective interventions for addictive disorders. However, the workshops have introduced new information and critical knowledge of the AIDS epidemic into the informal but pervasive social network that addicts share, and there is some hope that ultimately, safe sex and safe needle-use behaviors will become normative behaviors for addicts in much the same way that safe sex behaviors have become the norm for gay men in San Francisco.

II. Intervention with Families

Case 1

HW* is a 32-year-old Black man who is exclusively homosexual in his sexual orientation and activity. He lives alone. Although he has a wide circle of friends, he has not had a stable, long-term sexual relationship. For many years his sexual activity has consisted of casual sexual encounters. In mid-1986 he was tested for HIV antibody and discovered he was seronegative. He described this as a wonderful experience. "I was so sure I was positive," he said, "that I felt like it wouldn't make any difference to try to change my behavior. But after I found out I was negative, I felt like I had a new start in life. I made a lot of changes."

Although HW was able to make substantial changes in his behav-

---

*HW and CG are not real people. Given the sensitive nature of the subject matter, we developed these composite cases in order to convey the usefulness of psychoeducation as a family intervention.

ior, he continued to have unprotected anal intercourse. These episodes seemed to be precipitated by holidays and other "family" times. HW described a great deal of anxiety on these occasions and used the sexual activity to deal with his emotions. In part, he was trying to ease the pain of a long and bitter estrangement from his family of origin, which had never been supportive of him but which had been even more rejecting since learning of his homosexuality.

Family therapy was begun to assist HW in controlling his sexual behavior. Psychoeducation with the family of origin helped them understand about the AIDS epidemic, and recognize their homophobia. Central to the psychoeducation process was teaching this hostile unit the means for expressing positive thoughts and feelings. This task proved to be extremely difficult as family members were habitually critical of each other. The psychoeducation format allowed the therapist to address the role of hostility and criticism in illnesses like schizophrenia and to suggest that it might be related to the life-threatening behaviors that troubled HW. The family — united in wanting to protect HW's health — was able to relinquish some of its hostility. The new tenor of the family relationship gave HW significant support for behavior change.

Case 2

CG* is a 30-year-old Latin man with a ten-year history of drug abuse. He is married and lives with his wife. They have no children. Through the media CG's wife learned that AIDS was transmitted through sharing needles. She became very upset that CG might become infected. CG and his wife came to psychoeducation sessions with his counselor. The counselor gave the wife more information about the AIDS epidemic and about the risks that CG faced when he shared needles. The counselor stressed to CG the need for "staying clean" — trying to stay off drugs altogether and using clean needles when he slipped. Although CG's wife had previously shown many of the attitudes and behaviors associated with co-addiction, as she became more educated about AIDS, she became more and more supportive of CG's "staying clean." With her support, CG made a deeper commitment to treatment, attending clinic sessions and meetings of Narcotics Anonymous on a regular basis.

The treatment also helped the couple to discuss whether or not they needed to use condoms. CG was able to state that he was not yet confident that he would not slip. His wife became clear that, even if he became infected, she did not want to become infected also. This was a difficult conclusion for the couple to reach as both worried that this level of honesty might threaten their relationship. The counselor helped the couple to express their affection and loyalty on a regular basis. As the couple was able to face the dilemma of possible infection, they agreed that it was important to use condoms until CG's sobriety had become more stable. Both CG and his wife learned not to express anger and hostility about the need to use condoms, but rather to see it as an expression of their mutual caring and concern.

Commentary

Both HW and CG were able to make some significant changes during the course of treatment. The two vignettes highlight an important feature of psychoeducation which is the power implied in the premise, "Your knowledge and behavior can prevent (or ameliorate) illness." Families are moved by that hope and will struggle to implement behavior changes that they would have refused to accept given any other presentation of the need for change.

Despite the power of the method, and the changes it can initiate, "slips" — i.e. relapses to high risk behavior — remain a possibility. Neither HW nor CG has been "cured" of high risk behavior. Maintenance of behavior changes has been recognized as a field of study in its own right. Since the virus will be present in the environment for decades to come, it is imperative that we develop and implement methods to reduce the numbers of those who suffer a relapse in behavior change.

THE NEED FOR COALITION

The AIDS epidemic poses a unique challenge to our society and to the world. The state of our biomedical technology has allowed us to unravel the mysteries of this complex illness with a speed that would have been unimaginable ten years ago. Yet the only effective strategy for combatting AIDS does not emerge from our technology but rather from our ability to influence human behavior. For the foreseeable future, our ability to talk to each other and to shape the nature of our group life will be critical to our ability to contain this epidemic. In this paper we have reviewed theoretical and practical evidence which suggests that psychoeducation is a useful model for intervention and one that can be adapted to many situations.

In this section, we raise a final issue, which is implied in the earlier sections of this paper. Implicit in the "curative" aspects of psychoeducation interventions is the affect of acceptance and tolerance that these interventions promote (Leff et al., 1983). AIDS — the "dirty" disease — stirs many emotions of hostility and rejection. These emotions only serve to increase the burden of disease on society. First of all, the stress of anger and hostility may make individuals more susceptible to infection with the virus. Second, the hostility acts to erect barriers between those who most need to change their behavior and the larger society. While alienated groups may succeed in saving themselves, it is more likely that a concerted, unified societal effort will succeed in achieving this goal.

At its most fundamental level, this implies that all those in society who are concerned with stopping the epidemic need to put aside other differences in order to combat the disease. The experience at BVHPF has been that coalitions are powerful. Such coalitions operate on many levels. On one level, the coalition expedites the sharing of knowledge from one community to another. For example, the gay community has implemented a variety of AIDS-prevention strategies. Through coalition efforts, BVHPF has attempted to extract those solutions found to be most effective and to adapt them for use in the minority community. Similarly, BVHPF is an acknowledged expert in working with San Francisco minority communities. This knowledge has proven to be critical to those members of the scientific community who wish to study the effects of AIDS on minorities and to develop effective prevention strategies.

Beyond the sharing of knowledge, however, coalitions offer participants an opportunity to explore and test conceptions and *mis*conceptions that each holds about the other. For example, AIDS researchers initially viewed minority collaborators as "go-betweens" in their efforts to gain access to the minority communities. Through coalition activities, they have learned to appreciate (and more importantly, to use) the knowledge and expertise that minority researchers possess in a wide range of programs and projects. Similarly, it has been helpful for minority leaders to work closely with white and minority gay men and lesbian women in the design of effective intervention programs. Each group has been able to make a more realistic appraisal of the other's knowledge, attitudes and behaviors and to use this appraisal in their programs. Certainly, those who have participated in these coalition efforts have come to believe that they have an essential role to play in "psychoeducation" about AIDS.

SUMMARY

AIDS is a new, fatal, incurable and contagious disease. Prevention must address both the fears of the general public and the behavior change needs of those at risk for HIV infection. Because of its association with addicts and homosexual men, it is seen by the general public as a "dirty" disease that arouses fear, anger, rejection and repulsion. For those at risk for HIV infection, prevention will necessitate change in behaviors; for those at risk because of addiction, prevention also means control of a chronic, relapsing disease process that has defied the forms of treatment currently available.

While "education" is universally viewed as the only weapon against AIDS, this paper argues that "psychoeducation" is actually the more appropriate model. Developed for the treatment of schizophrenia, psychoeducation helps the patient by directing behavioral change and information transfer at key social networks. As applied to AIDS, psychoeducation will take a variety of forms.

For minority communities, the AIDS epidemic poses specific risks, both because of the heavy burden their members share and because of the social backlash that will be directed against minority community members if they are perceived by society to be carriers of disease. Further, minority communities have limited resources with which to deal with the spread of HIV. The development of coalitions with others dedicated to defeating the AIDS epidemic is seen as critical for minority survival. Among groups that are deeply involved in such coalitions are: minorities, gay men and lesbian women, scientists, and public health officials.

Interestingly, psychoeducation is a strategy that was developed by psychotherapists. While this paper has suggested some broader applications for the model, the general nature of the AIDS epidemic is such that therapists concerned with behavior change have an important role to play in preventing further extension of the AIDS epidemic. Many of the people unable to change their behavior will be those that therapists see in treatment: acting-out adolescents who are experimenting with drugs and sex, alienated adults isolated from their families of origin, and drug abusers aided and abetted by their loved ones. Through the use of psychoeducation, therapists can play a critical role in assisting these highly vulnerable individuals and families to learn new — and safer — ways to live together.

REFERENCES

Bakeman, R., McCray, E., et al. (1987). The incidence of AIDS among Blacks and Hispanics. *Journal of the National Medical Association, 79*, 921-928.

Bayview-Hunter's Point Foundation Staff. (1985, June). *Consolidated financial statement.* Unpublished document.

Bowser, B.P. (1985). Community and economic context of Black families: A critical review of the literature, 1909-1985. *The American Journal of Social Psychiatry, 6*, 17-27.

Brown, G.W., Birley, J.L.T., & Wing, J.L. (1972). Influence of family life on the course of schizophrenic disorders: A replication. *British Journal of Psychiatry, 121*, 241-258.

Browning, E., Lambert, L., & Deveres, F. (1987). *Understanding differences: A manual for families of children with developmental delay.* San Francisco: MCFPP.

Center for Disease Control. (1987, October 5). *Weekly AIDS Surveillance* (Available from [Center for Disease Control, Atlanta, Georgia]).

Chesney, M.A. (1987, September). *Applying a health education model.* Paper presented at the NIMH/NIDA workshop on "Women and AIDS: Promoting healthy behaviors," Washington, D.C.

Franks, P. (1987, September). *Federal and state AIDS activities.* Unpublished manuscript.

Freedman, B. (1987, September). *Marketing and advertising: Techniques for influencing behaviors.* Paper presented at the NIMH/NIDA workshop on "Women and AIDS: Promoting healthy behaviors," Washington, D.C.

Fullilove, R.E. (1987). *Images of science in the media: Their impact on the*

160   *MINORITIES AND FAMILY THERAPY*

choice of science as a career. Washington, D.C.: Office of Technology Assessment.

Gilber, F.S., & Bailis, K.L. (1980). Sex education in the home: An empirical task analysis. *The Journal of Sex Research, 16,* 148-161.

Lange, W.R., Primm, B.J., et al. (1987). The geographic distribution of Human Immunodeficiency Virus (HIV) antibodies in parenteral drug abusers (PDAs). *Abstracts Volume: Third International Conference on AIDS.* Abstract No. TP.54.

Leff, J.P., Kuipers, L., & Berkowitz, R. (1983). Intervention in families of schizophrenics and its effect on relapse rate. In W.R. MacFarlane (Ed.), *Family therapy in schizophrenia* (pp. 173-187). New York: The Guilford Press.

MIRA Research Staff (1987, Summer). The third international conference on AIDS. *MIRA Newsletter.* (Available from [Multicultural Inquiry and Research on AIDS (MIRA), San Francisco, California]).

MMWR Staff (1986). Human T-Lymphotropic Virus Type III/Lymphadenopathy-Associated Virus antibody prevalence in U.S. military recruit applicants. *Morbidity and Mortality Weekly Report, 35,* 421-424.

MMWR Staff (1987). Antibody to Human Immunodeficiency Virus in female prostitutes. *Journal of American Medical Association, 257,* 2011-2012.

Mullings, L. (1985). Anthropological perspective on the Afro-American family. *The Journal of Social Psychiatry, 6,* 11-16.

Wermuth, L., & Scheidt, S. (1986). Enlisting family support in drug treatment. *Family Process, 25,* 25-34.

Multi-Impact Family Therapy:
An Approach to Working
with Multi-Problem Families

Paulette M. Hines
Deborah Richman
Karen Maxim
Hillary Hays

Poor families span the continuum with regard to ethnic background, type of family structure, level of functioning, and the number of generations embedded in poverty. Some are working poor, some are temporarily unemployed while others are chronically unemployed. The poor families referred to in this paper are African-American families who face the triple jeopardy of being economically poor, politically weak and discriminated against because of race. They face frequent crises (e.g. inadequate housing, untimely deaths) and stress is persistent. They have insufficient concrete resources and must rely extensively on governmental institutions to help meet basic needs.

Family therapy is far from a panacea for the problems that multi-problem poor families encounter. Both poverty and racism are conditions that extend beyond the personal experience of most helping professionals; all therapists lack the capacity to ameliorate these conditions within the context of therapy. Nonetheless, family transactions are influenced by external stressors and the ways that fam-

Paulette M. Hines, PhD, Deborah Richman, ACSW, and Karen Maxim, RN, MS, are on the faculty, University of Medicine and Dentistry, Community Mental Health Center at Piscataway, NJ.

Hillary Hays, PhD, is on the faculty, Princeton University Counseling Center, Princeton, NJ.

161

ilies adapt to the circumstances that they face are not always optimal (Pinderhughes, 1982; Lefever, 1977). The odds are greatest that multi-problem poor families will be thwarted in their abilities to function effectively when external stressors occur at points of transition in the family life cycle and when these normative stressors intersect with unresolved emotional conflicts. However, family therapy can be useful in assisting the poor in differentiating the sources of their distress, learning to avoid collusion with oppressive forces, and exercising their limited options in ways that are most constructive for the family unit and its individual members.

The reality in most mental health systems, however, is that multi-problem poor families often terminate prematurely or fail to show for therapy appointments. Countless hours are wasted as clinicians sit and wait with estimated rates of no-show as high as 50% after the first visit. Many families never request services even when they receive multiple recommendations from school and other professionals to do so.

If multi-problem families are to benefit from involvement in a therapeutic program, a radical change must be made in the traditional model of mental health service delivery. To be effective, treatment must be planned and delivered within the framework of a family's cultural, ethnic and social system. Factors contributing to resistance must be addressed not only at the level of the family but at the levels of the therapist and larger helping system as well (Anderson & Stewart, 1983).

It was in response to these concerns that a group of family therapists collaborated in an effort to develop an alternative model to address the needs of multi-problem, primarily Black families which we called Multi-Impact Family Therapy (MIFT).

DESCRIPTION OF THE MIFT MODEL

Our initial formulation of the MIFT program was derived in part from the "Multi-Impact Therapy Project" developed in 1956 by Robert MacGregor and his colleagues at the University of Texas Medical Branch Hospital in Galveston (MacGregor, Ritchie, Serraro, & Schuster, 1964). Their program was developed due to the need to provide services to families living a great distance from mental health facilities. The families traveled to Galveston and stayed for the two or three day duration of the treatment program. A multi-disciplinary team met with families who were referred because of difficulties with an adolescent family member. A battery of tests was routinely administered. The team assessed problem areas and promoted change through opening blocked communication channels, challenging resistances, making interpretations, and suggesting ways for families to make changes after they returned home. Treatment included follow-up six months later. MacGregor reported that the success rate of their treatment was at least comparable to that attained by more conventional therapeutic methods.

While geographic distance was the barrier for treatment for the clients for whom the MacGregor model was designed, our clients seemed reluctant to seek treatment for a variety of other reasons (Hines & Boyd-Franklin, 1982). We decided that at least four modifications (three of which were adapted from MacGregor et al., 1964) needed to be made in the traditional evaluation and treatment approach if the poor multi-problem, largely Black, population in our catchment area was to be engaged:

1. The need for immediate and brief intervention was considered important if not crucial. This has been amply demonstrated in the work of Pittman, Langsley and Kaplan (1971) and others. Individuals and families in crisis are ready to make important shifts such as structural realignments and behavioral changes more quickly than when they have stabilized and already begun to accept their difficulties as a part of everyday life.

2. The use of a treatment team was believed to have significant advantages over the use of an individual therapist model. In spite of the creativity, skills and dedication required to work with the poor, most systems offer no special incentives to therapists who take on this work. Caseloads can become overwhelming. Individual therapists are likely to have particular difficulty remaining focused on salient issues with multi-problem families. Far too often, therapists are penalized by the insufficient allotment of time for outreach, advocacy, referral, paperwork, etc. Therapists may unwittingly act out their resentment at these circumstances in ways that further distance

clients. With the use of a team, chances are greatly increased that therapists will not be inducted into the pathology of the family system. The varying personalities, skills, and characteristics of the team members increase the potential for supportive alliances to be formed with each family member. The impact of necessary feedback to the family can be amplified. A therapist team supports the emotional needs of its members while enhancing clear and effective cognitive functioning. Also the supportive environment created among the clinical team members greatly reduces the risk of clinician burn-out.

3. The notion of assessing the family in relation to its larger context is basic to systems thinking. Thus, we deem it of critical importance to consider if not to consult or actually include, in the therapy all persons involved with the problem or its solution. This includes persons from the formal "helping system" who influence decision-making. We accordingly, expanded our usual phone intake to clarify before seeing a family, those persons outside the natural kinship system who could help or, if ignored, hinder the problem-solving process.

4. An extended single session format is one of the cornerstones of the MIFT model. Multi-problem poor Black families are generally, at best, ambivalent about involvement in therapy. Stress and suffering are an expected part of life; they value "being strong," and changes dictated by crises are quickly consolidated into everyday life. Talk is not seen as a solution to problems; they are unlikely to understand the nature of mental health services or to perceive them as relevant. These families are not likely to expect that their concerns will be addressed by persons who are sensitive to the realities of their world. They may not only feel ashamed to share their life difficulties, but believe that to do so only reinforces society's pejorative evaluation and rejection of them. The combination of ambivalence about the value of therapy, frequent crises, and conflicting job, school, and childcare responsibilities can make it difficult to engage key family members at any given time, day or evening (Hines & Boyd-Franklin, 1982; Hines, 1988).

We have found a minimum of six hours to be essential to hypothesize, assess, and intervene in the problems presented by multiproblem families. The devotion of a single block of time increases the potential for relevant persons to be present for the family session. It facilitates joining, and permits greater impact than is afforded by weekly therapy sessions which are often intertwined with new crises, cancellations, and no-shows. Family members feel comfortable that they have ample time to be heard, individually and collectively.

Essentially, the MIFT model combines: (1) immediate response to a request for service, (2) a brief, problem-solving treatment approach, (3) use of a team of therapists who all work face-to-face with the family, (4) the inclusion, as necessary, of significant others from the informal network and the multiple agencies involved with the family, and (5) the devotion of a day to the initial family contact. A six week follow-up session is conducted. Families are seen at the clinic unless the physical illness of a significant member requires a home visit. Transportation is arranged, if necessary. While we recognize the benefits of seeing families in their homes, our experience suggested that better results would be realized from a day-long session if we exercised greater control over factors (e.g. intrusion by neighbors, noise level) that can detract from everyone's ability to focus on the identified problems.

METHOD

Cases selected for the MIFT project are chosen on the basis of the following criteria: complexity of their problems, resistance to referral, and need for prompt service. The first is defined as any combination of economic, behavioral, relationship, academic, job and health problems. Resistance to referral pertains to the family having terminated mental health services prematurely in the past and/or to their actual or anticipated failure to follow-up on a referral for mental health services. We define the need for prompt service to mean simply that the family's problems have escalated. Since our staff can not work on the project on a full-time basis, it is not possible often to see families on the same day they call or are referred for service. However, we assume that families would have a greater receptivity to change if seen as soon as possible (generally within a week).

The appropriateness of a family for MIFT intervention is determined from a review of referral and initial contact data. This includes demographic data on those living in the home, significant persons in the informal network, information regarding past contacts for service, and information from any representatives of other agencies who referred the family. If a family is judged to be one that can benefit from the model, more detailed intake information is gathered. Our aim is not to conduct a full telephone interview but to gather sufficient information to reasonably determine who should be present and/or what information should be attained prior to the day of contact. Families are presented with details about the day-long program and given the option of being seen by the team or in the traditional weekly session model. Most families have opted for the day-long program. Working parents have been willing to come since they are advised that any additional services that might be required will be planned around their work schedules. The family spokesperson is encouraged to invite those persons considered critical to understanding or solving the identified problems and a session is scheduled only after their availability has been considered.

The day-long session is divided into four phases: (1) pre-session strategizing, (2) assessment, (3) treatment planning, and (4) intervention. Varying from the MacGregor model, a visit is scheduled six weeks later and subsequent assistance (e.g. systems advocacy) is provided as needed. The Team, consisting of three to four therapists, determines who will serve as the lead therapist for a given family prior to the session; this person orchestrates the session and is identified for the family as the person to contact if the need arises before and after the six week follow-up.

A more detailed description of the process involved when families are seen in the MIFT model follows.

Pre-Session Strategizing

Upon arrival at the clinic, the family is registered and assisted in completing questionnaires to facilitate the team's evaluation. Meanwhile, the team reviews all available data about the family and develops hypotheses to guide the initial exploration of the family's difficulties. The team draws upon the family life cycle (Carter & McGoldrick, 1988), eco-structural (Aponte, 1974; 1976), and Bowenian (1976) frameworks to zero in on why the symptoms have developed or become worse, and why the family has decided to seek help at this particular time. The goal of hypothesizing is to narrow the field of inquiry to prevent becoming overwhelmed by information from the family and other agencies. It increases the chance of effecting meaningful change by reducing the chance of getting sidetracked by the family's multiple problems and multiple storytellers.

Assessment Phase

During the assessment phase, the team meets with the family for approximately 1 to 1 1/2 hours. The decision about whether and at what point to include the agency representatives in the session is based on whether their input seems critical to understanding or resolving the family's difficulties. In one case, for example, a 13-year-old girl was referred for school avoidance and disruptive behavior at home and school. Workers from a number of agencies (e.g. school, child welfare, social services) were actively involved in delivering services to the family. Each had tried to refer the family for mental health services without success. The mother asserted that she was calling for an appointment at their insistence. The workers were contacted to clarify their concerns and it became obvious that they were beginning to overwhelm the family and to sabotage each other's efforts.

When agency representatives are invited, they are scheduled to come into the session about 30 minutes after the session begins. This allows the team to have sufficient time to engage the family, clarify their ideas about therapy, orient them to the services provided at the agency, and clarify the boundaries between the mental health center and other agencies. During the interview, the genogram data gathered during the initial phone intake is expanded. Relationships between the family members, between the family and agency representatives, and among the agency representatives (Imber-Coppersmith, 1983) are explored as these relate to the presenting problems. Every person is given a chance to share his/her perspective on the problems, efforts already made to resolve the problems, ideas about why these failed, and ideas about what would help the family to address the problem(s) more effectively. The information gathered during the interview may support or refute the Team's original hypothesis; the field of inquiry is expanded as needed. Interventions (e.g. reframing) are made to shift the family's perceptions of the identified problems and identified client, as well as to emphasize the benefits of change. During the interview, the team members model open communication and heighten awareness of any polarization in the family by strategically discussing our differences while in the family's presence. This process may occur without prior planning; the team is situated in the room so that each member can more easily observe the other's nonverbal signals. We may choose to take a break and confer outside of the therapy room at any point during the day.

The family is subsequently seen in individual and/or sub-system groupings for approximately 45 minutes. The sub-group meetings are an important component of the model's application to multi-problem, poor families. As a result of the joining afforded by the one on one interaction, greater rapport is established with family members thus enhancing the climate for change. The team is able to develop a clearer view of each individual's strengths and can clarify/expand upon any differences in viewpoints among the family. Family members are able to share information they might withhold or not expand upon otherwise. Thus, the mother who is viewed as a hostile and withdrawn person, who beats her children can be appreciated as an overwhelmed, anxious mother who was abused as a child. The sub-system interviews are conducted concurrently with a prearranged time for everyone to reassemble. Divisions of the family into sub-groups are made dependent upon the size of the family group, the number of team members present, generational boundaries, roles, power, and how the family appears to be organized in relation to the identified problems.

Treatment Planning

At mid-day the family takes a lunch break of 1 to 1 1/2 hours. The team meets to share information gathered during the sub-system interviews. The brief questionnaires that are completed by the family members during the pre-assessment phase are reviewed. The team refines or reformulates the working hypothesis and develops a plan of action for assisting the family. Interventions may involve a combination of educational, behavioral, eco-structural, strategic and communication approaches.

Treatment Phase

The treatment phase begins with reconvening the family and, when appropriate, other agency representatives. The team share their assessment of why the family has had difficulty in resolving the identified problem(s). Generally, we offer families a straightforward, consumer-oriented reframing of the problem(s) presented; these are systemically and benevolently framed. We always begin by pointing out family strengths and crediting them for all attempted solutions. We focus on those issues that are within the family's ability to change and zero in on the central emotional issues which are crucial to the family's ability to proceed developmentally. Empowerment (Pinderhughes, 1982), opening up communication, acknowledging and using family strengths and resistances have been cornerstones upon which all strategies are built.

The lead therapist from the team assumes administrative responsibility for the case and any follow-up services that are needed. Occasionally, additional family or individual sessions may be necessary (e.g. suicidal family member).

FOLLOW-UP

Six weeks following the all-day session, a two-hour interview is scheduled with the family and any appropriate agency representatives. The status of the problems that were targeted for intervention is reviewed. If the family has achieved or moved towards resolution of the identified problems, the family is advised to call should any further problems arise. If a family does not call within a three month period, a follow-up call is made to review the status of their presenting concerns. If there has been little or no change in the identified problems or if new problems have arisen for which the family desires help, a date and time for follow-up is established.

CASE EXAMPLE

Fifteen-year-old Sandra, a Black teenager, had been hospitalized for a week after having her third "seizure" for which attending physicians could find no medical basis. The family had been referred several times by the social service department of the local hospital to the Community Mental Health Center (CMHC) for a psychiatric evaluation. They never followed through on this recommendation.

A staff person from the hospital's social service department contacted the CMHC for suggestions of ways to persuade the family to apply for service. She provided the following information about the family. The family was headed by a single parent and lived in a low income housing project. Sandra's father lived in the South and was remarried; her mother, Ms. Brown and a 16-year-old brother, Sam, lived with Sandra in the household. Ms. Brown was unemployed and the family was dependent upon welfare subsidies. Neither adolescent was attending school on a regular basis. Another brother, Charles, age 23, lived in a nearby neighborhood and visited the family daily. He was receiving disability payments because of severe sickle cell illness.

After considerable efforts at outreach including the special provision of transportation, the family agreed to come to the center to participate in the MIFT project. Since the family had not developed a relationship with personnel at the school, welfare agency, and hospital, the team decided against inclusion of representatives from these agencies; tentative arrangements were made for Sandra's school counselor to come if the need arose.

During the pre-assessment phase the team met to review the available data while the family members completed several questionnaires. Because a medical basis for Sandra's "seizures" had been ruled out and neither adolescent was attending school the team hypothesized that the family members might be having difficulty with separation related to unspoken anxieties about the older son's

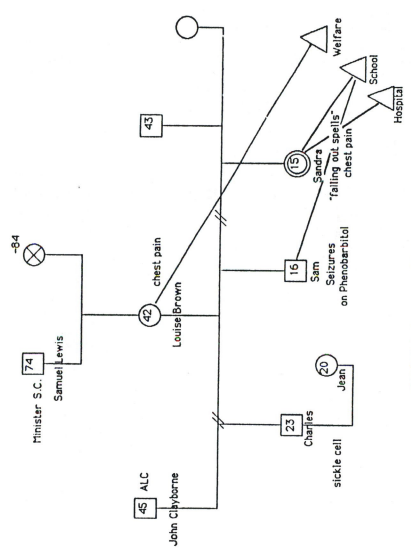

FIGURE 1. Genogram: The Brown Family

life threatening illness. This pre-assessment hypothesis served as a guide for initial information gathering.

During the Assessment Phase the team learned that the family described Sandra's seizures as "falling out" spells. They explained that during these spells Sandra appeared to be unconscious with her eyes fixed on the ceiling. Mrs. Brown reported that Sandra seemed depressed; she frequently stayed in her room, refused to socialize with friends and family and used physical complaints to avoid school.

Ms. Brown reported that she had suffered from similar "falling out" spells when she was a child. They would occur whenever a particular aunt came to visit. Her mother solved this problem by having the aunt call before she visited so Ms. Brown could leave the house. It was also learned that Ms. Brown was periodically experiencing "heart pains" that had intensified since the death of her mother three years earlier. She described them as so painful that sometimes "I think it is my last go round." Ms. Brown had been to the hospital several times but had not been found to have anything wrong with her heart. She had experienced great difficulty dealing with her mother's death and would call her mother's old telephone number and allow the phone to ring.

Issues of unresolved grief and anticipated losses emerged repeatedly during the family and sub-system interviews. It was learned that Sam had a seizure disorder which had been controlled by phenobarbital for four years. Charles had experienced great difficulty in separating from the parental home. Each family member reported seldom leaving home because of concerns about each other's health. They also feared the lack of safety in their housing project and school environment.

At mid-day the family left for lunch while the team met for information sharing and treatment planning. (The break in the day has generally proven useful for families as they have tended to discuss their reactions to the morning's events with one another thus facilitating shifts in their perception of the presenting problem(s) and one another.) The team members met over lunch and summarized the information gathered during the individual and family interviews. We reached consensus on a series of interventions based on the following observations:

1. The family members shared a style of coping with stress through somatization; mutual overprotectiveness among the family members inhibited individuation and the accomplishment of normal developmental tasks.
2. Each family member, but in particular Ms. Brown, evidenced unresolved grief over the death of Ms. Brown's mother.
3. The family's continuing experience with death, serious illness, and environmental hazards had resulted in overly rigid boundaries which limited their movement.

The first strategy in the Treatment Phase was to reframe the problem as one of the family being so loving and close that unknowingly they prevented each other's growth. We emphasized our belief that the family tradition of sticking together was a valuable part of their heritage that was very important to continue. The team pointed out that the ongoing threat to Charles' health and the dangerousness of the family's neighborhood rendered them prone to be even more protective of one another. (Note that the family's genogram had been drawn on a chalkboard during the treatment planning phase. The lead therapist emphasized the family's construction of a wall around themselves by drawing a heavy dark circle around their symbols on the genogram as she spoke.) We suggested that they had become even closer and more inclined to try and protect one another as a result of the daily threats posed by the older son's life threatening illness and the family's immediate environment. At that point, Charles expressed agreement with the Team's analysis and shared his effort not to worry his mother with his problems because he feared she might end up "like a neighbor who died because her children nagged her to death."

We expressed great admiration for their desire to be supportive and available to one another but questioned the necessity of demonstrating their concern by sacrificing fulfillment of their individual needs (e.g. social, educational, vocational). The long-term benefits of changing their behavior based on their individual and collective concerns were emphasized. During this process the family listened while nodding emphatically in agreement as points were made.

We perceived Ms. Brown to be pivotal in effecting change in the family's functioning. She was surprised to learn how fragile she was perceived as being by her children and to learn that they avoided communicating various concerns to her out of fear that she might die. By redefining Ms. Brown's illness, more appropriately as the expression of her mourning, we helped to shift her children's misperception of her alleged fragility. We encouraged her throughout the session to talk about her past accomplishments as a way of beginning to correct the family's misconceptions of her as in need of protection.

Thirdly, we reframed Sandra's school avoidance and "seizures." Analogies were drawn between her effort and those of each of the other family members to make the noble but unhelpful sacrifice of always being available to try to protect each other from the hostile world outside their apartment. The team supported and emphasized Ms. Brown's belief that she must be very involved in her children's lives. We suggested that she could be quite helpful in convincing her children that her health complaints were not life threatening by beginning to pursue some activities outside the family. She responded positively to the suggestion that she might help her children avoid the pain of an overly close relationship with a parent. We suggested that Ms. Brown knew best what to pursue amongst many endeavors she had often considered but deferred (e.g. work, bowling, evening classes). Ms. Brown accepted the task of helping her children reconnect with school guidance counselors to learn about vocational schools or other options.

The family did not return for the scheduled follow-up session. Mrs. Brown left a message that the family was doing well and she saw no reason to return to the clinic at that time. She was no longer concerned about Sandra being depressed and there had been no return of the seizures. She was agreeable to the notion of Sandra stopping by the clinic to pick up follow-up questionnaires. Sandra was reluctant to walk to the clinic but accepted the therapist's offer to meet in a local coffee shop. Her depression had lifted noticeably. Her dress and hair were definitively more feminine and she informed the therapist that she had started a course at a local modeling school where she was socializing with her peers. Six months later, Ms. Brown had taken a job outside the home and Sam had entered a job training program. Two years after the initial contact Sandra reported having had no seizures and Ms. Brown had remarried.

CONCLUDING STATEMENT

Brief, yet intense, the MIFT model is not meant to be a Band-Aid, but rather is an alternative to the traditional approach to therapy that allows a family to work on limited but significant goals. Diagnostic and treatment formulations are conceptualized keeping in mind a family's cultural values, socioeconomic and political context. Our basic assumption is that a family's feelings of powerlessness can lead to difficulties in perceiving and exercising the limited options that may exist for them. The aim of the MIFT model is not to prevent all future problems for the family system nor to induce major personality changes in individual family members. The goal is to maximize a family's chances for success in solving present life difficulties while strengthening their overall functioning. We neither dismiss nor overfocus on external stressors and systems beyond a family's control. The MIFT model permits therapists to draw upon a range of therapeutic approaches but emphasizes offering respect for a family's history of struggle and survival, adaptive behaviors and resistances. We emphasize family strengths, offer hope and seek to facilitate change at the cognitive, emotional, and behavioral levels.

Our pilot effort did not include empirical evaluation beyond consumer satisfaction data. These results are promising but are not generalizable since data were collected from only 12 of the 25 families seen. Our subjective impression is that the model is better received and more effective than the traditional approach with multi-problem poor families. However, empirical evaluation of the model's efficacy is sorely needed.

REFERENCES

Anderson, C.M., & Stewart, S. (1983). *Mastering resistance: A practical guide to family therapy*. New York: Guilford Press.

Aponte, H. (1976). Underorganization in the poor family. In P.J. Guerin, Jr. (Ed.), *Family therapy: Theory and practice* (pp. 433-434). New York: Gardner Press.

Aponte, H. (1974). Psychotherapy for the poor: An eco-structural approach to treatment. *Delaware Medical Journal, 46*, 432-448.

Bowen, M. (1976). Theory in the practice of psychotherapy. In P.J. Guerin, Jr.

(Ed.), *Family therapy: Theory and practice* (pp. 42-90). New York: Gardner Press.

Carter, E.A., & McGoldrick, M. (Eds.). (1988). *The changing family life cycle: A framework for family therapy*. New York: Gardner Press.

Hines, P. (1988). The family life cycle of poor black families. In E.A. Carter & M. McGoldrick (Eds.), *The changing family life cycle: A framework for family therapy* (pp. 515-543). New York: Gardner Press.

Hines, P., & Boyd-Franklin, N. (1982). Black families. In M. Mcgoldrick, J. Pearce, & J. Giordano (Eds.), *Ethnicity and family therapy* (pp. 84-107). New York: Guilford Press.

Imber-Coppersmith, E. (1983). The family and public sector systems: Interviewing and interventions. *Journal of Strategic and System Therapies, 2,* 38-47.

Lefever, H. (1977). The religion of the poor: Escape or creative force. *Journal of the Scientific Study of Religion, 16*(3), 225-236.

MacGregor, R., Ritchie, A., Serrano, A., & Schuster, F. (1964). *Multiple impact therapy with families*. New York: McGraw-Hill Book Co.

Pinderhughes, E. (1982). Afro-American families and the victim system. In M. McGoldrick, J. Pierce, & J. Giordano (Eds.), *Ethnicity and family therapy* (pp. 108-122). New York: Guilford Press.

Pittman, F.S., Langsley, D., & Kaplan, D. (1971). Therapy techniques of the family treatment unit. In J. Haley (Ed.), *A family therapy reader* (pp. 99-107). New York: Grune & Stratton.

Discrimination in Urban Family Practice: Lessons from Minority Poor Families

George W. Saba
Denise V. Rodgers

A few years ago, a Cambodian father brought his son to the emergency room of a large city hospital. The child was lethargic and had a fever of 103 degrees. During the exam, the physician noticed severe bruising over the boy's body. The family spoke only Cambodian, and there was no translator available in the hospital. The language barrier made it difficult to verify what had happened. However, the doctor noted that the father seemed suspicious and anxious. Suspecting foul play, the physician called Child Protective Services (CPS) to report possible child abuse. The doctor admitted the child for observation and sent the father home. The next morning, the father was found hung in his bedroom. Only after speaking with the family's refugee worker did the physician discover that the bruises were not from abuse. They resulted from an ancient healing called "coin rubbing."[1] He also learned the father was ashamed that he had lost his son, and that the authorities thought badly of him.

This father had attempted to help his son with a respected, and often effective, healing ritual. When that failed, he brought the sick

George W. Saba, PhD, is Director of Behavioral Sciences, Family Practice Residency, San Francisco General Hospital, and Assistant Adjunct Clinical Professor, Department of Family and Community Medicine, School of Medicine, University of California, San Francisco.

Denise V. Rodgers, MD, is Associate Director, Family Practice Residency Program, San Francisco General Hospital, and Assistant Clinical Professor, Department of Family and Community Medicine, School of Medicine, University of California, San Francisco.

Both authors have contributed equally to this work. We would like to thank the following people: Teresa Rebeiro Saba, Virginia Rodgers, and Kathy Thompson.

child for the powerful medicines of American doctors.

This dramatic anecdote demonstrates an extreme outcome due to the ignorance of well-intentioned health care providers.[2] Obviously, the availability of a Cambodian translator could have saved their father's life and prevented the family's pain. In many ways, the error is too obvious. Most providers upon hearing this story reflect, "I doubt I would ever make such a mistake." However, in such situations, one can easily feel caught in a whirlwind of considerations (e.g., "Must I call CPS?"; "Might these bruises represent something other than abuse?"; "Are bruises, inflicted for the sake of healing, abuse none the less?").

In lieu of an interpreter, the above provider made an assumption and acted upon it. He assumed that the bruises were the result of possible abuse. In an effort to protect the child, he admitted him. The father also made an assumption. He viewed the hospitalization and his dismissal as punishment. Thus the provider misinterpreted the effects of attempted healing (coin-rubbing) as evidence of abuse, and the father misinterpreted the actions of the physician as punishment. Perhaps most disturbing about this situation is that all the people involved were acting out of concern for the child, and yet such caring resulted in tragedy.

In examining our work and that of others, we have seen how narrow assumptions can lead to unintentional disasters. Problems can occur when we assume that we "know" certain truths. For example, we have learned that when a child presents with multiple fresh bruises, we must consider this evidence of child abuse until proven otherwise. However, the aggressive pursuit to determine child abuse often depends on one's assumptions about the patient s/he is treating (e.g., "Child abuse leaves scars like these." "Child abusing families have characteristics like these."). If these assumptions are rigid and narrow, they can often blind providers to the possibility of alternate explanations and lead to disastrous, discriminatory results.

DISCRIMINATION:
A TOOL FOR HEALING AND HARMING

Providers and patients alike naturally develop assumptions about all aspects of their experience (e.g., life, death, health, illness).

These assumptions help sort through experiences, ascribe meaning to events, and define realities. In the everyday applicaton of these assumptions, discrimination is an indispensable tool.

As discrimination will serve as a focus for this paper, let us explore its various meanings. *Discrimination* is defined as *"the act of distinguishing; the act of making or observing a difference; distinction; as, the discrimination between right and wrong. The ability to make or perceive distinctions; penetration; judgment; perception; discernment"* (Morris, 1969, p. 376).

In addition to these denotations, discrimination carries a variety of connotations. At first glance, many consider discrimination a "negative" activity. Negative discrimination involves the unfair treatment of a non-dominant subset of the population. Such treatment discriminates "against" people and is, in part, based on ignorance and fear. For example, health care providers can unwittingly discriminate against their patients. Providers may assume that Black patients lack insight and can benefit only from behavioral models of therapy.

Providers can practice another type of negative discrimination by discriminating "for" patients. This perspective leads health care providers to prevent patients from reaching their full potential believing further development may "just be too hard." Thus, providers can underestimate the abilities of patients and/or excuse them from responsibility for their problems. Based on paternalism and protectionism, this underestimation encourages an attitude of "I'm doing this for your own good." This is more subtle and insidious than discriminating "against," since the provider-patient relationship is supportive and trusting rather than adversarial. The patient is at greater risk of believing and incorporating the discriminatory message.

Finally, one can consider a third kind of discrimination, "positive" or appropriate. From this perspective, providers treat people differently because, as a member of a particular ethnic group, differences do exist. For example, adult Anglo patients may enjoy being personally close to their providers (e.g., calling each other by first names). On the other hand, for a provider to speak informally to an adult Latino patient may be disrespectful (e.g., to use the "tu" [familiar] rather than the "usted" [formal] form of address). To assume patients of different cultures have similar expectations can represent a failure to appropriately discriminate. Providers most often encounter problems when they try to obscure the boundaries between their own and different cultures.

While certain discrimination is essential to our clinical practice, misperception, failure to differentiate, and poor judgment can quickly become unwelcomed guests. Also, differences in assumptions between providers and minority poor patients set the stage for discriminatory mistakes. Without a clear sense of their biases and prejudices, providers will often deliver suboptimal care.

Some have recommended that clinicians examine their assumptions as a way of clarifying their models of therapy (Liddle, 1982; Schwartzman, 1983) and medicine (Saba and Fink, 1985). Similarly, we suggest that providers explore their assumptions about working with minority poor people and identify discriminatory patterns in their practice.

This article represents our attempts to examine assumptions that we have found operative in our own work and that of our colleagues.[3] To focus this examination, we will identify common discriminatory pitfalls that can occur in the treatment of minority poor families in an urban medical center.[4] We will discuss how best to avoid these pitfalls and recover when they are unwittingly encountered. This article is intended for family-oriented health care providers (e.g., family physicians, family therapists, family nurse practitioners) practicing in the inner city. A brief look at our context and clinical perspective will ground the discussion of discriminatory patterns.

CONTEXT

San Francisco General Hospital is the setting for the work we will discuss. The Family Health Center of this county hospital provides outpatient care and serves as a training site for Family Practice residents (Sommers & Massad, 1987). The patient population is ethnically diverse: 28% Asian (mainly Chinese, Filipino, and Southeast Asian); 25% Latino (mainly Mexican and Central American); 10% Black; 10% White; and 27% Other. While these categories help to group patients, they can eliminate the wide variety of geographical areas and cultures from which our patients have originated. Most of the patients are poor, their care paid for by state/federal programs. While patients have similar incomes, their class backgrounds and attitudes vary. In addition, we see a variety of family structures in our setting (e.g., single parent families; large, extended networks; families containing a number of non-biologically related members; and lesbian/gay families).[5]

The health care providers in our clinic include family physicians, nurse practitioners and family therapists, as well as trainees for each of these disciplines. The majority of care is provided by family physician residents and faculty.

PERSPECTIVE

The Hipbone's Connected to the Welfare Office

Montalvo and Gutierrez (1983) suggest an inter-institutional perspective when working with minority poor people. We find this broad lens essential and expand it to include the patients' physiological lives. We have found a perspective of both "internal" and "external" medicine to be invaluable. Thus, we practice a systems-oriented model of medicine (Bloch, 1983; Saba & Fink, 1985) which appreciates the interconnections of a patient's physiological functioning with other systems such as family, community, the economy, and society.

Our patients seem to inherently share this view. For instance, when one family member is ill, the whole family often visits the doctor knowing that the illness of one affects all. In addition, they also "feel" or "are aware of" institutional involvement and its control in their lives. Their "extended family" includes the welfare system, the health department, the immigration service, the courts, and the schools.

A classic example of this interdependence involves a mother receiving Aid to Families with Dependent Children (AFDC) who becomes ill at the end of the month and refuses admission to the hospital until the first of the month when her welfare check comes. This woman knows that unless she is able to cash the check, her children will suffer while she is away. In this situation, a provider must balance the medical needs of the mother with her need to know her children are cared for and secure.

Clearly a broad systems perspective can aid a clinician regardless of his/her patient's race and class. In addition, minority poor families can experience the ever-present instability in their interconnected world, requiring a heightened sensitivity to one's perspective.

For example, in many ways, poor families are analogous to the frail elderly. A frail elderly person who catches the flu can become dehydrated and dizzy. This dizziness can precipitate a fall and resultant hip fracture. Pneumonia can develop secondary to the associated immobility, with death following soon. Just as the aging biological systems become increasingly vulnerable to shifts in their functioning, the social systems of the poor are susceptible to changes in the delicate web of interdependence. When one institution involved in the life of a poor family fails, the results can become catastrophic. For example, a missed welfare check can lead to unpaid bills. Vital services such as heat and electricity can be discontinued. If such conditions persist, the family is at increased risk for physical and emotional stress which endangers health. As we know, sick children are more likely to miss a significant amount of school, leading to poor school performance, and the demise of opportunity. It is hard to imagine such far reaching consequences of a seemingly simple disruption of a missed welfare check. However, when a family repeatedly faces minor crises, a missed welfare check can precipitate a cascade of catastrophic events. Appreciating the fragility of interconnections has forced us to sharpen our systemic focus.

Comprehensive Care

The family physicians, the primary deliverers of care in our setting, are trained in the fundamentals of family therapy. This occurs for various reasons: (1) Philosophically, systems-oriented family practitioners want the option to intervene at multi-system levels in order to optimize patient care; (2) People often present providers a complex picture of multiple psychosomatic problems. For example, somatic symptoms are often linked to psychological, familial and/or social difficulties. People from so-called "primitive" societies fail to understand our notion of the "specialized healer" (e.g., physician, psychotherapist, priest), and initially seek help from a provider who they expect to care for the whole person, body and soul; (3) Language barriers hamper adequate care in many mental health clinics; (4) In general, mental health services are inadequate, underfunded, and less available to the poor in this country. Rarely can these resources afford the luxury of addressing "minor" concerns such as school problems, marital discord, parenting difficulties, or the anxiety that often accompanies living in an inner-city environment; and (5) For many people, acceptable behavior excludes seeking help from mental health professionals for problem-resolution. Therapy is reserved for those who are truly "crazy" or as an alternative to imprisonment.

In the ideal setting, family physicians and family therapists work together to comprehensively treat the whole person/family. Unfortunately, only a few clinics can achieve this goal. Until this model of care becomes a reality, minority poor families will continue to turn to the health care setting for relief of a variety of problems, even primarily emotional, economic, or familial ones.

Arenas of Interventions

We commonly intervene at the individual and family (nuclear and extended) levels. However, we remain cognizant of those institutions which seem out of reach, and thus consider interventions at the *legislative* (e.g., health policy, National Health Program), *community* (e.g., educational programs), and/or *inter-institutional* (e.g., school, welfare office, probation department) levels.

LESSONS, PITFALLS, AND STRATEGIES

The field of systems medicine is relatively new. In addition, insufficient research exists to guide providers' work with minority poor families. Previous study has generally been done by non-minority providers with non-minority, middle class families. In our work, we have filled this vacuum of information with instruction from experts, the families themselves. In an effort to share our education, we will present a number of lessons which result from challenges to our assumptions, discuss related discriminatory pitfalls, and offer strategies to avoid them.[6]

Understanding the Importance of Class: The Color of Money

Lesson

Providers must learn to discriminate appropriately by understanding the role of class in the lives of minority families.

Pitfall 1

Providers who fail to make such discriminations may assume that families of the same race will act similarly regardless of class. Much of the literature lumps minority families together based on ethnicity and ignores the complexity of socio-economic class. When assuming race is more influential than class, a provider may apply theories and techniques to a family of one racial background which were designed for families of the same racial background but of another class. This assumption will be increasingly problematic as more minority people enter the middle class.

Pitfall 2

Providers may assume that poor families have always been poor. For instance, some refugees (particularly those who emigrated for political rather than economic reasons) enjoyed a higher standard of living in their country than they find here and must adjust to a lower income and reduced access in society. Families who had servants must shift roles and hold several jobs to make ends meet. To assume an El Salvadoran peasant and a Nicaraguan physician will have similar attitudes, expectations, and behaviors simply because they are Latino, currently poor, and utilizing a public hospital is a serious mistake.

In addition, some of the non-refugee families we treat have not always been impoverished. Some families were better off economically because of the "War on Poverty" programs of the 1960s and

1970s. However, given current economic difficulties, greater numbers of these families are downwardly mobile. After a period of increased hope, they are forced to the underclass. Also, many retired elderly patients now face increased medical bills along with a higher than expected cost of living at a time when they were anticipating a more secure economic life.

Strategy

To focus on race exclusive of class and current economic status can skew one's attention from significant issues and potential obstacles to change. For this reason we recommend taking an economic history once a certain degree of trust is established. Sample questions include: What jobs have you held? What is your current occupation? Who contributes to the economic resources of your family? From what social service agencies do you get financial support? Do you and your family have enough money to meet your basic needs (e.g., rent, food, clothes)? What are your future career dreams for yourself and your children?

Resisting the Ease of Simplification: Throwing the Family Out with the Bathwater

Lesson

In an attempt to care for a variety of families, all clinicians tend to identify rules of thumb to guide them through considerable diversity. However, when treating minority poor families, providers are at risk of accepting socially-sanctioned, discriminatory short-cuts to care. In an attempt to neatly categorize complex families, we can lose sight of the uniqueness of the specific family being treated (Lappin, 1983).

Pitfall

The minority poor families one treats will bear certain similarities to families in general and to one's own family. Conversely, significant differences will exist among minority families of the same race and class, and between those families and the dominant culture. In the family studies field, two ways of conceptualizing the care of minority poor families have emerged: One is to assume that essentially all people are alike; specific focus on their culturally idiosyncratic characteristics is extra baggage and serves to confuse (monotyping). At the other extreme, some believe that providers should not work with minority families without in-depth knowledge about the particular minority group, because of the potential for a great deal of harm (stereotyping). Both of these simplifying perspectives can be problematic; the first can be reckless, while the second, too confining and inaccurate. At another level, they replicate society's discriminatory patterns (i.e., "We are all the same. Let us minimize our differences"; or "We are fundamentally different. I can share few of your experiences.").

We have struggled to develop a view which accepts the existence of both similarities and differences. An example of this dilemma involves a single parent who is concerned about the friends her 11-year old plays with at school. Her son stays out late, smells of marijuana, and acts rudely, She feels he needs to be physically disciplined. However, the provider feels that corporal punishment is inappropriate. The provider's challenge is to balance advocacy of her/his viewpoint with cultural sensitivity for the mother's position. The pitfalls include either educating the parent to the "correct" view (since "we are all the same") or referring to a minority provider (since "we are too different").

Strategy

The following perspective embodies a strategy we have found useful: "There are many ways to care for children. The family and I may have different opinions; however, we may be unaware of each other's rationale. We must share our opinions and expertise, and then collaborate to help the child."

We find a number of advantages to this strategy. First, it allows the family to guide the provider to a better understanding of its culture (Lappin, 1983, Montalvo & Gutierrez, 1983). Second, both the family and provider have an equal opportunity to offer possible solutions, thus respecting time-honored beliefs while evaluating new alternatives. Finally, a more overt decision making process can occur which increases trust.

Assuming with Care: To Assume Otherwise Can Make an "Ass" Out of "U" and "Me"

Lesson

All clinicians must make assumptions about families, health and illness, and the clinical process. However, the provider's and patient's assumptions regarding roles, the assessment, and process of treatment may vary considerably. Therefore, these assumptions must be made with great care.

Pitfall

Perhaps the biggest obstacle to identifying discriminatory assumptions is that our "world views" trick us into thinking that we "know," when in fact we do not. Augmenting the deception, assumptions tend to be unspoken and operate at a covert level.

For example, a student received a graded test which he had failed. The teacher wrote on the test, "You did not follow directions." Shocked, the student approached the teacher only to hear, "Well, if you didn't understand, you should have asked me for clarification during the test!" The student replied, "I didn't think I misunderstood. I didn't have any questions."

When we enter a situation believing we already know the answer, we close ourselves off to the possibility that perhaps we really do not know at all. At a clinical level, differing assumptions may lead minority poor families to act in ways that bewilder non-minority providers. Rather than exploring alternate assumptions, providers may attribute this behavior to ignorance, passivity, or hostility.

The following example highlights the potential dilemma: A provider consulted a psychologist about a patient with multiple physical complaints and questionable mental status. The patient was a 68-year-old Black woman without close family. The provider, who had interviewed the patient twice, was confused by the complex medical picture presented. She was unable to understand why this seemingly intelligent woman took multiple medications and made frequent drop-in visits to the clinic. In addition, the provider had concerns about the patient's stability since she often got rambling, disjointed answers in response to pointed questions.

The consultant observed the first part of the interview, as the provider and patient discussed the latter's past. The consultant saw a woman who had survived many difficulties in her life, without a great deal of support. She had energy, intelligence and a strong will. Because of illness, she was unable to work. She had lost much of her identity in the past three years, being unemployed and watching her body begin to "fail." After listening for a while, the consultant concluded that the woman was indeed of "sound mind." He wanted to establish this fact by focusing on her strengths (Minuchin & Fishman, 1981). The consultant interrupted the discussion, "Could I ask a few questions? It might help me to help you if I got to know you a little better." The patient consented. "So, your Doctor tells me you completed college?" In the consultant's mind, this question would begin the process of strength identification. The patient replied, "Why do you want to know that? Don't you think Black people can go to college? Do you think all we want is to grow up and work in your White kitchens?" The consultant was stunned. Initially he thought, "How dare you accuse *me* of being a racist!" He wondered why his question evoked such an angry response. Even if the woman had considered the question inappropriate, she could have educated rather than attacked him.

Clearly, the question was a loaded one for her. Perhaps she feared that once he established her as a college graduate, he would look down upon her or at least question why she had not fared better in life. While she seemed displeased with the consultant's assumption that "Blacks don't go to college," she may have been equally displeased with her life. Perhaps, she had assumed that graduating from college should have protected her from her current situation.

The consultant realized that he had assumed his question to be benign. He apologized for any rudeness and clarified why he was asking the question. Once the patient felt less threatened, she was able to examine her own behavior. She discussed how her life had changed and what she could do to regain some control. By the end of the session, she decided to eliminate half of her 23 medications, believing she could do without them. She no longer comes for drop-in visits, and her health has improved.

The consultant constructed his initial question on the assumption that it would be viewed as affirming rather than patronizing. The patient filtered the consultant's questioning through her mistrust of White doctors. Both parties engaged in a discrimination "against" pattern assuming the other fit into a certain mold.

Strategy

A number of strategies are generalizable from this example: (1) A willingness to question oneself can facilitate escape from a discriminatory cul-de-sac. A systems-oriented provider might assume that s/he and the patient have co-created many of their interactions. Thus, when a conflictual episode occurs, the provider could quickly assess his/her part of the dance. One can stop the action to examine the precipitants of the conflict. While this skill is helpful regardless of who the patient is, a special sensitivity is valuable when the provider and patient differ along dimensions of race, class, age, religion and/or gender; (2) Honest, non-defensive disclosure of the provider's intentions can demonstrate that what one said, poorly represented what one meant. Such a disclosure can open dialogue and point to differing assumptions between the provider and patient. This process can also validate patient's feelings of being attacked and clarify for the provider how her/his behavior could be viewed as discriminatory; (3) To prevent problems, one could preamble reasons for a line of questioning, tests ordered, and course of treatment. These interventions should be tied to improving the patient's general well being as well as addressing the patient's specific needs; (4) A provider must be willing to be fallible and vulnerable. An admission of unintentional discrimination will be more healing than a defensive assertion of one's worthwhile character or an inquisition of why the patient responded so angrily; and (5) The patient-provider relationship needs to be the top priority rather than the pursuit of particular data. When part of the therapeutic goal is the creation of a healing, continuity context, a rupture in the relationship requires immediate repair.

Developing an Inclusive Picture:
Avoid Cropping the Family
to Fit the Frame

A 27-year-old Black man came to the emergency room with severe nausea and vomiting. He was admitted to the hospital. He had visited the ER on numerous occasions with the same problem, often being admitted. Due to the chronicity of the problem, the physician feared that the man might have a very serious illness. However, after an extensive workup, the cause for his illness remained elusive. As time progressed, the patient presented an increasingly complex picture. A family session was convened during one of his hospital admissions. During this interview, a wide spectrum of diagnoses emerged. The patient believed he had a severe illness; his mother thought his girlfriend had put a voodoo curse on him; his sister thought his symptoms resulted from psychological stress caused by the parents' divorce; and his father insisted that his son was lazy and had induced an illness to prevent him from working. Given the variety of family-generated explanations, to pick any one of the partial diagnoses was risky. Doing so could alienate an important person in the system and lose a potential avenue for change.

Lesson 1

A provider must realize that family members and health care providers may differ considerably in their explanation of symptoms. The framing of the problem needs to be sensitive to this complexity.

Pitfall 1

According to Kleinman (1980), a single medical encounter can contain a multitude of explanatory models for the illness under consideration (e.g., the larger society's, the subculture's [when appropriate], the patient's, the family's, the health care system's, and the individual provider's). To add to the complexity, what the family and provider *think* about the illness may differ from how they concretely *deal* with it.

Even when a provider offers a diagnosis, patients and family members may retain their original beliefs about an illness. A provider's search for a working medical or interactional diagnosis may neglect the variety of explanations the family entertains. The potential clash of assessments can be considerable. A provider may discriminate "against" the family by narrowly defining the problem.

Strategy 1

The fine discriminatory line which providers need to walk is to know when to incorporate varying belief systems into the treatment, when to respect and leave them alone, and finally when to reject them because of their negative impact on the family. Simple rules for making the above distinctions elude our grasp. The challenge includes recognizing that varying belief systems are in operation and selectively attending to them according to the family's clinical needs. To elicit and clarify all of the operant explanatory models may decrease the likelihood of discriminating by narrowly defining illness.

In treating the above family, one could incorporate the competing perspectives into a treatment approach which includes medical surveillance, parental teamwork to support the son's independence, individual sessions with the patient to facilitate job acquisition, and curse-removing healing rituals. The provider could move freely among and prioritize such modes of treatment, depending on the clinical requirements.

Pitfall 2

Another discriminatory trap involves how one gathers information. The very act of asking the family's views will have an effect. If the provider treats the patient as if they have given the "wrong" answer, the patient can feel invalidated, and care will suffer. For example, many of our patients find meaning in concepts such as the evil eye, curses, powerful spirits, and misalignment with the cosmos. Providers can label these beliefs as crazy since they differ so radically from those of biomedicine.[7]

Strategy 2

Providers need to discover how patients construct their universe, to respect views which differ from their own and be willing to co-construct a workable frame.

Lesson 2

The discrimination caused by narrowly defining the problem can result from a reluctance to consider, or an ignorance of, the families' broader definitions. It can also result from a refusal to frame the symptoms and family in context.

Pitfall

The technique of positively reframing a problem is often quite effective and powerful (Watzlawick, Weakland, & Fisch, 1974). Generally, providers can offer fresh perspectives which may yield novel solutions. Many families, minority poor and otherwise, have benefited from reframing problems in creative ways.

However, negative consequences related to such relabeling can occur. That is, commonly a provider may reframe a symptom (e.g., drinking, asthma) as part of the family pattern which emphasizes mutual love and protection. As systems-oriented providers, we can agree that the lives of all families are interconnected with their biological and societal subsystems. However, we tend to exclude the influences of such micro and macro systems when constructing a reframe. Families often follow suit.

Consider the reframe: "You are letting your husband drink because you love him"; and "You drink to give your wife someone to take care of." Is it clear to this couple that the pattern of drinking is also reinforced and maintained by societal patterns, economic factors, environmental influences, and genetic predispositions? Generally, we think, the family accepts the provider's incomplete reframe and fails to see the involvement of other systems. Additionally, the therapeutic process reinforces this narrow reality as it tends to focus primarily on the intrafamilial. One might hypothesize that some families leave treatment because they disagree with the limited assessment and feel misunderstood.

The feminist critique of family therapy has raised similar concerns. Goldner (1987) discussed the "blaming the victim" nature of defining spouse abuse as an interactional phenomenon. When one looks for cause within the narrow lens of the family, s/he can easily blame the participants regardless of the larger institutional influences in their lives. When one reframes intrafamilially, symptoms become defined as modes of communication among family members. Providers often ignore the larger societal underpinnings of symptom and family functioning. In the interest of finding that working "diagnostic" handle, a provider can mistake the size of the cup.

Strategy

The family therapy field has worked diligently to demonstrate that individual patients are not the center of the pathology. Many, however, have unintentionally replaced the individual with the family as the locus of pathology. Clearly, the next step is to broaden one's frame to view society as part of the puzzle when constructing a reframe (Minuchin, 1984). Thus a provider should acknowledge the role of society (e.g., poverty, politics) in the family's troubles when presenting an assessment.

**Emphasizing the Family's Strengths:
Competency is in the Eye
of the Beholder**

Lesson 1

Providers can optimize care from a perspective of acknowledging and utilizing family strengths.

Pitfall 1

Emphasizing family strengths, however, is easier said than done. Many Americans view minority poor families as incompetent. In this country, the dominant belief is that hard work yields success. Being poor represents laziness. The general literature is replete with subtle, and not so subtle, references which lead many to infer the "lack of health," if not downright pathology, of minority poor people.

In addition, capitalizing on a family's strengths carries a relatively recent and minor history in the health care field. The social and medical science literature provides ample allusions to specific problems found more commonly in minorities; minority status, in itself, emerges as a risk factor for disease. Again, most of this literature fails to examine socio-economic class as an added significant variable influencing health and illness. In the family therapy field, Salvador Minuchin, a pioneer in caring for minority poor people, represents one of the few advocates for accentuating a family's competency (Minuchin & Fishman, 1981). However, much of the family literature labels minority poor families as "underorganized," "disorganized," "disadvantaged," and "multi-problem" (Fullilove, Carter, & Eversley, 1985). Such descriptors discourage clinicians from celebrating the competencies of these families.

In addition, the clinical context encourages a focus on "what is wrong." Hospitals are sites where diseases are cured and problems are fixed. Thus, providers concentrate on the symptoms presented, search for etiology, and diagnose diseases. The gravest mistake is to miss an important diagnosis. As a metaphor of these problem-oriented efforts, the Joint Commission on Accreditation of Hospitals has required that every patient chart must include an easily accessible Problem List. They do not require a comparable list of how well the patient functions. Shaped by the context, providers rarely tell patients what is positive and healthy about their bodies, their minds, or their relationships.

Patients share this problem-oriented bias. Many middle class families visit doctors *both* for prevention and treatment of illness. However, many minority poor people can envision coming to the doctor *only* when sick. A trip to the doctor may mean taking time off work (which may jeopardize a job), paying considerable money for transportation and the visit, and/or delaying attention to important household business.

A potentially dangerous cycle can occur in busy urban medical clinics. A minority poor patient with a chronic problem (e.g., diabetes, alcoholism) visits a pathology-focused provider. Treating the problem takes the spotlight for both parties. Over time, the provider views the patient only through this problem-oriented lens, unwittingly neglecting strengths. The likelihood of considering family and social relationships diminishes in the process. Conversely, the patient provides information about what is wrong with her/his body and life. This interchange supports the patient's view of the purpose of clinic visits as *only* problem-oriented. This mutually reinforcing pattern becomes discriminatory not by malice, but by virtue of its inattention to strengths.

Pitfall 2

Even when providers acknowledge strengths, differences may exist between how s/he and the family define them. A provider may assess a family's degree of open communication, the assertiveness of individual members, and the sense of control members feel in the world. If the provider finds the family lacking in any of the above, s/he may define them as dysfunctional. However, the family may value secrets, personal sacrifice, and acceptance of the status quo. A failure to appropriately discriminate between one's own and the family's values may result in the provider attempting to change characteristics that the family holds sacred.

Pitfall 3

In addition, while the provider may have his/her checklist for strengths, s/he may be unaware of what escapes the list. For instance, some providers place little emphasis on religion in their lives. However, many patients organize their lives around a strong and active belief in God. A provider who fails to assess faith as a resource for the family may miss considerable opportunities for care-giving. For example, a Latino man, near death, was brought to the hospital on Friday. His wife declined any heroic measures to keep him alive. He recuperated and went home. A few weeks later, he returned to the hospital, on a Sunday. The wife requested that the physicians do all they could to keep him alive. Her change in position baffled the staff. In talking with the family, the primary provider discovered they were devout Catholics. Both the husband and wife hoped the husband would die on Saturday, because they believed any Catholic who dies on Saturday, wearing a scapular, will directly enter heaven. This fervently religious couple was able to accept death on a Saturday but not on a Tuesday. The provider sidestepped the trap of assessing this family as crazy. Instead, she utilized their devotion by helping them reconcile their wishes with God's will.

Strategy

Providers must accurately assess the internal and spiritual resources available to patients. Asking directly what family members see as their own competencies and what strengths they observe in each other can yield profound insights. This inquiry can avoid misidentifying strengths. Suggested areas of exploration include: (1) coping strategies of various family members, (2) family's evaluation of the success of these strategies, and (3) rich, intergenerational myths and legacies (e.g., "We are survivors," "We are a close family.").

Lesson 2

Not only do providers evaluate patients, but a systems perspective requires the complement (i.e., minority patients evaluate providers). Years of being poorly treated contribute to distrust and a reluctance to disclose. If patients risk discussing what they find valuable in themselves, they will at the same time judge the provider's response. Thus, reinforcement of the patient's strengths by the provider is critical.

Pitfall

For this reason, the usual methods of affirmation (e.g., nodding the head, looking interested, or attending to the issue) are often insufficient.

Strategy

The provider's response must reflect respect for the patient. Often times, what providers view as needless commentary on one's accomplishments can be reinforcing (e.g., "You've survived; your family is quite strong to have made it through all you have."). This affirmation strengthens the healing relationship and fosters the identification of more competencies by both the provider and the family.

Lesson 3

To elicit strengths without cultivating them into tools for healing is insufficient. The following example demonstrates how to transform an in-session experience of a family's positive aspects into a prescription for change. A young Mexican-American couple asked their physician's help with the husband's "drug problem." This couple trusted the provider who had delivered their second child. In the initial interview, the drama unfolded fairly quickly. The wife reported that the husband took drugs, stayed out late, and resented her return to school. He needed to change. The husband apologetically agreed. As the session progressed the cycle of incrimination (by the wife) and self incrimination (by the husband) increased. This occurred despite the provider's attempts to explore if anyone thought the wife should change, and/or if the husband was at all competent. To break this cycle, the provider shifted gears in the interview to help elicit strengths. He wanted to hear about their courtship. He requested they discuss together what attracted them. For the first time, the wife discovered how much her husband appreciated her waiting for him while in jail. In his words, "I never had anybody care for me like that; I've had a pretty shitty life." Similarly, the husband learned that the wife saw this "macho" guy both as protective and vulnerable.

Pitfall

As these 22-year olds began to cuddle in the room, the provider realized that this initial declaration of strengths was necessary but insufficient to catalyze change.

Strategy

The provider asked them to decide together what might be a first step to resolving their concerns. As they talked, they experienced a renewed sense of hope and affection. They both agreed that just holding hands and kissing more would herald a change. Noting that they had designed their own task, the provider ended the session. On the way out the door, the husband told his wife, "I think we're going to lick this problem." While the larger concerns still remained, this brief session served as a positive foundation for the next phase of therapy with the provider.

Lesson 4

A provider must be ready to redefine seemingly inappropriate behaviors as positive when those behaviors are representative of a patient's strengths. For example, a severely depressed Filipino man came to the clinic and described himself as someone who had sacrificed himself in relationships. He gave to others, never looking after his own interests. The provider identified this sacrificial tendency as valuable. While agreeing, the patient felt that too much of a good thing had complicated his life. The treatment began to focus on helping this man gain more control in his relationships.

Pitfall

In a subsequent session, the provider casually remarked that the man was still failing to stand up for himself at home. The patient took immediate offense, saying, "You know that is bullshit; it's superficial bullshit. I don't want you to waste my time if you can't be real with me." The provider, taken aback, continued on his train of thought, defending his original statement. However, he stopped mid-sentence, realizing that the patient was demonstrating a desired assertive behavior. The provider said, "Wait a minute; you are right. I need to make sure I'm saying things that are real for you and not bullshit. I'm glad you told me so clearly and honestly." The patient, shocked that he had acted so disrespectfully, apologized. The provider replied, "If there is anyone who should apologize, it's me. I want you to keep me honest. I like that strong part of you. That's what we're working for."

Strategy

Initially in this case, the provider discriminated against this patient, believing that strong, negative emotions directed toward a clinician are unacceptable. Fortunately, the provider recognized that the patient had demonstrated the desirable behavior and could positively reinforce him.

Lesson 5

A provider may find it difficult to convince a family it has strengths.

Pitfall

Unfortunately, many patients have accepted the societal myth that they are worthless. If providers adopt a stance of "discovering what strengths exist" rather than "determining if any do," they can set a more productive tone. However, this posture may still fail to convince a family of its worth.

Strategy

Providers should persist and convey this message on verbal and non-verbal levels. The identification and confirmation of strength cannot be done with patronizing platitudes (e.g., "You are a strong person"). Statements must be tied to data that are grafted to the family's experience and that the family can agree demonstrates competency.

Helping Families Cope: Against All Odds

Minority poor families have developed various methods of coping with the considerable adversity they face. One common strategy employed is that of acceptance. Many find accepting what the external world offers easier than attempting to control it.

Some families realize that fighting against an oppressive context can be dangerous and disappointing. For example, consider the mother whose 16-year-old son helps pay the rent but does so by selling drugs from their home. She accepts her situation, feeling incapable of controlling her son. Such continual patterns of "passive acceptance" can handicap families from identifying or taking advantage of opportunities for change. Low esteem, increased depression, and general hopelessness may result.

Other families value the notion of harmonious co-existence with the world. They "actively accept" their defined role in life. For example, a mother whose 16-year-old son is mentally retarded, may view her son's affliction as God's will. She may have worked since his birth to optimize his functioning and provide a meaningful life for him.

Lesson

As providers, we must learn to differentiate between a family's *active* and *passive* acceptance in order to recognize when to acquiesce and when to challenge their patterns.

We will explore some of the common pitfalls in providers' and patients' search for solutions to adversity.

Pitfall 1

A family may ask a provider to help resolve some of their difficulties (e.g., health, economic, immigration and housing). The family seems overwhelmed, having accepted their lot in life. The provider is at risk of adopting the hopelessness of the family and taking a stance of "There's not much I can do to help you." While paradoxically this may stimulate a family to change, more often it can extinguish a flickering hope.

Pitfall 2

Similarly, the provider, feeling overwhelmed, could explore only a narrow range of solutions. Such remedies might include filling out general assistance forms, thus declaring able-bodied people unfit for employment, and prescribing psychopharmacologic agents to deal with the stress (e.g., anxiolytics, anti-depressants). Obviously, for some people these strategies prove useful. However, providers will often prematurely initiate such solutions when they feel helpless to improve the family's situation. In these instances, palliative rather than curative goals preside.

Pitfall 3

Providers can also challenge people to change beyond "what seems reasonable and possible." For example, "You *must* leave your abusive husband"; "You have to stop drinking and go to AA"; or "You must get a job." One can term this approach to change: "Pull yourself up by your bootstraps." Acontextual and peppered with "should" statements, this perspective assumes that "By living in the United States, everything is possible if you only work for it." Such an approach can replicate societal propaganda: "With hard work, the world is out there for your choosing, and you have complete choice." When this approach succeeds, the family is empowered. When it fails, as it often does, providers begin to feel cynical, declare the family unmotivated, and distance themselves.

Pitfall 4

The provider may assume the role of the "white knight." Unless s/he gets and keeps the ball rolling, the family will continue to be overwhelmed. This stance can prompt calling for and arranging job interviews, driving people to AA meetings, lending money, continually visiting other professionals involved with the family, and arranging multiple support services (e.g., homemakers). While providers sometimes need to engage in these activities, primary responsibility should rest with the family. Risks of this approach include family infantilization and provider burn-out.

Strategy

A balance we try to strike is to help a family determine what it can accept and what it can change in their life. The serenity prayer most succinctly expresses the tasks to be accomplished: "Lord, help me change the things I can, accept the things I cannot, and grant me the wisdom to know the difference." This framework has many advantages:

1. It can provide a context for evaluating a family's present circumstances, deciding what battles are worth fighting, and setting priorities.
2. It helps us assume that families want to change but find it

somewhat difficult. This view acknowledges a family's desire to change, but respects the contextual constraints in which it operates. Regardless of race and class, families and providers must explore the negative as well as the positive consequences of change. However, it must be noted that the material resources available to poor people for effecting change are unquestionably different from those available to middle class families. For example, an illegal alien cannot simply apply for jobs, move to better housing, or borrow money from relatives. To attempt to empower poor families in one narrow area of their lives when they have little power elsewhere may have unexpected negative consequences. For example, we often encourage patients to take charge of their own health care. This advice can be confusing and demoralizing, when all the other institutions with whom they deal squelch, at best, and punish, at worst, any attempts at autonomy or self-determination. Discrimination can be averted by assessing a family's resources and constraints, thereby preventing over- or underestimation of the difficulties change would entail.

3. It can help a provider to activate a system to resolve its own problems without making major, all-encompassing changes. Simple, well-focused interventions can be more effective than total systemic ones. For example, a couple with marital problems seek help. They live with their five children in a one-room apartment. Without question, a provider can best serve this family by facilitating their move to better housing. A larger apartment may provide a context in which less tension exists, so that the couple may themselves resolve their marital discord.

4. Finally this framework can enable a provider to clarify what s/he is able and unable to do. Overt negotiation about roles can reduce fantasies and disappointments in both patients and providers.

One application of this strategy involves an older El Salvadoran couple concerned that the wife might have a heart attack. Five months ago, the husband had had a heart attack and triple bypass. Compounding this, the wife had recently lost her job. Suddenly, the family was without income. During the first session, the provider observed the couple's understandable absorption with their problems. The couple's mutual fear for the other's health paralyzed any thinking about the wife returning to work. Nonetheless, the provider challenged them to worry less and consider the wife healthy and still employable. In an effort to shift from such a negative focus, he suggested they should go out on a date.

At the next session, they reported applying for Disability through Social Security and had failed to go on the date. Additionally, the husband's cardiologist discovered a chest mass on x-ray. Visibly distraught, the couple complained they lived under a black cloud. Feeling overwhelmed and helpless, the provider wondered to himself if they were not correct.

To avert a maelstrom of hopelessness, the provider attempted to help the couple take control of the situation while also accepting the recent turn of events. He asked them to discuss together what each could do to make the best of a horrible situation. The husband told the wife, "I can best help you by not telling you when I am in pain." The wife adamantly replied, "That makes matters worse. I know when you don't feel well. And I worry, but I can't tell you." She continued to surprise the husband by revealing that she calls his cardiologist to inquire about his health since her husband bars her from the exam room. She asked him to inform her when he hurts so they can do something about it. He agreed.

At the next session, the couple was visibly happy and talkative. Still unaware of the biopsy results, they had gone to a carnival. They worried less, believing they could handle whatever the result. Before the session ended, the couple admitted concerns about the cardiologist's insensitivity to their needs. The provider encouraged them to express their displeasure, offering assistance if desired. While the provider had intended for the wife to return to work, he nonetheless supported the couple's new-found energy to alter some aspects of their life while holding others constant.

At the six month followup, the couple seemed quite content with their lives. The husband's chest mass was benign. They had confronted the cardiologist, and found improvement in that relationship. Their contentment shocked the provider because they remained on Disability, and the wife did not work. His formula for their happiness included the wife's getting a job evidencing that they could tolerate less proximity and worry. In his words, "I guess I just have to redefine what success means for them."

This example demonstrates a strategy to effectively work with apparently overwhelming situations. What seemed unalterable (i.e., the heart attack and abnormal chest x-ray) was accepted; while the initial intrafamilial patterns (e.g., worry, overprotection) shifted just enough to allow the couple to improve their communication and rely on each other's strengths. Additional change in these arenas appeared unnecessary. Finally, the provider needed to realign his sights to avoid discriminating against this couple by either accepting their hopelessness or asking them to change beyond their needs.

"How Is Discrimination Affecting Your Work?"

Lesson

Discrimination is a necessary partner in clinical practice. As we have seen, this tool can heal or harm as it helps to differentiate our perceptions of our patients. The direction it takes relates, in part, to the provider who uses it. We believe providers must examine how discrimination operates in their work in order to prevent suboptimal care for their patients.

Pitfall

Too often, discrimination fails to receive attention as a critical process in caring for minority poor families. For some providers, an inward search for prejudice can be very threatening as it may reintroduce latent discriminatory beliefs acquired merely by growing up in this society. Other providers may mistakenly believe that race and ethnicity have no role in treating families. We hope that the lessons we present serve as an adequate rebuttal to this latter contention.

Still others assume that their good intentions will shelter their work from harmful discrimination. However, the danger does not end by declaring, "I do not and will not discriminate against my patients." Returning to the case example at the beginning of the paper, few would conclude that the father was killed by negative discrimination. Yet, unintentional discrimination by well meaning providers can have devastating effects on a family. While many in our society are purposely prejudicial, most health care providers who choose to work with the poor do so for positive altruistic reasons. However, these motivations can trick clinicians to consider themselves immune from discriminatory patterns.

Strategies

We have identified some specific strategies to better care for minority poor families. Clearly, many of these strategies apply to all families. We hope, however, to have sensitized the reader to the nuances, and subtleties, of unwitting discrimination. To remain vigilant, we recommend the following guidelines: (1) Clarify your assumptions about minority poor families; (2) Realize that your perceptions may vary considerably from the family's; (3) Accept that a climate of mistrust exists; (4) Understand that mutual stereotypes enter the interview room first; (5) Be conscious of the power relationships between you and the family; (6) When uncommon events occur, consider alternate explanations in addition to the obvious ones; (7) Accept and admit your fallibility; (8) When you discover your discriminatory behaviors, do not give up. Make changes and continue to work; (9) Explore your setting for structures that foster prejudice; (10) Cultivate safe collegial relationships which will permit discussion of clinical discrimination; and (11) Most importantly, be open to learning from the families you treat.

NOTES

1. "Coin rubbing" or cao-gio is a practice in which one applies liniment or balm to another's skin. The skin can then be rubbed with an implement (e.g., coin, spoon, bamboo) or pinched with one's fingers until a sensation of well-being is felt. The practice has no known negative consequences (Duong, 1987).

2. In this article, we will discuss the work of health care providers (e.g., family physicians, family therapists and family nurse practitioners). The issues we address similarly affect providers regardless of discipline. Thus, we will use the term "health care provider" to refer to any clinician who treats some subsystem of families in a health context.

3. We have selected case examples from our practices and those of our colleagues. We want to thank the patients who have provided us an opportunity to learn. We also acknowledge the noble efforts of our colleagues who have allowed us a window into their work. In particular, we thank Jill Ginsberg, MD, Jonathon Gray, PhD, Jonathon Rapp, MD, Robin Serrahn, MD, Alistair Smith, MD, Greg Stern, MD, and Katherine Weiser, MD.

4. We treat individuals, couples, families, and larger systems. Frequently, we will use the term "family" since we commonly work with the subsystems (e.g., individual, family, community) of people we serve.

5. Many view these "alternative" family structures at best, as adaptations to stressful environments; they represent aberrant solutions to be accepted rather than valued. However, we lose sight that the "desirable" nuclear family is itself a recent adaptation to a changing society in which industrialization and mobility have considerably altered family structure. Society has trained us to consider the two-parent, nuclear family as ideal, and we must guard against forcing others, even subtly, into this mold.

6. Clearly, health care context, society, and patient population modify discriminatory patterns. However in this paper, we will primarily focus on the provider. We do not blame providers for discriminatory behavior, but rather hope to highlight a context for exploring some manageable avenues for change. Thus, we ask the reader to remain cognizant of how provider attitudes and behaviors interact with other systems.

7. Some interpreters have told us about their reluctance to translate patients' traditional explanations of the illness. They may fail to translate patient statements about the "mal de ojo" (evil eye), visits to traditional healers (e.g., curanderos), or evil winds in the body. The interpreters usually represent a higher social class than the patients and worry that providers may view the patient and themselves as primitive. We have found it useful to (a) form good relationships with interpreters, (b) express a need to know everything the patient says, and (c) over time, address the filters translators use to censor information. Faust and Drickey (1986) and Sluzki (1979) provide useful suggestions for work with interpreters.

REFERENCES

Bernal, G., & Alvarez, A.A. (1983). Culture and class in the study of families. In C.J. Falicov (Ed.), *Cultural perspectives in family therapy* (pp. 33-50). Rockville, MD: Aspen.

Bloch, D. (1983). (Ed.). *Family systems medicine*. New York: Brunner/Mazel.

Duong, V.H. (1987). The Indochinese patient. In R.B. Birrer (Ed.), *Urban family medicine* (pp. 238-242). New York: Springer-Verlag.

Faust, S., & Drickey, R. (1986). Working with interpreters. *Journal of Family Practice, 22,* 131-138.

Fullilove, M.T., Carter, K.O., & Eversley, R. (1985). Family therapy and Black patients. In M.T. Fullilove (Ed.), *The Black family: Mental health perspectives* (pp. 122-134). San Francisco: UCSF School of Medicine, Black Task Force.

Goldner, V. (1987). Instrumentalism, feminism, and the limits of family therapy. *Journal of Family Psychology, 1*, 109-116.

Kleinman, A. (1980). *Patients and healers in the context of culture: An exploration of the borderland between anthropology, medicine, and psychiatry.* Berkeley, CA: University of California Press.

Lappin, J. (1983). On becoming a culturally conscious family therapist. In C.J. Falicov (Ed.), *Cultural perspectives in family therapy* (pp. 122-136). Rockville, MD: Aspen.

Liddle, H.A. (1982). On problems of eclecticism: A call for epistemologic clarification and human-scale theories. *Family Process, 21*, 243-250.

Minuchin, S. (1984). *Family kaleidoscope*. Cambridge, MA: Harvard Press.

Minuchin, S., & Fishman, H.C. (1981). *Family therapy techniques*. Cambridge, MA: Harvard Press.

Montalvo, B., & Gutierrez, M. (1983). A perspective for the use of the cultural dimension. In C.J. Falicov (Ed.), *Cultural perspectives in family therapy* (pp. 15-32). Rockville, MD: Aspen.

Morris, W. (Ed.). (1969). *The American heritage dictionary of the English language*. New York: American Heritage Publishing Co., Inc.

Saba, G., & Fink, D. (1985). Systems medicine and systems therapy: A call to a natural collaboration. *Journal of Strategic and Systemic Therapies, 4*(2), 15-31.

Schwartzman, J. (1983). Family ethnography: A tool for clinicians. In C.J. Falicov (Ed.), *Cultural perspectives in family therapy* (pp. 137-149). Rockville, MD: Aspen.

Sluzki, C.E. (1984). The patient-provider-translator triad: A note for providers. *Family Systems Medicine, 2*(4), 397-400.

Sommers, P.S., & Massad, R.J. (1987). Graduate training for urban family practice. In R.B. Birrer (Ed.), *Urban family medicine* (pp. 243-247). New York: Springer-Verlag.

Watzlawick, P., Weakland, J.H., & Fisch, R. (1974). *Change: Principles of problem formation and problem resolution*. New York: Norton.

The Sound of Two Hands Clapping: Cultural Interactions of the Minority Family and the Therapist

Betty M. Karrer

Mrs. B. sank into her chair and rolled her eyes as she recalled her first impressions of her arrival to Chicago.

> What surprised me the most was the dreary, dark sense the city had. I came to Chicago in February! The wrong time to come. It was dark so early! I was confused about the time for the rest of winter and part of spring. It was so different from Bogota . . . no mountains, no green. . . . That was my first impression, one that remained with me for quite a while until I was able to find the beauty that I couldn't see at first.

Mrs. B. concentrated on the next question and continued with the interview. . . .

> As I look back, it seems that the next difficult step was being seen by others in very different ways than I saw myself. It was as if all of a sudden I had become someone else! My identity and beliefs were all put through a different filter and came out unrecognizable, limited, and above all dissonant with my pre-

Betty M. Karrer, MA, is on the faculty, Family Systems Program, Institute for Juvenile Research, Chicago, IL.

The author wishes to thank: Nancy Burgoyne for her valuable contributions to the development of this chapter; Rathe Karrer for editorial help; and the staff and trainees of the Family Systems Program of the Institute for Juvenile Research for their continued support and validation of the ideas developed in this chapter.

209

vious views of myself. For some time I questioned my ability
to view myself in a clear way. Was I this person I thought I
was? Or the person they said I was? I struggled with this dilemma for many years . . . in time I was able to see the difference between limited and limiting. Although I had no control
of how limited these perceptions were, I had control of how
limiting they could be . . . .

Mrs. B.'s poignant comments well describe the process of becoming a member of a minority group in a culture where the majority defines who you ought to be. Her struggle is representative of
the struggle that immigrants of a variety of ethnic groups experience
in their contacts with the host culture. Her words illustrate the oppression minorities experience when their identity and beliefs are all
put through a limiting (majority-constructed) filter.

The systemic view requires that we view behaviors in a complementary way; that is, the recursive context of minorities in relation
to the majority, the family's values in relation to the therapist's
values, and distinctions made in relation to those that make the
distinctions. When we focus on the majority's view without considering the minority, our descriptions are like "the sound of one hand
clapping" (Reps, P. 1961).[1] What we need to remember is that the
distinctions that we make about the cultural values of others say as
much about ourselves as they do about others.

This chapter attempts to provide the sound of two hands clapping
(Bateson, 1972) by taking into consideration the cultural values of
the family in interaction with the therapist's values. To do so, I first
will briefly review the evolution of cultural perspectives in the family therapy field. Second, I will discuss the usefulness of viewing
cultural values multidimensionally, and having various interrelated
dimensions that evolve over time. Each dimension will be illustrated by vignettes that will help therapists consider points of connection and understanding and make appropriate distinctions as to
the course of treatment. The vignettes are taken from the Transition
Research Study,[2] training, and clinical case histories.

THE EVOLUTION OF CULTURAL VIEWS
IN THE FAMILY THERAPY FIELD

Gould's (1983) concept of the evolution of ideas was applied by Schwartz (1987) to the different models in family therapy and their stages of evolution. This concept is useful for understanding the evolution of ideas regarding culture in the family therapy field. Schwartz proposed three stages in the evolution of ideas: the essentialistic, the transitional and the relativistic stages. The essentialistic stage is the discovery stage. During this time, an idea is viewed as the most useful (and perhaps the most truthful) irrespective of changing circumstances. The transitional stage begins when critical questioning is possible and limitations to the original ideas are considered. The relativistic stage emerges gradually. In it ideas are considered in relation to timing, context, and variation, and this stage results in the elaboration of a complex multidimensional model. Each of these stages is necessary for ideas to evolve and arise in response to their historical context. It is the task of the essentialistic stage to bring ideas to the fore in order to sensitize us to their importance. This stage also provides the necessary stability for change to continue. The task of the transitional stage is to perturb the system by introducing new information into the field, and thus beginning the process of elaboration of ideas. The relativistic stage allows the integrated usage of a broad range of ideas and moves us to a different level of abstraction.

Over the last decade views of culture in the family therapy field have evolved from the essentialistic to the relativistic. The essentialistic stage has been characterized by an overemphasis on ethnicity at the expense of other cultural dimensions. This stage is highlighted by statements such as "Irish families are . . .," "Polish families tend to . . ." etc. While sensitizing us to cultural differences, this thinking was monolithic and tended to ignore within-culture variations. The transitional stage in the evolution of thinking about culture, has been advanced by many authors (e.g., Falicov, 1982; Friedman, 1982; Lappin, 1982; Karrer, 1986; McGoldrick, 1982; Montalvo, 1983; Sluzki, 1979; 1982; Schwartzmann, 1983; also see Saba and Rodgers, this volume). These authors have questioned monolithic views of culture, and have focused on the interaction between ethnicity and other (within and across) cultural dimensions. They have also raised questions about the complementarity of the therapist's values. Their questioning has opened up new possibilities for looking at cultural values from a multidimensional (relativistic) perspective.

The relativistic stage validates a variety of ways of being human which cultures teach us. It considers the therapist's cultural values as double descriptors of the values of the family, and as potentially overlapping with those of the family along some cultural dimensions. For example, the therapist and the family may indeed vary in nationality or socioeconomic background, but they may share in religious affiliation, or they may all have been raised in small, rural towns. Focusing on overlapping cultural contexts between the therapist and the family reduces the constraint that therapists initially experience when confronted with someone's "differentness." Movement towards a relativistic perspective about culture affords the expanded option of focusing on both similarities *and* differences between families and therapists.

CONTEXTUAL DIMENSIONS OF VALUES

When discussing cultural values we need to consider the domain of values itself, and the domain of social organization in which these values are embedded. Values cut across all levels of social organization.[3] For example, religious values, are played out predominantly within the individual, the family (both nuclear and extended) and the neighborhood. However, issues such as birth control may bring into contact all levels of social organization such as, the family, the community, normative groups of a particular religious denomination, and the predominant religious views of each society about birth control.

Cultural values are social norms about relationships between individuals and families with the levels of social organization in which they are embedded. Society provides a general blueprint for the family; in turn, the family provides guidelines for interpreting these rules and expectations for its members. Reciprocally, the individual's influence is seen across all levels of social organization.

Thus, a recursive cycle evolves among society, its institutions, the community, the family, and the individual.

Families and individuals interpret cultural values in a variety of ways, and develop lifestyles that represent a punctuation in the recursive cycle. Each punctuation is unique by virtue of the variations in historical experience. From this interplay of cultural dimensions, a sense of fit among the individual, the family, and society develops, characterized by recurring periods of oscillation between a good fit, dissonance, and/or alienation. When individuals are unable to achieve a comfortable fit with their environment, they may challenge some of the contexts that they perceive as constraining. The challenge of some individuals can be creative contributions to society's evolution. Other individuals may be weakened by lack of fit and end up losing contact with their environment.

A definition of culture which both reflects the move toward relativistic thinking, and allows for an ecological explanation of adaptation, is offered by Falicov (1988) "... those sets of shared world views and adaptive behaviors derived from simultaneous membership *in a variety of contexts*" (emphasis my own). Expanding on this definition I will discuss those dimensions that illustrate the potential for shared world views and adaptive behaviors across the various contexts within which one may have simultaneous membership. *These dimensions are: economics, education, ethnicity, religion, gender, generation, race, minority status, and regional background*. In addition, for immigrants, the added dimension of *cultural transition* must also be considered.

These dimensions are systemic in their organization. Rather than being simply mechanistic aggregates, they are inevitably intertwined, and over time, either become salient or recede into the background. The degree of salience of each of these dimensions varies due to the sociopolitical history of a generation. For example, gender currently is salient in the family therapy field, reflective of this generation's sociopolitical history, whereas ethnicity and poverty were emphasized in the seventies and first part of the eighties.

Therapists will likely differ as to the number of dimensions they consider, and their relative influence. The goal of relativistic thinking is to emphasize the necessity of conceptualizing culture from a multidimensional perspective, not to create a series of "true" dimensions. The validity and potential influence of each dimension becomes clear, when discussed separately.

Economics

The impact of poverty on families, individuals, and societies is severe. Describing the attitudes and behaviors of the urban poor from the outside, reflects a level of distinction that at best, is an approximation. Nevertheless there are eloquent voices in the field that have managed to surpass these constraints and have given us an image of both the overwhelming reality of poverty, and the strengths that poor families show in their everyday coping with poverty (Aponte, 1976; Auerswald, 1968; Minuchin et al., 1969; Montalvo, 1976; also see Saba & Rogers, this volume).

The middle class has received attention by default rather than by design, and tends to be seen as a monolithic group. This group serves as a reference for value orientations that we contrast within and across groups. In fact, the poor, the rich, and the middle class are actually heterogeneous groups with different lifestyles and aspirations stemming from their membership in other groups, e.g., rural, urban, religion, ethnic, etc. Economic groups also have to be considered as embedded within and across all levels of social organization. Those attitudes and behaviors that regulate, and maintain them operate simultaneously at the family, community, institutional, national, and international levels.

The following vignette illustrates the dilemmas that many therapists experience when working with poor families. The C. family consisted of a single mother age 28, and 6 children ages 10, 8, 7, 5 years, and 5-month-old twins. She was referred by the school because her oldest son was frequently truant. Mrs. C. was a second generation American of Puerto Rican descent. In her earlier childbearing years she had been on and off welfare, but after the 5-year old was born, she had made the decision to go back to school and had received a certificate as a nurse's aid. She had worked at a community hospital for two years, and had been able to support her family. This brief, trouble-free time, ended when she met the father of the twins, a non-documented Mexican. They married after a few months so that Mr. C. could file for legal residency status. He left her soon after he got his documents, a few months before the birth of the twins. With the addition of two more children, Mrs. C.'s salary at the hospital plus childcare, was insufficient for taking care of her family (a common "catch-22" with poor families. She actually made more money by being on welfare.) Thus, the institutional system supported her staying home, but undermined her sense of competency. The family was part of an early intervention program that was designed to work with poor families in an inner-city community of Chicago. The case was assigned to one of our paraprofessional staff. These women (Mothers of Intervention, or MOIs) all lived in the same community. When the MOI visited Mrs. C. at home she expressed several feelings; anger and sadness about the loss of her husband, and impotence about raising her family as a single parent. She also expressed sadness about not being able to work. Her job had become a source of satisfaction to her and she missed being in charge of her own life. A prevailing theme expressed by Mrs. C., was what she called "irrational" feelings of sadness when looking at the walls in her apartment. They reminded her of her misery, because they were too dirty and needed paint. The walls in her apartment became a metaphor for her present situation. The MOI began her therapeutic work by utilizing all available community resources to help Mrs. C. begin the process of regaining her sense of competency. Initially a homemaker was made available to help Mrs. C. take care of the twins. The MOI worked with the homemaker in setting goals for gradual inclusion of Mrs. C. in the caretaking of all of the children. In addition, the MOI recruited a group of volunteers (high school girls and boys) to come and paint Mrs. C.'s apartment under her direction. This seemingly mild intervention was tremendously powerful in changing Mrs. C.'s feelings of impotence. She took charge of the task, describing herself as "having my old energy back." After the end of treatment, during a follow-up interview, she reported that this single event shifted her outlook, and began giving her hope about the future. After six months the homemaker was taken away but Mrs. C. was able to resume total care of the twins with the support of the MOI. Therapy progressed and in time Mrs. C. went back to work.

The progress with this family was the result of many agencies and many people working in collaboration. Initially, the main thrust of the therapy was to counteract the destructive context of poverty by providing situations that included hope, and competence. At the programmatic level, the role of the MOI was planned as a bridge between the traditional therapeutic Institute and the community. The MOI's familiarity with the community, her ability to convene resources for this family and her experiences as a working woman, were invaluable points of connection for Mrs. C. who was isolated, and valued work. The MOI's many creative ideas taught the supervisor important ways of working with the poor.

Education

Education also influences attitudes and behaviors and can be a powerful value and organizing cultural dimension. Education refers to the amount of schooling that an individual has (grammar school, high school, college), and the content of study (profession) as well level of general knowledge (as in "cultured"). Interests can also be considered education since they expand the content of knowledge that the individual acquires.

Generally, the language that the family utilizes, a product and function of education, can serve as a point of entry for the therapist, whose own cultural background may overlap with this dimension. The language that is utilized within each profession, interest, and/or trade has greater semantic consensus for that group, and therefore, can serve as a point of entry for therapists. There are also differences across groups. Engineers, for example, conceptualize stress in very different ways than do mental health practitioners. Terms such as stress have multiple meanings with objective as well as metaphorical referents. The therapist has the option to use one or both referents.

The following vignette illustrates how education served as a point of entry with a very difficult case. The V. family were originally from Afghanistan, but had moved to Iran as a result of the Soviet intervention, only to be further dislocated during the Iraq-Iran war. They emigrated to the U.S. 5 years before they came to therapy. Father was a physician, and mother, a housewife. They had 5 girls ages 13, 12, 10, 9 and 8 years. The IP was the oldest daughter, who

was reported to have suddenly dropped her level of academic performance. The family described themselves as very close and saw
the oldest daughter as quiet and separate from them. Father reported
that he and his daughter had been particularly close until recently
when he had been unavailable because he was preparing for the
Boards in general medicine. The female therapist, a Fellow in child
psychiatry, originally from Italy, had considerable difficulty engaging father, who asked her to take care of his family and let him
concentrate on studying so that he could regain his professional
status. There was a training team behind the mirror consisting of
three child psychiatry Fellows, one from Thailand, one from the
Philippines and one from Argentina, and the supervisor (myself)
from Mexico. Four women and a man. The cultural differences
between the family and the rest of us were substantial. It was seduc-
tive to view the father's behavior as an expression of a typically
male oriented society. Though clearly relevant, this context emphasized the family's differentness and provided little opportunity to
connect with, and therefore move the family forward. The team
elected to focus on the father-daughter relationship. Our task was to
find ways to keep him involved in the treatment and with his family. A useful class of information to focus upon was the commonality of our immigrant status, and the fact that, like father, each of us
had faced the task of regaining our professional affiliation in this
country. We were lucky to have had such a ready-made context for
connection! One by one, starting with the male Fellow, each team
member (except for the supervisor, who was not a physician) entered the room and talked with the father about the difficulties, and
resources that each of them had encountered when preparing for
Medical Boards. Focusing on education as the overlapping context
between us and the family was an important point of entry into this
family. After this session, the treatment was able to progress with
father present.

Ethnicity

Ethnicity has been defined by Shibutani and Kwan (1965) as
"those who conceive of themselves as alike by virtue of their common ancestry, real or fictitious and who are so regarded by oth-

ers.''[4] Ethnicity is one of the most powerful cultural dimensions played out in family relationships. Ethnic patterns express themselves in subtle ways, are frequently out of the domain of our awareness, and have a strong emotional base that is easily polarized.

Ethnicity has frequently been viewed in relation to minority status. The process of ascribing minority status is usually based on attitudes and behaviors not valued by the dominant society (see ''Minority Status'' for further discussion). Ethnicity has been at the forefront of the family therapy field. Its overemphasis has organized therapists to think that ethnic groups are this way but not that way. This narrowing of context is dangerous when we consider that the goals of therapy are to expand options. How can therapists expand options if they perceive cultures as having limited options?

Ethnicity seems to have been described as a characteristic of the families we serve, but not of the therapist. When describing therapists it seems as though by virtue of their training, they have transcended their ethnic affiliation. Rotheran and Phinney (1987) provide us with a less ethnocentric definition of ethnicity. They consider all groups (minority or majority) as ethnic, whether they are families or therapists.

Individuals and families experience their ethnic affiliation with different degrees of intensity. Some may have lost contact with the background of their ancestors, while others may experience a strong ethnic affiliation. Each generation contributes their own perceptions about the ethnicity of the family. These perceptions can represent idealized notions about the native culture, projections, and/or dissatisfactions with the host society. Some are alliances with one parent's ethnic affiliation over the other, others are adaptations to what the dominant society considers acceptable. At times, these perceptions become cultural myths which are adopted by families or entire ethnic networks.

Ethnic loyalties and the feelings they evoke seem to become stronger as a result of cultural transition. The degree of ethnic loyalty and affiliation is frequently not experienced as strongly in the native land, and emerges as immigrants experience the loss of their native land. While these traditions are evolving in the native culture they are maintained in the host culture as rituals for connection between the native and host cultures. In a way you can say that Italians are more "Italian" in this country than in Italy.

The following vignette illustrates how a family therapist and supervisor utilized their ethnic backgrounds and phases of acculturation to develop a series of therapeutic stages to fit the family's dilemma. The R. family came to therapy because the wife had recently discovered that her husband had an affair several years back. The first stage of treatment addressed this problem by utilizing the religious language the family had made available (this stage of therapy will be described in the next section). Once the presenting problem was ameliorated, the developmental stage of leaving home became the focus of therapy. The R. family consisted of the father (age 54) the mother (age 52) and five children. The two oldest children were married and living in the same community. One daughter had left in an abrupt way and was living in a commune. The two younger children were in process of leaving, but had not yet been successful. All three phases of the acculturation process were experienced simultaneously by the R. family (see Karrer, 1986). The parents were Mexicans-in-America, the older children Mexican-Americans, and the younger children were Americans of Mexican descent. As is frequently the case during developmental transitions, some cultural dimensions became involved in the conflict, and some aided in the resolution. The traditional value of familism, common to many traditional populations across societies, was used by the parents to argue that the children needed to stay nearby. The children, having adopted to a greater degree the modern value of independence, were struggling to become more autonomous. This situation polarized the family into cultural splits, isomorphic of their generational stage.

The therapist, a young American male of Polish descent, had successfully separated from a traditional Polish family. The supervisor (myself) shared ethnic affiliation with the family (Mexican-American) was also an immigrant, and had recently completed the same developmental task as the family now faced.

The R. family shared with other immigrant groups the American dream of better educational and economic opportunities for their children. Although this was a dream shared by all members of the R. family, the parents had perceived their children as indifferent to their dream. The first stage of treatment was to discuss the differences in perception about the dream. By exploring the parents' leaving Mexico to pursue their dream, validation of the idea of leaving home was introduced. The parents and the supervisor exchanged impressions about the costs of leaving home in pursuit of dreams. The children and the therapist shared perceptions about leaving home. By introducing new information, the meaning about leaving home gradually shifted. The parents saw their children's goals as fulfilling their dream. The children on the other hand, gave testimony to the sound upbringing which they had received from their traditional parents. The shift in meaning allowed the family to move to another level of organization, from a "split" family with different views, to a "together" family with a common dream.

Religion

The influence of religion has varied within and across societies throughout history. All religions share a belief in a God(s). What varies across religious groups are specific beliefs, and the way these beliefs are expressed. Catholics of the world are similar in many of their basic beliefs, so are Protestants, Jews, Hindus, and Moslems. At the same time, there are significant within group differences.

Within each religious group, there are different levels of understanding and adherence to beliefs. Some groups become extreme in response to outside challenges or perceived internal destructuralization (e.g., the Shiites of Iran, or some of the fundamentalist groups within the U.S.). Others are reformers and evolve their religious beliefs in consonance with modern ideologies.

Strong religiosity influences the way individuals and families interpret actions and ascribe meaning to universal ideas. If therapists are not aware of the variation of beliefs, not only across but within religions, they need a consultant who can suggest possibilities for healing and change that all religions have in their ideology.

The R. family discussed in the previous section was Catholic, although typically Mexican Catholic (i.e., sometimes practicing, sometimes not). The presenting problem was the mother's feelings of betrayal because of the affair her husband had 15 years prior to coming to therapy. The mother expressed the religious values for most of the family (common in traditional families). She came to the first session with a bible which she held on her lap. She spoke about "God's help in forgiving and forgetting," as well as ways for the husband to atone. The husband also spoke about atonement and the necessary time for his wife's wounds to heal. The therapist was also Catholic and observant of his religious beliefs. Consequently, the religious themes presented by mother gave the therapist, who was conversant with this language, the perfect point of entry. A task was given to the family to develop religious rituals for the husband's atonement which would allow mother time to begin forgetting and forgiving. The utilization of the overlapping religious dimension between the family and the therapist provided an initial healing context until the couple were ready to move to the next stage of treatment.

Gender

Although feminism has been evolving throughout society for many generations, views on gender have only recently begun to impact the family therapy field. It is just ten years since Hare-Mustin's (1978) historical article on feminism began to sensitize family therapists to the impact of gender inequalities in family life. The Women's Project in Family Therapy (Carter, Papp, Silverstein, & Walters, 1984) raised questions about our role as therapists in maintaining these inequalities in the therapeutic context. The systemic and the feminist perspectives have been critically reviewed, and contrasted (McKinnon & Miller, 1987; Taggart, 1985). The current challenge for the field of family therapy is whether the systemic view will be expanded to include the feminist's view. There are groups in the field (Rampage, MacKinnon, James, & McIntyre, 1988; Goldner & Walker, 1988) who are in the process of developing an integration of theory and practice, rather than continuing the either/or position characteristic of recent years.

Clearly, gender values are a cultural dimension with great potential to enhance or undermine the common ground which the therapist and family may share. Differences in values about gender between therapists and families vary in at least three possible ways. Some families are traditional and adhere to a complementary view of gender. Some are in the process of transition, questioning roles, gains, losses and costs. Some are contemporary and view gender roles as adaptations to historical contexts that are ethically immoral, and no longer adaptive to our current social structure. Therapists also vary from traditional to contemporary in relation to gender issues.

Understanding the family's values is a priority. Problems are embedded in relationships, and it is impossible to talk about relationships and not address gender inequalities. In my experience (most likely because I see this perspective as central to my own growth as a person and a therapist) gender issues are almost always relevant to the treatment process. At a basic level, the impact of the therapist's gender on the therapeutic context needs to be addressed. What does the wife/mother experience with a male therapist? Conversely, what does the husband/father experience with a female therapist? Furthermore, if the family is traditional and the therapist contemporary, clarification of, and respect for their difference should be acknowledged.

Deciding when to utilize gender sensitive interventions with a traditional family was the central issue for the therapist in the following vignette. The G. family came to treatment because their oldest boy was rebellious and difficult to control. The family was originally from a small rural town in Northern Mexico. They were at the intermediate phase of acculturation (Mexican-American). The father worked as a butcher and the mother stayed home to care for the oldest boy, aged 3, and a 1-year-old girl. Their dream was to save money in order to go back to their native village and start a small business. Recently, their economic situation had become increasingly difficult because father's job had been reduced from fulltime to three days a week. Saving money became impossible, and prompted father to question the likelihood of fulfilling their dream. Why had they come, leaving family and friends, if not to make some money and return? What were the risks of returning home without enough money? Both of them were dedicated to this dream, but their traditional gender values (father as breadwinner, and mother as caretaker) were not economically adaptive to their present situation. Father wanted help, but was afraid to enter the contemporary world of two working parents. Mother, however, was beginning to question this patriarchal relationship, and initially in a timid way, was asking for a more flexible relationship, where both could be breadwinners and caretakers. Gradually, with the therapist's support, the wife felt more secure in her quest to gain a more balanced role in their partnership. The couple moved from discussing a two-career partnership (where mother added a career but maintained full responsibility for child rearing) to a more complete partnership, where they both shared many responsibilities of family life. This was accomplished gradually by exploring the meaning that the traditional marriage had for both spouses, and the possibilities for a more contemporary marriage, as well as the trade-offs and consequences of change. Since they were planning to return to their native village, not only did they need to consider each other, but to explore their views in regard to those of their extended families. Since the couple visited their native town to look for business opportunities, their new roles and aspirations were able to be checked out with the extended family. The wife's job allowed the couple to save the money they needed. After two years in therapy they went back to Mexico and opened a small store.

It is worth noting the impact of the therapist's relativistic stance in this case. Had the therapist taken an essentialistic stance, she might not have perceived the options for change that the family presented. Imagine, for example, a well-meaning therapist who, in an effort to be respectful of what she had either read or heard about Mexican families' traditional patriarchal structure, had either not seen, or supported a change in the couple's relationship. The couple, themselves in the process of evolving their own values with regard to gender roles, would have been stifled by an interaction with a therapist focused upon supporting traditionality. Relativistic thinking about cultural dimensions permits sensitivity to difference while recognizing that cultural differences are neither static, nor impenetrable.

Generation

Generation and gender are interrelated. Each generation provides very different experiences for men and women. Gender and generation, therefore, need to be considered equally, and in tandem when assessing attitudes about family life. Goldner (1988) has noted, that the field of family therapy has typically made gender incidental to generation which reduces the salience of the gender dimension.

The generation to which therapists and families belong points to common historical, and sociopolitical events that have many shared attitudinal and linguistic meanings within groups. Generation can also be viewed at many levels. At the societal level, there are many sanctioned values about the young and old, that influence therapists and families. At the familial level families have their own contextual markers about each of their generations. Examples of contextual markers for a given generation are; the Second World War, the assassination of John F. Kennedy, or the type of music one prefers.

Generation also imparts many subtle levels of experience. Temporal and spatial understanding, for example, changes significantly with age. For older people time "flies," for children time moves slowly. Older members of the family may expect a different level of proximity (space) from a young therapist than from an older therapist.

Whether therapists are young adults, recent spouses, at the beginning or at the end of the child rearing process will influence how they experience the family's values, as well as how the family experiences them. A therapist's credibility increases with age. Conversely, the therapist's perspective about the family changes as a result of age.

Generation also refers to shared historical events (for many years the question "where were you when Kennedy was assassinated" described one such an historical event). If therapists have a similar generational context with the family, there will be a commonality of history and language that can be utilized for connection and change. If the therapist and the family belong to different generations they have to learn from each other about their history and language.

The following vignette illustrates how the developmental stage of the supervisor helped a young therapist connect with a family who did not trust him because of his age. The M. family consisted of the father (age 56) the mother (age 54) and two adult male children ages 34 and 28. The presenting problem was the youngest son, who wanted to leave home and move to California. The traditional Jewish parents viewed the son's wish to move as rejecting the values of togetherness they expected from their children. The therapist, a young male age 24, had considerable difficulty being seen as potentially helpful by the parents. The complaints (expressed primarily by the father and supported by the mother), were that the therapist, like their younger son, was too young, and did not have enough wisdom about life to help them. This impasse was overcome when the supervisor, who was of the same generation as the parents, consulted with the therapist, and elicited the couple's help in teaching the therapist about life. A combination of sources of wisdom were utilized by the therapist; the family itself, the supervisor, and the therapist's own parents. Once Mr. and Mrs. M. realized that the therapist was respectful of their generation, they began trusting him with their problems. We knew we had surpassed the initial stage of therapy, when the father said to his son . . . "you should be as wise as this young man."

Race

Race cannot be viewed without considering minority status. The values of a minority are frequently a response to the distinctions that the majority makes about them. This is both an oppressive and a destructive process. In time, racial minorities modify their own identity, in some instances to accommodate to the majority of society, at other times in order to develop an acceptable identity. The time it takes, and the extent of the possibilities for self-redefinition depends on the level of evolution of a society.

The current white/non-white demographic descriptors present in this society are simplifications of a very complex, emotionally charged process. Modern societies are multiracial. There are all racial groups by themselves, plus all sorts of interracial variations. In many societies, racial descriptors are irrelevant, if not actually insulting. Definitions are more likely to be provided and accepted by the persons who are being defined themselves.

As this society continues to evolve towards interracial variations, the problem of definition becomes even more complex. Families who are interracial experience confusion when asked to define themselves, as for example, either non-white or white. Choosing one over the other has clear political implications in this society, but being defined in such a simplistic way, also does violence to people's identity. Must we consider someone's racial identity as an either/or? Or can we help to develop and accept the resolution the family has evolved about their racial identity through their history, without pressuring them to ignore or deny any part of their racial identity. The tendency to define people in "either/or" dichotomies is an isomorph of deep-seated prejudices that need to be overcome.

The following case illustrates the negative impact that this simplistic racial categorization can have on families of varied racial backgrounds. Mrs. L., a single mother with four children, was fourth-generation American of Irish descent. The father of the two oldest children was Black American, and the father of the two youngest children was a native American Indian. Both fathers were out of the home. The oldest children had opted for the Black American identity and the youngest for the native American identity. The tragedy in this family was the children's bind in identifying with their white part. This part represented their mother's identity, the parent they lived with and whose racial identity they did not respect. The family's internal conflict isomorphically replicated the community's and society's racial conflict, exacerbating the already polarized racial identity of each child. Through sibling therapy, the children were able to express their difficulty of even thinking that white was acceptable since it would be seen by some of their peers as "identifying with the oppressor" and by others as "denying their darkness." In reality this family could not win. They were moving towards premature disengagement. It took considerable time for the therapist (an American of Jewish descent) to help the children explore their white part and to see it as legitimate. At the end of therapy, however, their white part was accepted only at the family level. They all expressed the conviction that they needed to adopt a "political" stance of being black or native American Indians in public. Their solution is a reflection of our degree of cultural evolution as a society.

Minority Status

Consensus as to definition of the term minority has been plagued with controversy. Attempts at clarification have been at best ambiguous, at worst, misleading and representative of the prevailing dominant social order. This lack of clarity in regard to the term minority in the sociological literature prompts Meyers (1984) to conclude . . .

> It is suggested that the term carries the weight of a theory of prejudice that is hidden and that represents interests of the dominant sectors within the prevailing social order. It does this precisely by advancing a particular theory of power relations that conceals the actual dynamics of society and that erects a veiled defense of the status quo through the use of obscure language and the posing of misleading problems. (p. 8)

There seems to be, however, consensus as to what characteristics contribute to the inclusion of certain groups as minorities. Inclusion has traditionally been derived from visible aspects of the individual such as: race, religion, language, ethnicity, and dress. Greeley (1969) has poignantly described this phenomenon in his book *Why can't they be like us?*

Meyers (1984) reviews the prevailing theories about inclusion into a category of minority, from numerical, to pluralistic, then to Marxist, and lastly to nationalistic. Whether the term minority reflects a numerical description is highly questionable. There are minority groups, such as women, that are numerically in the majority, but have minority status. In addition, European groups, although a numerical minority in some countries, are widely represented among the rich, and powerful in several societies throughout Latin America. On the other hand, even though mestizos (combination of Indian and European) and other ethnic and racially mixed groups are a numerical majority in some countries, they are still widely represented among the poor and the disenfranchised.

The pluralistic definition of minority groups described the existence of minorities as inevitable in modern societies. This view takes an idealistic position and believes that through the evolution of the democratic process, minorities would eventually cease to exist. The Marxist definition considered prejudice and discrimination the natural concomitants of the economic social structure of nations. These structures create minorities as they divide workers inequitably along gender, national, and racial dimensions. The nationalistic definition described affiliations within each minority group, across national lines. For example: Malcolm X's belief that Black Americans needed to view themselves as a majority by identifying with Blacks throughout the world. This view alarms national leaders because it creates conflicts within nations (across groups) and across nations. Meyers concludes that the common denominator across these definitions is oppression. He proposes the term "oppressed group" instead of minority group.

There is considerable evidence that being a minority has detrimental implications for individual and family development (Asch 1952; DeVos, 1969). DeVos studied Japanese subjects, racially and ethnically consonant with the dominant culture, who were assigned the role of "outcast" on the basis of social acceptability. Once this label was adopted into the larger sociocultural context it became increasingly difficult for the group defined as outcast to perform at an acceptable level consonant with the rest of society. Predictably, the outcast's performance on achievement and intelligence tests consistently were below average level. Their ability to secure and maintain jobs was reduced and their overall adaptation level was considered below Japanese standards. Attitudes of alienation, bitterness, and peripherality were observed and proved difficult to ameliorate.

The context of oppression by a group has implications for therapy. Minority families will respond differentially to minority/majority therapists. Therapists, if representatives of the dominant society, are clearly part of the problem definition, and, therefore, need to be part of the problem resolution.

Regional Background

Within societies there is wide variation of values according to geographical regions, terrain (mountains, oceans, rivers, valleys, etc.) rural/urban settings, and climate. Regional differences between California and New York, between the North and the South, and/or the Midwest, between cities and rural environments, and between deserts and mountains are clearly visible, particularly in regard to orientation to time and space. Each region offers different possibilities and different constraints. The emotional attachment that most people show to their hometown, so clearly articulated by Mrs. B. in the beginning of this chapter, speaks to the strong affective bond that mountains, rivers, oceans, etc. hold for people.

Whether we live in a rural, urban, or suburban setting also colors our views of the world. Families raised in rural settings will experience an accelerated pace in urban settings, and will likely perceive their space as constricted. These dimensions are even more impactful when families relocate across two levels; within cultures (rural to urban) and across cultures. The struggle with cold and/or heat accounts to a degree for how we organize our lifestyle. Seasonal changes are influential on people's work pace, and recreation. Cloudy and cold weather have an impact on our moods, increasing the incidence of depression and/or suicide. Families who are used to warm climates that emigrate to Chicago have difficulties adjusting to the severe cold of winter. Some may initially act confused, unorganized, depressed, and/or lethargic, as a result of such extreme seasonal changes.

Therapists also come from a variety of regional settings. If they share any of these contexts with the family they may share a metaphorical language that refers to vertical and/or horizontal terrains. If they differ, therapists need to find out the meaning these areas have for families, and how it organizes their attitudes and behaviors about time and space.

The language a family uses to describe its setting is useful in developing interventions such as metaphors and rituals. The therapist's use of such a metaphor with such an individual, Mr. T., who emigrated from Cambodia three years ago, is instructive. Mr. T. was single, 24 years old, and lived in a port of entry community where a large proportion of immigrants from Cambodia had relocated. He was referred because of depression. Mr. T.'s broken English was just sufficient to express his sadness about losing his home as he spoke about missing his mountains. The therapist utilized a book of poems that had illustrations of beautiful mountains, rivers, valleys, and lakes to connect and communicate with Mr. T. about the loss of his native land (mountains) and about the regional possibilities in his new setting (in this case Lake Michigan). He was also asked to explore whether what he had learned about mountains could be applied to lakes. In this analogical way, the therapist began the process of connecting with, and validation of a very important context for this man. This was the first step in understanding the losses this man was experiencing through cultural transition.

Cultural Transition

Cultural transition is the process of bridging the values of the native culture and the values of the host culture. During cultural transition the goodness-of-fit that each individual and family has with their native culture undergoes a process of destructuralization (i.e., the loss of social referents such as roles, rules, and expectations). Restructuralization (the acquisition of new social referents) takes place gradually, but it requires a validating and supportive environment. During cultural transition immigrants experience a period of ambiguity where rules, roles and expectations are in a stage of flux. This is a difficult time when the rich get richer and the poor poorer. Like all transitions, cultural transition is also an opportunity for change. Figure 1 illustrates the bridging role of cultural transition.

The decision to immigrate begins the process of transition which lasts several generations (acculturation). The rate and ease of acculturation depends on the goodness-of-fit between the immigrant and the host society. Cultural fit, immigration and acculturation, and cultural evolution will be discussed separately for purposes of clarification.

Cultural Fit

Some immigrant groups have preferred status in the host culture. The assignment of preferred status seems to occur on the basis of fit with the host society. The more similar the immigrant is to the dominant majority, the better the fit. A white, middle class, urban, professional, for example, will experience a high degree of goodness-of-fit with the dominant society and will find it easier to acculturate, than a poor, dark, uneducated immigrant. Those families (and/or individuals within a family) experiencing less compatibility between themselves and the host society, will in turn adhere more to their native culture's values and will acculturate in a slower, more painful manner.

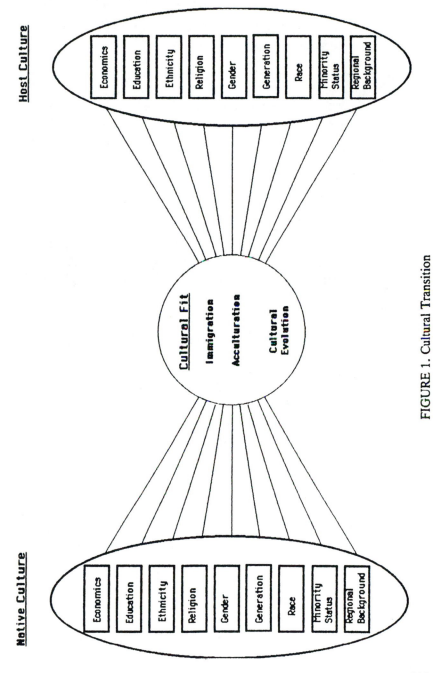

FIGURE 1. Cultural Transition

231

Immigration and Acculturation

Cultural transition begins with the decision to immigrate, and lasts several generations. Sluzki (1979) proposes five stages in the process of immigration. Acculturation begins when immigration ends, and the process of adaptation to the host society begins. Karrer (1986) has identified 3 phases in the acculturation process, each with specific stresses and opportunities for adaptation. Acculturation can be viewed as a transactional process where the immigrant's initial relationship with the host culture is either enhanced or impeded depending on the degree of mutuality or conflict experienced (Karrer, 1986). Therapists who work with families in the midst of the process of immigration and acculturation need to be sensitive to these stressors, as well as the opportunities that arise from each individual's experience of fit (or lack thereof) with the host society.

Cultural Evolution

Societies are fluid systems, continuously accommodating to their changing circumstances. All societies retain values in this process of transformation which may have had adaptive value in the past, but no longer fit the current historical context, and are therefore no longer fully adaptive. There are at least three concurrent phases of cultural evolution within societies: traditional, transitional and contemporary (Bernal, 1987). There are also periods of oscillation within each society where the pendulum swings either toward more traditional or more contemporary ideas. Traditional groups provide the necessary stability for the culture to grow. Transitional groups perturb society by critically evaluating ideas that no longer fit the context. Contemporary groups demand change, providing an opportunity for societies to continue their evolution. Together, these three levels regulate the social growth of a society.

Rates of cultural evolution vary across societies. Modern, industrialized societies such as the United States, are characterized by rapid cultural evolution. The immigrant who comes from a society where cultural evolution is slower (e.g., rural, small town settings and homogeneous societies) experiences considerable stress. The analogy of a time machine is applicable. Some immigrant groups find themselves as if "accelerating into the future" in regard to the host society, while experiencing being "frozen in time" in regard to their native culture. In addition, rates of cultural evolution frequently also vary for each member of a family.

Therapists may also have experiences with cultural transition. They may be immigrants themselves, or have contact with relatives who have immigrated. They may be minorities and, therefore, have a different goodness-of-fit with the majority. At the same time, they may be at different stages of cultural evolution, from traditional to contemporary.

THE THERAPIST'S FOCUS

Considering each of these dimensions may well seem overwhelming. Clearly, the wide angle perspective that the therapist needs to utilize in order to consider the ecology of minority populations has to be focused so that goals for therapy can be developed. The selection of a useful class of information (i.e., a particular cultural dimension) requires: (a) scanning all the contextual dimensions of values that impact the family, (b) scanning one's own contextual dimensions of values, and their interaction with those of the family, (c) participating with the family in the co-creation of a workable reality that will start the process of change, and (d) reading feedback.

Communication is the tool that the therapist will utilize to check for feedback from the family. Since communication, because of its many levels of meaning, is problematic, therapists need to include these levels of meaning when they check feedback. Pearce and Cronen's (1980) theory on coordination management of levels of meaning (CMM) is of relevance. CMM is explained in terms of interpersonal rules for meaning and action. The assumption is that people act on the basis of their interpretations of the meaning of actions, and that these interpretations have several referents. These authors describe several levels that connote meaning (content, speech act, episode, contract, lifescript and culture) which are all recursively related. Culture is the highest level, and is described as a matrix where perceived appropriateness of meaning is generated. A comprehensive description of this model is beyond the scope of this chapter. Of importance to our present discussion is the possibility for miscommunication at any level. Therefore, the therapist's task is not only difficult in selecting a class of information, but in interpreting this class of information in a manner congruent with the family's interpretation. It is important that consensus as to meaning between the family and the therapist be periodically checked (i.e., ask the family what their view is about the presenting problems, the solutions, the content of therapy, and the therapeutic relationship). Specific examples that access these differences are: "What do you think about what I just said?" . . . "about what I just did?" and, "what do you mean by 'intimate,' by 'respect,'" etc? The more dissimilar the cultural background of the family and the therapist the greater the possibilities for miscommunication. For example, the meaning of "wisdom" between the M. couple and the young therapist were highly incongruent (see "Generation"). On the other hand the meaning about "work" between the MOI and Mrs. C. (see "Economics") was congruent. These two examples are clear-cut cases, but most differences in meaning are more subtle. There-fore, it is recommended that therapists check for differences in meaning frequently. For an excellent description of ways to prevent misunderstandings see Montalvo (this volume).

In addition, therapists need to be prepared to occasionally chal-lenge those values that are constraining the family with outdated rules or expectations. Therapists will be empowered to do this, when they view culture as multidimensional and as validating both stability and change. When therapists are too organized by cultural preconceptions about what is possible and not possible for a given culture, they may focus on stability and give up their exploration of those cultural dimensions that sanction change. Cultural values are constantly in the process of stabilization and change. Therapists need to remember that stability and change are double descriptors of a recursive system, and that when a system is stabilizing, it is also showing potential for change.

SUMMARY

This chapter considers many sociocultural dimensions as sources of ideology for both the family and the therapist. Families and ther-apists have both shared values and value differences. Values are derived from membership in a variety of contexts, and are played out at all levels of social organization.

Therapists need to adopt a wide, relativistic perspective and consider all possible dimensions of culture as contexts within which they can join, understand, and intervene with families. At the same time, therapists (whether majority or minority) need to be aware of their role in co-creating therapeutic realities, especially realities that may maintain the status quo for minority families. The therapist's task are to first expand their own views and consider the ecology of the family, and then to choose a class of information that is useful at a given stage of treatment. This task requires checking for consensus of meaning attributed to actions by both the therapist and the family. The cultural values of the family need to be understood, validated and challenged. This is easier if therapists conceptualize all cultures as sanctioning both stability and change.

Ultimately, the therapist and family need to develop their own "cultural context." It is this relational context which has the potential for transforming the world views of both the family and the therapist.

NOTES

1. Bateson utilized the metaphor "The Sound of Two Hands Clapping" to illustrate the notion of double description. He based this idea on a zen story "The Sound of one Hand Clapping." The ancient story "The sound of one hand clapping" describes Mokurai, a zen master, and his young disciple Toyo, exploring various stages of awareness through meditation until he transcends all sounds. This story appears in a collection of stories compiled by Paul Reps, a student of comparative religion who spent his life studying pre-zen and zen writings.

2. For information on source of data please refer to the Center for the Study of Transition, at the Institute for Juvenile Research.

3. For a comprehensive description of levels of social organization, see Bronfenbrenner (1979).

4. The question of whether we can use the term "Hispanic" as an ethnic and/ or racial referent to Latin Americans, is controversial, and a misnomer. Its definition excludes, more groups than it includes. The term "Hispanic" refers to groups of Spanish descent (from Spain). However, groups of Spanish descent throughout Latin America are only one of the many ethnic groups that form part of these heterogenous societies. It is a particularly inappropriate term since it leaves out more groups such as Africans, other Europeans, Middle Easterners, and Asians, all groups who have immigrated to Latin America, as well as Indians who were

the first inhabitants of these regions. The term "Hispanic" is also not appropriate as a referent for race, since Latin Americans come in all races by themselves, and all combinations of races. The most accurate descriptor is nationality (i.e., Mexicans, Puerto Ricans, Argentineans, Chileans, etc.)

REFERENCES

Aponte, H.J., & VanDeusen, J.M. (1981). Structural family therapy. In A. Gurman, & D. Kniskern (Eds.), *Handbook of family therapy* (pp. 310-360). New York: Brunner/Mazel.

Asch, S.E. (1952). *Social psychology*. New York: Prentice-Hall, Inc.

Auerswald, E.H. (1968). Interdisciplinary versus ecological approach. *Family Process, 7,* 205-215.

Bateson, G. (1972). *Steps to an ecology of mind*. New York: Ballantine Books.

Bernal, G. (1983). Culture and class in the study of families. In C.J. Falicov (Ed.), *Cultural perspectives in family therapy* (pp. 33-50). Rockville, MD: Aspen Systems Corporation.

Bronfenbrenner, U. (1979). *The ecology of human development; experiment by nature and design*. Cambridge, MA: Harvard University Press.

DeVos, G., & Wagatsuma, H. (1969). *Japan's invisible race: Caste in culture and personality*. Berkeley: University of California Press.

Falicov, C.J. (1988). Learning to think culturally. In H. Liddle, D. Breunlin, & D. Schwartz (Eds.), *Handbook of family therapy training and supervision*. New York: The Guilford Press.

Friedman, E.H. (1982). The myth of the Shiksa. In M. McGoldrick, J.K. Pearce, & J. Giordano (Eds.), *Ethnicity and family therapy* (pp. 499-526). New York: The Guilford Press.

Goldner, V. (1988). Generation and gender. Normative and covert heirarchies. *Family Process, 27,* 17-32.

Goldner, V., & Walker, G. (1988 June). *Integrating feminist and systemic approaches to battering*. Brief presentation to the American Family Therapy Association, Montreal.

Gould, S.J. (1983). Of wasps and WASPS. *Natural History*, 8-15.

Greeley, A.M. (1969). *Why can't they be like us*? New York: Institute of Human Relations Press.

Hare-Mustin, R.T. (1978). A feminist approach to family therapy. *Family Process, 17,* 181-194.

Karrer, B. (1987). Families of Mexican descent: A contextual approach. In R.B. Birrer (Ed.), *Urban family medicine*. New York: Springer-Verlag.

Lappin, J. (1983). On becoming a culturally conscious family therapist. In C.J. Falicov (Ed.), *Cultural perspectives in family therapy* (pp. 122-136). Rockville, MD: Aspen Systems Corporation.

MacKinnon, L.K., & Miller, D. (1987). The new epistemology and the Milan approach: Feminist and sociopolitical considerations. *Journal of Marital and Family Therapy, 13*, 139-155.

Mayers, B. (1984). Minority group: An ideological formulation. *Social Problems, 32*, 1-15.

McGoldrick, M., Pearce, J.K., & Giordano, J. (1982). *Ethnicity and family therapy.* New York: The Guilford Press.

Minuchin, S., Montalvo, B., Guerney, B.G., Rosman, B.L., & Schumer, F. (1967). *Families of the slums.* New York: Basic Books.

Montalvo, B. (1986). Lessons from the past. *The Family Therapy Networker, 10*, 37-44.

Montalvo, B. (1989). Nine assumptions for work with ethnic minority families. In G. Saba, B.M. Karrer, & K. Hardy (Eds.,) *Minorities and family therapy.* New York: The Haworth Press, Inc.

Peace, W.B., & Cronen, V.E. (1980). *Communication, action, and meaning.* New York: Praeger Publishers.

Rampage, C., MacKinnon, L., James, K., & McIntyre, D. (1988, June). *Preventing abuse: An analysis of the social construction of masculinity and femininity.* Special International Presentation, to the American Association of Marriage and Family Therapy, Montreal.

Reps, P. (1961). *Zen flesh, zen bones.* New York: Double Day/Anchor Books.

Rotheran, M.J., & Phinney, J. (1987). Definitions and perspectives in the study of children's ethnic socialization. In J. Phinney & M. Rotheran (Eds.), *Children's ethnic socialization: Pluralism and development* (pp. 10-20). Beverly Hills, CA: Sage.

Saba, G.W., & Rodgers, D.V. (1989). Discrimination in urban family practice: Lessons from minority poor families. In G.W. Saba, B.M. Karrer, & K. Hardy (Eds.), *Minorities and family therapy.* New York: The Haworth Press, Inc.

Schwartz, R.C. (1985). Has family therapy reached the stage where it can appreciate the concept of stages? In D.C. Breunlin (Ed.), *Stages: Patterns of change over time* (pp. 88-94). Rockville, MD: Aspen Systems Corporation.

Schwartzmann, J. (1983). Family ethnography: A tool for clinicians. In C.J. Falicov (Ed.), *Cultural perspectives in family therapy* (pp. 137-149). Rockville, MD: Aspen Systems Corporation.

Shibutani, T., & Kwan, K.M. (1965). *Ethnic stratification.* New York: Macmillan.

Simon, R. (1984). From ideology to practice: The Women's Project in Family Therapy. *The Family Therapy Networker, 8*, 28-42.

Sluzki, C.E. (1979). Migration and family conflict. *Family Process, 18*, 379-390.

Sluzki, C.E. (1982). The Latin lover revisited. In M. McGoldrick, J.K. Pearce, & J. Giordano (Eds.), *Ethnicity and family therapy* (pp. 492-498). New York: The Guilford Press.

Taggart, M. (1985). The feminist critique in epistemological perspective: Questions of context in family therapy. *Journal of Marital and Family Therapy, 11*, 113-126.